WITHDRAWN
UTSA Libraries

Text and Culture

Theory and History of Literature
Edited by Wlad Godzich and Jochen Schulte-Sasse

For other books in the series, see p. 178.

Text and Culture
The Politics of
Interpretation

Daniel Cottom

Theory and History of Literature, Volume 62

University of Minnesota Press, Minneapolis

Copyright © 1989 by the University of Minnesota.

All rights reserved. No part of this publication may be reproduced,
stored in a retrieval system, or transmitted, in any form or by any
means, electronic, mechanical, photocopying, recording, or otherwise,
without the prior written permission of the publisher.

Published by the University of Minnesota Press
2037 University Avenue Southeast, Minneapolis MN 55414.
Published simultaneously in Canada
by Fitzhenry & Whiteside Limited, Markham.
Printed in the United States of America.

Library of Congress Cataloging-in-Publication Data

Cottom, Daniel.
  Text and culture: the politics of interpretation/Daniel Cottom.
    p. cm. — (Theory and history of literature; v. 62)
  Includes index.
  1. Literature—Philosophy. 2. Literature and society.
  3. Discourse analysis. 4. Dickens, Charles, 1812-1870. Great
  expectations. I. Title. II. Series.
  ISBN 0-8166-1762-7
  ISBN 0-8166-1763-5 (pbk.)
  PN49.C64 1989
  801—dc19   88-17341
                                                       CIP

The University of Minnesota
is an equal-opportunity
educator and employer.

Library
University of Texas
at San Antonio

For Mary Childers
who likes a good joke

Contents

Preface

This is a study of the politics of interpretation. I approach this topic through the relation between text and culture in contemporary disciplines of interpretation. In the first chapter I discuss the cultural meanings of a form of discourse, in the second the concept of culture, and in the third a specific text, Charles Dickens's *Great Expectations*, which I use to illustrate and further develop the arguments of the preceding chapters.

Broadly speaking, one could say the issues of literary genre, context, and reception are treated successively in these three chapters. However, readers will find this way of classifying things antithetical to the argument I pursue here. These essays overlap to such an extent that they might be seen just as well as three critical meditations on the politics of interpretation. For instance, problems of community, identity, mastery, deviancy, repression, violence, desire, reading and writing, teaching, and power are addressed in every chapter. I believe this redundancy leads to a more satisfactory understanding of the topic, but then of course I must leave this judgment to the reader.

Although this work is directed to issues especially important to my own discipline of literary studies, I deal with material from a number of other disciplines as well. Anthropology, sociology, sociolinguistics, history, philosophy, and psychology are among these other fields of study. My argument needs this extension since one of its claims is that the discourse of culture goes beyond the conventional boundaries of disciplines and carries political implications that are not boxed within particular texts, oeuvres, or areas of knowledge. I have tried to avoid egregious errors and misrepresentations in dealing with works from traditions with which I am less well acquainted than my own discipline, but even in matters of literary theory and criticism I have not been concerned to maintain traditions or to discuss works within traditions. One reason for this approach is the pragmatic need to focus on the politics of interpretation rather than on the arcane histories, disputes, feuds, and complexities involved in this or that matter of interpretation in the work of figures such as Wittgenstein or Freud. An even more important reason is that my argument challenges the concept of tradition along with the prevailing conception of academic disciplines.

In the first chapter, "What Is a Joke?" the example of the joke as a form of discourse enables me to begin discussing the perplexities involved in the act of interpretation. Intellectuals have viewed jokes from various angles: anthropological, historical, psychoanalytic, semiotic, and so on. In almost all these approaches they have relied on a normative concept of culture to support their interpretations. Although I am concerned to note differences, such as those that separate Kant's idea of the joke as play, Freud's idea of the joke as a representation of unconscious relationships and actions, and A. R. Radcliffe-Brown's idea of joking relationships as a means of maintaining social cohesion, I analyze the significance of these differences in terms of the politics of identity and community played out in these theories. My argument is not simply that politics always is implicated in such theories—although I try to show that this is not as simple a point as it may seem. My argument is that interpretation is situated historically in a way that does not allow for neutrality in its description. Therefore, we cannot be justified in giving any text, even the simplest joke, an interpretation that excludes the possibility of differing and contradictory readings. I conclude this chapter by identifying one traditional way of limiting readings as "the dialectic of the wise fool" and by trying to summarize the faults of this kind of approach through a discussion of *King Lear*.

The second chapter, "*Ethnographia Mundi*," is a study of what anthropologists call "the culture concept." In contrast to a history-of-ideas approach to the tradition and revision of this concept, I analyze culture as a discourse that developed in the twentieth century as a ground for interpretation in the social sciences and humanities. Recently this ground has become especially important for literary theory and semiotics as intellectuals have tried to formulate a general basis for explanation that is not smuggled into texts arbitrarily and yet is not determined by a biased notion of tradition (or "culture" in an old-fashioned sense). Although this discourse has its virtues, I am concerned to analyze the assumptions that go into it and the significance of the way these assumptions operate in interpretations made on the basis of culture. In considering works by intellectuals such as Bronislaw Malinowski, Clifford Geertz, Dell Hymes, Jacques Derrida, and Basil Bernstein, I concentrate especially on the part played in the discourse of culture by the ethnographic boundary, the metaphor of totality, the relation of text to context, and the figure of the deviant. In doing so, I argue for an emphasis on heterogeneity that would open the discourse of culture to the realities of historical conflict, desire, and change.

The concluding chapter, "Paranomasia, Identity, and the Power of Meaning," considers the various ways of making sense dramatized in *Great Expectations* and their relation to the different ways readers may make sense of this novel. By focusing on the issue of Pip's inexplicable love for Estella, I argue that a rule of irony is of key importance if we are to see this novel as a coherent whole. By this argument, rhetorical figures like irony are not simply formal or technical devices. They are practices through which readers appropriate texts in a way that both asserts and represses from recognition a panoply of assumptions about the constitution of such things as feeling, character, ideology, truth, nature, transcendence, and history. By showing the politics of rhetoric in this way—by showing what interpretive assumptions are entailed in a reading of *Great Expectations* as a coherent whole—I argue for the value of a historical approach to literary studies. At the same time I argue for the importance of going beyond the historical reification of culture as a ground for understanding by exploring the conflicts that always exist in readings of texts and by considering the possibility of reading them in ways that do not presume the necessity of unified forms. In this way I try to show how a recognition of the politics of interpretation may lead us toward a power of meaning that idealist types of interpretation can imagine only in the guilty forms of deviancy, violence, silence, absence, or mystifying desire.

Acknowledgments

I would like to express my appreciation to John Franzosa, Ross Pudaloff, Michael Bell, Mary Childers, Len Tennenhouse, Nancy Armstrong, Jerry Herron, and Henry Golemba, whose comments on various drafts of this work have helped me a great deal. The late Dennis Turner also provided a helpful reading of an early draft—he is missed.

Charlie Baxter provided especially detailed criticism of the second chapter, which led to major changes—thanks.

I appreciate as well the hospitality of the editors of *Critical Inquiry*, especially W. J. T. Mitchell, to the shorter version of Chapter 1 that originally appeared in that journal.

Stanley Fish gave generous encouragement to this project, for which I am grateful; Jochen Schulte-Sasse's editorial advice and support were again valuable; Terry Cochran continues to be a patient and supportive editor, without whom this book etc.

Many other friends and acquaintances, in addition to those just named, have helped me out by telling me jokes—I would like to acknowledge their contribution, too. Keep 'em coming.

Text and Culture

Chapter 1
What Is a Joke?

I

Our laughter is always the laughter of a group.
—Bergson[1]

A melting sermon being preached in a country church, all fell a weeping but one man, who being asked, why he did not weep with the rest? O! said he, I belong to another parish.
—*Joe Miller's Jests*[2]

Consider a joke that circulated among academics a few years ago:

> A Texan is walking across Harvard Yard. He stops a guy and asks him, in his nasal drawl, "Can you tell me where the library's at?" The guy looks him up and down, pauses, and says, "At Harvard we do not end our sentences with prepositions." The Texan apologizes, saying, "Excuse me. Can you tell me where the library's at, asshole?"

This joke may seem far removed from the subject of this book, which is supposed to be a serious one. But then what is the joke about if not the seriousness of language, its power, and the demystification of that power by our native brand of deconstructionist, the shrewd rube?

A friend thought this joke would be a great pedagogical tool. Tell it to your students, she suggested, and then ask them, "Which character would you rather be?" Later, I used the joke in this way, and it worked. The students laughed, they

3

got the point, and our discussion of prestige dialects or of "Standard English" could proceed. Of course, no one wants to be the city slicker; everyone wants to be the cowboy who deftly shows the Easterner's learning to be so much doodly squat.

If we find the joke funny, I imagine this is the attitude with which we identify. We all want the gumption to reject an arrogant cultural authority. This attitude may be especially appealing to students, who are bound to be alienated, in one way or another, from the obnoxious ways authority speaks to them in our educational system.[3] However, it may also appeal to intellectuals who feel befuddled by the complex relations between power and knowledge. After all, as we are all *placed* in a profession—chosen or passed over for distinction, rewarded, ranked, regarded, or simply liked and disliked according to an authority that ultimately lies beyond us—we all remain students who may be as resentful of our knowledge as we are proud of it. There is a reason for the existence of the academic novel as a comic form; there is a reason professors are broad targets for humor even among themselves. There is also a reason for professors to be especially vulnerable on the subject of language, authority in this subject being so equivocal that its very assertion may be its betrayal. Long before I had heard the joke about the Texan and the Harvard man, George Meredith noted this circumstance when he gave an example of those who fail to attain to the comic spirit: "A very learned English professor crushed an argument in a political discussion, by asking his adversary angrily: 'Are you aware, sir, that I am a philologer?' "[4]

Nietzsche suggested that grammar is a metaphysical discipline comparable to the reign of God. If we follow his suggestion, the pleasure of the joke with which I began may seem to lie in its humiliation of law of all sorts. Something like this conclusion was drawn by Wittgenstein when he raised the following question— "Let us ask ourselves: why do we feel a grammatical joke is *deep?*"—adding, "And that is what the depth of philosophy is."[5] Walter Benjamin saw the joke as a quasi-revolutionary action that "puts forth its own image and exists, absorbing and consuming it," so as to establish a kind of "dialectical justice."[6] Mikhail Bakhtin is another who saw laughter as a kind of liberation.[7] Freud, of course, suggested that jokes represent a fundamental rebellion against all the social laws extorted from our unconscious drives.

Following these suggestions, we could see enjoyment of this joke as a momentary rejection of every form of culture "imposed on our nature," as the saying goes. From this perspective, even the way I am discussing this joke must seem ridiculously at odds with the spirit of the thing. No wonder academic psychologists today, like Cicero in his time, should make defensive remarks about the risibility of people who seriously analyze jokes.[8] Perhaps the old joke that one is better off not knowing how some things are made, such as sausages and laws, should caution us against going too far in analyzing the laws jokes humiliate and the laws they represent.

But there is more to liberation than the feeling of release—fascists have orgasms, too—and there is more to this joke than the reading I imagined to be the first one.[9] After all, this Texan might just as well be a Californian who exercises by chopping wood on his ranch and then goes back East to counter the windy fulminations of intellectuals with his homespun tales of people buying vodka with food stamps, with a cowboyish enthusiasm for murdering people in Central America, and with an aw-shucks approach to nuclear weaponry. In other words (to explain this joke to readers for whom it may no longer be topical), this Texan might just as well be a particularly loathsome President of the United States named Ronald Reagan.

This is the enchantment of the joke: the fact that this humiliation of culture can be as charming to a vicious reactionary like Reagan as it can be to leftists, philosophers, bored students, and disaffected academics. (Remember how Reagan was said to charm the media with his fondness for humorous storytelling?) Whatever we may be, once we identify with one of the figures in the joke, we are enchanted by it. In our identification, we lose sight of the fact that these figures form a comedy team. In our pleasure, we forget that the natural man and the man corrupted by civilization are given birth by the same joke. In our understanding of the joke as a form of discourse, we ignore our understanding that these textual figures come into conflict only because they are cooperating to produce the effect of native truth. We fail to analyze the law that goes into breaking the law.

This process of identification may be necessary if we are to enjoy the joke or even to understand it as a joke. However, this enjoyment—this linguistic competence—is potentially a form of political servility. In seeming to free ourselves of grammar, we may be hornswoggled by rhetoric.

I follow a long literary tradition in calling this situation "enchantment," although I take issue with the usual definitions of this term and this tradition. This enchantment is a kind of mastery all forms of discourse, including academic writing and jokes, may enjoy over us. It is comparable to the "fascination which forms of expression exert upon us" that Wittgenstein set out to counter.[10] It is a mastery that takes place through our enjoyment and all our other feelings: sadness, pathos, horror, ecstasy, whatever. Like the archetypal frontiersman, this mastery is especially powerful because its origin is obscure. As a result of our identification with forms of discourse, this mastery seems to come of the blue, godlike. It seems to be the very frontier of intelligibility. It seems unsolicited, spontaneous, unquestionably authoritative, natural . . . and therefore it seems to have a universal appeal.

Because of this enchantment, texts may appear to be most in our possession when we are most possessed by them. For instance, through this process genres are formally defined, along with terms such as *competence, community, convention, context*, and, to mention one of the two terms on which I concentrate in this study, *culture*.

Through this enchanting effect of language, cultural objects escape the social conditions of their meaning. They come to appear authoritatively natural, transcendent, magical, or even professional, like the "Great Communicator" himself, as the media have dubbed Reagan (who, of course, only represents the fix American society is in as I write this book). Through this escape meaning is indeed liberated, but only as one speaks of a liberated territory, implying by this phrase a controversy over its rightful possession. The meaning is up for grabs; and so it seems all cultural objects might be epitomized by amphibology (sentences having two or more different meanings) or by equivocal verse (the humorous poetic form that expresses diametrically opposed attitudes, depending on how it is read).[11] But then even these models would be inadequate. When all objects seem characterized by the intimacy of seriousness and parody often noted in roasts and in carnival, the result is no longer a doubleness of values that can be neatly categorized, described, and analyzed.

Given this situation, a critic's task is difficult. If I want to trace the social relations implicated in the terms of enchantment and yet displaced from its overpowering appearance, how can I avoid being a fancy-pants Easterner who is betrayed by his own citation of the law—a law that operates, of course, only through the necessity of such betrayal? (One can never perfectly identify with a law: law is impersonal and so must differ from individuals, who cannot possess themselves in it.) On the other hand, if I try to play the fool, flaunting a personal disenchantment with authority, how can I hope to communicate with an audience unprepared to take jokes seriously—unprepared, for instance, to find the protocols of scholarly writing violated by emotional references to Ronald Reagan that will not be topical by the time this study is published? (Not to mention the consideration that this betrayal of scholarly law, this unserious style of the joke, could still be seen as an oblique citation of the law.)

It would be acceptable, I know, to touch on the intersection of politics, topicality, and joking and serious writing through the use of appropriate scholarly examples. For instance, I might mention the character of Mr. Dick in *David Copperfield*, with his endless writing of a "Memorial" of his life that always fails because the figure of Charles I somehow sneaks into it. (In fact, I refer to this character's problem in my concluding chapter.) To refer only to such *proper* material, though, must seem the silliness of an academic thinking about jokes without ever cracking a smile, writing about politics in a lexicon that excludes the expression of feelings like anger and disgust. Why bother?

And yet, again, an attempt to reject all law in this writing about law would be narcissistic or dictatorial. Insults heaped on a creep like Reagan, say, would not appear as insults to Reagan. They would insult the audience I evidently expect to indulge my capriciousness. In this stylistic bind, searching to avoid incapacitating alternatives that are not really alternatives at all, one's best hope is to insist on the relation between poetics and politics and thus to concentrate on the issue of rhetorical authority.

The issue of rhetorical authority, for instance, in my choice of the joke about the Texan and the Harvard man as an exemplary text. It might be objected that this joke is a special case among jokes or that the joke is a relatively simple form of discourse too easily turned to my purposes. Other works, it might be said, especially works more commonly treated as literature, could not be given readings so radically different from each other.

While part of my purpose throughout this book is to demonstrate that this objection does not hold, consider again the case that has received precisely this criticism. Once, when I discussed this joke as part of a presentation to an academic audience, several members of the audience responded by telling me variant versions they had heard. These involved blacks in the role of the Texan, and one member of the audience suggested I could not have "turned the joke around" so easily if I had told it in that form.

To be sure, it would not have been the same joke. Nor could it have been given the readings I have imagined here. One has to be stunningly blind to racism, though, to believe no telling of this joke with a black in the role of the Texan could make the black out to be an oppressive rather than a liberating figure, a vicious antagonist rather than a playful rube.

Consider, first of all, what happens when a white academic laughs at this form of the joke. Does this laughter signify approval of this challenge to academic authority, or does it rather signify a nervousness about this alien figure, a fear displayed even as it is denied or symbolically mastered, a liberation that is really the repression of comedic form? Is this black Amiri Baraka or Stepin Fetchit or, perhaps, an intersection of the two within the white imagination? One need only consider how the white academic would react if a comparable situation were to occur in the classroom — one need only remember the 1960s — to see that the joke in this form is no less equivocal than it is when the Texan is in the role of the sympathetic protagonist.

This is not the end of the matter. Imagine how the identification involving the speaker and the audience would be altered in other situations in which this joke might be told. What would it mean if told by one staunchly pro-government Afrikaner to another? Or what would it mean if told among a group of whites in a room in which a black man was within earshot? (One of my white colleagues, teaching a class of black students, was asked by one student, "Do you know what has eight legs and goes 'Ho dee doh, ho dee doh, ho dee doh, ho dee doh?'" So he had to wonder: what does it mean if he admits that he knows the answer, four black guys hurrying for the elevator? Or, if he pretends not to know the answer, what is the appropriate response for him to make when the students tell it to him? And, in either case, how will the situation be affected by the way he looks, holds his head, stands . . . ?)

Still other questions might be raised. In noting that " 'the Harvard man' has linguistic recognition," Michael Gregory and Susanne Carroll have asked, "Does anyone speak of 'the Alabama State man'?"[12] What would this joke about the Texan or the black man mean if told to someone unaware of the enchanting effect of the key words *Harvard*, *Texan*, and *black?* It would have to be explained, you might say; and the question then would be, who would explain it, and to what end?

As it happens, in his study of laughter Henri Bergson inquired, "why does one laugh at a black man?"[13] In a sense this was the most important question he asked, although he did not recognize how crucial it was and certainly did not give it an adequate response.[14] One might also ask why Jews are funny, as in the version of my joke recounted by Stephen Leacock. The dialect humor of this joke may suggest rebellion against "proper" English, but then again it may be interpreted as suggesting, "humorously," the danger of contaminating the proprieties of language, education, and ethnic heritage:

> A certain wealthy Jew came to Harvard University to enter his son as a student. He was especially anxious to have him taught to speak English correctly and without a Yiddish accent. "I vant him taught the way you spigg here," he said, "and I vant you should take him in hand yourself and give him brivate instructions." "Well," said the Harvard professor of English, speaking with that large, cultivated accent that marks the place and the subject, "I shall certainly be glad to do so. We rather flatter ourselves here on our English."
>
> The Jew went away and returned a few months later.
>
> "Vell," he asked, "and how is my boy getting on mid his English?"
>
> "Oh," said the professor, "he is megging brogress, goot brogress. I togg mid him effery day."[15]

William Labov has touched on this subject in noting how a stigmatized pattern of speech, such as Sam Weller's *v/w* alterations in *The Pickwick Papers*, can become a joke. "Long after it is actually extinct in speech," Labov writes, "a linguistic variable can survive as a stereotyped use of certain words, then as a standard joke, and finally as a fossil form whose meaning has been entirely forgotten."[16] In tracing such changes, Labov's work also shows that we are never simply dealing with historical changes in the interpretation of language. The question is not whether an expression is a stereotype, a joke, or a meaningless inheritance (what anthropologists call a "survival"), because in a particular society these and other characterizations may coexist. Political differences, such as whether one belongs to a stigmatized speech group, are likely to determine how a particular expression or form of speech is classified.

The same point may be made by considering how different my initial joke would be if the Texan or the Harvard man were women. For instance, if the Texan is a man and the Harvard student a woman, is he clever, clever and macho, vulgar and violent, or what?[17] If we do not impose an arbitrary closure on reading, there is no way to put an end to these differing interpretations. One cannot attribute a formal reality to texts, much less a meaning, apart from their political construction. It is only by reference to other groups of speakers, after all, that Sam Weller's way with *v*'s and *w*'s can be isolated as a variable in the first place.

Consider in this respect another joke I recently heard:

Why do women have vaginas?
So men will talk to them.

One way of reading this joke would analyze the ambiguity of the pronoun and the complex grammar of *have* in order to evaluate the significance of the sexual attitudes implied in this question and response. Even assuming such a thorough cultural analysis has been performed, though, am I to consider this joke to be brutally sexist, wisely feminist, or something else entirely?

It was told to me, I believe, as both a sexist and a feminist joke. That is, I was entrusted with a certain degree of irony. I was talking to a friend; the joke was not told "straight"; and yet it would not have been as funny to us if the straight meaning had not been as strong as the critical, cynical, feminist sense it could have. Jews, like friends, are famous for telling jokes about themselves formally identical to those that might be told by their enemies, and yet very different. Other groups, like blacks, families, and cliques that share "in jokes," trust each other with meaning they would find betrayed if it were translated into another context. Understandably, then, in telling this joke about women to others, I have received the strongest response from the people to whom I am closest and more nervous responses from casual friends. And, of course, there were any number of people to whom I did not feel I could tell it at all, even if I framed it as a part of an essay on which I was working, for fear they would not take it, as the saying goes, in the right spirit. In other words, for fear they would not consider it to be a joke at all, much as Russian officials claimed to find no joke in the way Reagan once tested a microphone by announcing the imminent nuclear destruction of the Soviet Union. ("This was really no joke," Gregor Samsa thinks, somewhere between bemusement and terror, when his father drives him back into his room.[18]) And what would my joke be if not a joke? Or which telling is the joke, if it is a joke?

There is no text beyond these questions. There is no text that can be read outside the historical play of political differences. As J. G. A. Pocock puts it,

At any given moment . . . the "meanings" (one cannot avoid the
plural) of a given utterance must be found by locating it in a
paradigmatic texture, a multiplicity of contexts,which the verbal force of
the utterance itself cannot completely determine; and if we wish to trace

some aspect of its history by making statements of our own, we must, by our own deployments of language, isolate the context or universe in which we say this piece of history took place. Speech is not self-locating.[19]

Of course, this description of my experiences with these two jokes is only a very rough sketch of the variety of contingencies that can disturb the interpretation of texts. But the questions I have raised should indicate that every possible condition of a text, including even its nonexistence, must be conceivable within a theory of literature if that theory is not to be a tool of political oppression.[20] The situation of theory is that simple and that complicated. Any theory that puts an end to readings, that disqualifies any readings unconditionally—as is the case with all traditional literary theories and even with much of the theory that passes under the labels of structuralism and poststructuralism—represents an abject identification with an imaginary law. This condition of theory is ridiculous, a joke; it is as serious as a joke.

II

> There is a recognized class of jokes about institutions which lose sight of the interests of the clientele who constitute the sole reason for their existence, centering round the basic theme of 'this would be a splendid place to work if it wasn't for the . . . (pupils, guests, etc.).'
>
> —Halliday[21]

In *The Pursuit of Signs*, Jonathan Culler brushes away an irritation to theory:

> We have little difficulty setting aside the idiosyncratic response whose causes are personal and anecdotal (simple discussion with other readers can eliminate these). The problem is to make explicit the operations and conventions which will account for a range of readings and exclude any we would agree to place outside the normal procedures of reading.[22]

Generous readers might make excuses for the writer who produced these two sentences in the midst of a substantial and distinguished book, but the idea that a teacher might actually believe them is scary. "We would agree," the professor says; and readers, comfortable in the professor's genial assurance, nestling within the circle of agreement, may swallow this poisonous distinction between the "personal and anecdotal" and the institutionally approved. No matter that this fantasy of a natural consensus, this quintessentially liberal belief in the teleology of discourse, makes it seem as if the distinction between normality and deviancy descends upon us from the heavens of an institution, from a history we are compelled to follow:[23] who would be so idiosyncratic as to reject the trust the professor is offering us? "One can only determine a correct reading," he says, "in relation to a standard, and such standards are ultimately imposed by varying sorts of cultural authority" (*PS*, 77). Before this ideal of "cultural authority," which is "imposed" upon one's nature, who would dare suggest that authority is always a source and a product of struggle, which may be irrational as well as inequitable in its social effects?

Not that Culler is unaware of possible objections:

> One could, of course, scrap the term "literary competence" to avoid
> the appearance of presuming agreement among readers on the existence
> of a normative, "competent" interpretation, but this would involve a
> loss, since "competence" does indicate that one is dealing with an
> ability involving norms. Not only does interpretation employ repeatable
> operations, but in one's attempt to interpret a text one is always
> implicitly appealing to norms. When one wonders whether a particular
> line of thought will work out, whether one will succeed in elucidating
> an obscure passage, one posits norms of successful interpretation,
> adequate clarity, sufficient coherence. These norms may remain vague
> and they may vary greatly from one interpretive community to another,
> but the process of interpretation is incomprehensible without them, and
> one is usefully reminded of this by the allusion to norms implicit in the
> concept of "literary competence." (*PS*, 51)

Still, even if one accepts the academic form of interpretation Culler assumes is exclusively governing "literary competence," his description of this competence mystifies the academy as an essentially neutral and systematic institution. It mystifies the ways success actually occurs and is measured. No wonder, then, that he can write, "A primary task of the study of reading is to describe the operations responsible for interpretations we find plausible," as if it is a complex of *operations* (neutral, impersonal, descended from on high) that determines plausibility, not the material force of institutions, the accidents of personality and personal influence, and similar historical contingencies. Historical considerations are secondary, we are told, to these enchanting operations: "Questions such as to what extent individual readers perform the same operations or how far these operations are confined to a tiny community of professional critics can not really be answered until we are better able to describe the operations in question" (*PS*, 73).

Stanley Fish presents another interesting case in this regard, especially since *Is There a Text in This Class?* specifically deals, in part, with the institution of the university. At one point Fish describes a colleague and a student who are talking from a shared understanding of the classroom situation:

> That shared understanding is the basis of the confidence with which
> they speak and reason, but its categories are their own only in the sense

that as actors within an institution they automatically fall heir to the institution's way of making sense, its systems of intelligibility. That is why it is so hard for someone whose very being is defined by his position within an institution (and if not this one, then some other) to explain to someone outside it a practice or a meaning that seems to him to require no explanation, because he regards it as natural. Such a person, when pressed, is likely to say, "but that's just the way it's done" or "but isn't it obvious" and so testify that the practice of meaning in question is community property as, in a sense, he is too.[24]

Although Fish describes M. H. Abrams's fear of rampant subjectivity and relativism by saying there is "something of the police state in Abrams's vision" (*ITT*, 337), he evidently does not recognize that utopias like the institution he describes might also be considered police states. It is "automatically" that Fish's persons "fall heir to the institution's way of making sense," which presumably descends upon them like a spirit. No violence, coercion, inequity, history, or materiality of any sort appears within the confines of Fish's institution to disturb its abstract "members." Instead, this institution or interpretive community, like Culler's, is composed of free consensual discourse. "What I finally came to see was that the . . . business of criticism . . . was not to decide between interpretations by subjecting them to the test of disinterested evidence but to establish by political and persuasive means (they are the same thing) the set of interpretive assumptions from the vantage of which the evidence (and the facts and the intentions and everything else) will hereafter be specifiable" (*ITT*, 15–16). *Eloquentia*, it seems, is what moves history: no police states but in words. Only an academic and, probably, only an American could have such a jolly sense of satisfaction in the submission of human beings to forms of authority. One would not suspect that this is a man who has actually made fun of Harvard.[25]

Even more remarkable is Fish's seeming inability to see the possibility that individuals might owe allegiance to a variety of institutions, with said allegiances often conflicting in ways that cannot be rationally predicted or resolved. No, for Fish "sentences emerge only in situations, and within these situations, the normative meaning of an utterance will always be obvious or at least accessible, although within another situation that same utterance, no longer the same, will have another normative meaning that will be no less obvious and accessible" (*ITT*, 307). Not only is there no ambiguity, indeterminacy, or unconsciousness in Fish's institution: there is simply no contest. One voice holds power, and Fish's persons either submit to that voice or else become the master voice by virtue of their eloquence. "The greatest rewards of our profession are reserved for those who challenge the assumptions within which ordinary [interpretive] practices go on, not so much in order to eliminate this category of the ordinary but in order to redefine it and reshape its configurations" (*ITT*, 366). Although we cannot be sure exactly what "rewards" are in Fish's institution, it would appear they can be fairly characterized as the placement within the institution that accrues to those who prove most skilled at entertaining authority without challenging it. In other words, as Fish portrays his situation within his institution, he is just an innocent joker unsettling the fancy-pants professionals who unthinkingly follow the laws given to them. Indeed, the title of his book refers to such a situation—which he takes as a joke—involving a student, another professor, and himself.

In making this criticism of Fish and Culler, I do not argue that a reading of literature on grounds other than those of sociohistorical understanding is in any way illegitimate. On the contrary, the point is that no way of reading is wrong except as it may become so under specific political conditions. Therefore, these conditions must be treated as the subject of sociohistorical differences within any literary theory that would not blindly identify itself with an imaginary law. One cannot admit that the individual is a social and historical being and so incapable of founding theory as a *res cogitans* and then resurrect this pure ego in the form of an institution. There is no ideal political authority in *eloquentia*, institutions, contexts, communities of readers, or anywhere else, but rather a complexly over-determined conflict over authority that cannot be described adequately as long as one isolates students in a classroom or members in an institution from the historical contingencies involved in differences such as those of race, class, wealth, and gender. Despite all the work that has been done by feminist and leftist critical theory, it still may seem crude to demand the inclusion of such contingencies within the protocols of literary theory. However, the effect of this demand is to restore to institutions a real historical complexity erased from their every aspect when they are assumed to be utopias of consensus. It is not enough simply to note differences that have existed in the past along with the possibility of future differences. The demand of theory should be to recognize the relations between poetics and politics implicated in the very conception of the cultural institutions within which the act of reading takes place.[26]

Interpretation in all the humanistic disciplines is affected by the failure to heed this demand. Literary criticism and theory are by no means the only offenders in this regard. In philosophy, the speech-act theory developed by John Searle is a subtle instance of this failure. Searle is aware that a speech act, such as promising, can be a very complex matter. He says, ''it is important to realize that one and the same utterance may constitute the performance of several different illocutionary acts'' because the utterance may be related differently to different people.[27] In the case of promises, he also acknowledges the possibility that an utterance may be affected by other obligations that conflict with it and so may overrule it (*SA*, 180 n). Still, one could say he does not begin to fathom the philosophical implications of the most common American proverb on this topic: ''Promises are made to be broken.''

Searle's analysis of speech acts is thoroughly compromised by his assumption that we all come before language as equals, at least in ordinary or ''non-defective'' circumstances. He can idealize the promise as a categorical act because he assumes society is composed of individuals who are categorically equal. His most frequent image for speech is participation in a game, an image that implies we all freely choose our places in society and in its systems of communication. As J. O. Urmson says of Austin's approach to philosophy, which is the inspiration for Searle's, ''one can employ the technique only for a language of which one is a master''[28] (a point, incidentally, also made by Humpty Dumpty in *Alice in Wonderland*).

Searle can disambiguate speech—''a non-defective promise must be intended as a promise and not as a threat or a warning'' (*SA*, 58)—because he has taken speech in the first place to be an institution constituted by neutral conventions. It does not matter, it seems, that the decision as to whether a promise has been uttered often is made by the material institutions of the judiciary, not the ideal conventions of language. It does not seem to matter, either, that not everyone has equal access to the courts or, access having been gained, equal means to pursue a case. It does not matter that courts at different times and in different places make decisions in very different ways.[29] Nor does it seem to matter that, when a child makes a promise to a parent, say, or a president makes one to a nation, the utterances are defined and judged in very different ways, to say the least. Sitting in the chair of reason and peering out the windows of his institution, Searle can overlook such inconvenient details to see all of society making sense. He simply takes for granted that games have winners and losers; that some games demand the most trivial involvement whereas others may involve matters of life and death; that some people are unable or unwilling to play some games and that some people are prevented from playing others. As the joke says, the people who actually participate in institutions appear as nothing but impediments to the smooth functioning of those institutions.

Promises are even more complex than Searle allows, then; and they are not unique in this complexity, which touches all forms of discourse. Consider again the case of jokes. Many theorists, such as Geoffrey Bateson and Erving Goffman, speak of a framing or cueing one performs so as to establish the genre of one's utterance. However, a joke also requires an audience, and not just any audience. It requires an audience that recognizes it as a joke.[30] The audience need not laugh—it may take the text in question to be a bad or a failed joke—but if it does not hear the joke as such, if it will not perceive the kind of performance intended by the speaker, one can expect trouble. The same text may still be a joke for its teller and yet at the very same time not a joke at all for the audience, as Milan Kundera's protagonist discovers in his novel *The Joke*.

At one point in this novel, Ludvik Jahn writes a postcard to his girlfriend Marketa. The postcard says, ''Optimism is the opium of the people!''[31] When he is called before the Party University Committee to explain this text, which the committee believes has broken the law, Ludvik finds that politics are not ''the same thing" as persuasive discourse, that "the same utterance" does not simply acquire "another normative meaning" in a different situation, and that one cannot always be included within the warm agreement of a community. "They said I'd written what I had to say on an open postcard, that it was there for everyone to see, that my words had an *objective* significance which could not be explained away by my mood at the time" (*J*, 29). His protests that it was a private joke, a trivial remark, an innocent bit of *eloquentia*, go for nought. In other words, he finds one cannot necessarily know in what institution one is reading, writing, and interpreting.[32] He finds an authority one cannot pin down so neatly may decide the meaning of a text, and in fact decide it in such a way that the meaning one once thought it had is totally erased from history, as Kundera's *The Book of Laughter and Forgetting* and *The Unbearable Lightness of Being* further illustrate.

In the last work, in fact, Kundera returns to the subject of jokes. In describing a woman who stands before the narrator almost naked and puts a bowler hat on her head, Kundera suggests how political differences may affect interpretation in the most intimate aspects of life as well as in the more impersonal relations between individuals and states. As he writes, "But suddenly, the comic became veiled by excitement: the bowler hat no longer signified a joke; it signified violence; violence against Sabina, against her dignity as a woman."[33] Although I presume Searle would say this is a defective instance of a joke, a reader of Freud might have more difficulty in rejecting out of hand the idea that a form of humor could also be a form of violence and desire and so could differ radically from itself.

True, in his preface to *The Joke* Kundera seems to think a joke, or a text, does have a meaning beyond the permutations of authority that may be applied to it. He says, quoting a saying attributed to Terence (though not so noted here, where it seems to come out of the mists of time, godlike),

> *Habent sua fata libelli.* Books have their fates. The fate of the book called *The Joke* coincided with a time when the combined inanity of ideological dictatorship (in the Communist countries) and journalistic oversimplification (in the West) was able to prevent a work of art from telling its own truth in its own words. The ideologues in Prague took *The Joke* for a pamphlet against socialism and banned it; the foreign publisher took it for a political fantasy that became reality for a few weeks and rewrote it accordingly. (*J*, xvi)

However, in a novel that describes in great detail the disillusionment of a man who believes in just this conception of meaning, it is difficult to credit the resounding idealism in this phrase about a text "telling its own truth in its own words." The fate of *The Joke* and the fate of the joke it recounts show that our words are never entirely owned, even when they may seem to be so. According to Kundera's novel, there is no utopia outside the forces of politics, which go beyond individuals and consensual communities. Kundera's characterization of textual truth in this preface is more comprehensible as a function of the preface as a generic form, a form that seems to establish a utopia beyond the text in which the vicissitudes to which it is fated can be transcended, than as a statement of his "real" opinion about the nature of works of art. Jacques Derrida has written about this form of the preface as a kind of compulsion that must deconstruct itself; but it does not seem to have occurred to the likes of Fish, Culler, and Searle that the innocent description of institutional operations might be the preface to the oppression of those who are "in a sense" the property of the institutions. In other words, it does not seem to have occurred to them that a text is never the "same" even within the "same" situation, that the very act of drawing the boundary of the situation must be the source and product of conflict.

The same consideration applies to all theories of the joke based on the idea of formal context. Cognitive psychologists may speak of incongruity as the basis of humor, Gestalt psychologists of figure—ground relationships, and others of the effects of surprise, disparagement, or some other trigger to psychophysical release. The problem is that all such theories finally describe the deciding context in terms of cultural norms or conventions that repress the reality of political differences.[34]

I might now revise my first description by saying a joke must be successfully presented as such in order to be a joke, but then a problem would still arise. For if the initial description neglected the power of social relations, this one would identify with particular forms of that power. It would accept uncritically the criterion of success or dominance. I point a gun at you as I tell you a story, which I frame as a joke: you laugh. Or, less melodramatically, "culture" tells us blacks, Texans, and women under certain conditions are funny, and we laugh. As these examples indicate, unless we preserve the possibility of not accepting the joke as such, the possibility of seeing the joke as radically differing from itself even within the same situation, our definition of the joke becomes a form of coercion. It serves to institute the very culture within which it is judged by us to be appropriate. And this consideration is just as important in the case of the Texan as it is in the more sensitive cases of blacks and women, for one way culture is instituted is precisely by means of differentiations between innocent and touchy subjects.

The work of Erving Goffman, which has been immensely influential in the fields of sociology, social psychology, and folklore, exemplifies the consequences of the failure to take into account considerations such as this, just as do the works of Culler and Fish in the field of literary theory and Searle in philosophy. Consider what happens when Goffman writes of deviancy:

> In the analysis of deviancy it is sometimes argued that the issue is not
> so much what an individual has done, but rather the perspective brought

to bear upon the deed by those empowered to act in regard to it. When alternative perspectives are examined in detail, it becomes apparent that judgment about the case will consist of making a choice among available perspectives or frames and sometimes using one as mitigation or exacerbation of the applicability of another. The framework of frameworks can be taken as given, and the creative element in the labelling process restricted to that of pressing the applicability of a particular primary framework or a particular transformation.[35]

In the opening of this book, Goffman allows, disarmingly, that his terms and distinctions are flawed, that his work is limited by accident as well as intention, and that he is looking less for epistemological sophistication than for a pragmatic means of obtaining useful results. Moreover, he specifically disclaims any concern with "the core matters of sociology—social organization and social structure," even though he acknowledges that his focus on personal experience to the exclusion of society "is itself a standpoint with marked political implications, and that these are conservative ones" (*FA*, 13–14). However, as his description of deviancy makes clear, this preface is not simply a frame that organizes the nature and scope of his work. This frame creates the institution of normal interpretation that it describes as the topic of Goffman's study.

First, Goffman identifies himself with a certain conception of the normal (we are all flawed, limited, pragmatic creatures). He then idealizes this normality, which becomes the "framework of frameworks" within which deviancy appears merely as the subject of formal transformations. There is no notion that the category of deviancy might be so implicated in the category of normality that individual "choice" might not be the best term for the basis of its construction. Similarly, there is no notion that such categories, even within an individual's experience, might not appear within a coherent "framework of frameworks" that "can be taken as given," godlike, out of the blue (an objection raised by a slogan that appeared during May 1968 in Paris: "*Une structure ne descend pas dans la rue*"[36]). Nor is there any recognition that the nature of deviancy as a historical invention might intrude on its phenomenological classification. For Goffman, it appears, a deviant, like a joke, is simply a matter of form, even though his writing shows there is no description of form that is not an enactment of a specific scheme of social relations.

A similar situation arises in the work of Mary Douglas, the anthropologist. Putting aside her formal definition of the joke, which represents an acknowledged and rather simplistic Freudianism, one finds this description of its significance:

It represents a temporary suspension of the social structure, or rather it makes a little disturbance in which the particular structure of society becomes less relevant than another. But the strength of its attack is entirely restricted by the consensus on which it depends for recognition.[37]

Within this interpretation, society is imagined as a homogenous field of relations in its norms as in its rebellion against norms. Just as there is no recognition that jokes might be as serious as any other form of discourse—the joker is "a humble, poor brother of the mystic" and "distinctly gimmicky" ("SCC," 373)—so there is no recognition that one cannot adequately describe social conflict simply through the binary oppositions of *unofficial* and *official values*, of *rite* and *antirite*, or of *society* and *community* ("SCC," 366, 369, 370). In other words, there is no recognition that the situation of the joke might be something less—and more—than society as a whole. Douglas fails to see that jokes might call into question this idea of social consensus, even the very idea of the social "situation," as much as they do the social structure. Instead, the anthropologist simply identifies with society as an ideal boundary to the understanding surrounded by the mystic country of potential change. Society appears as a boundary within which there is no fundamental conflict, difference, or ongoing struggle. It is a boundary constituted by a "social structure" that appears as a coherent framework of frameworks. The result is a kind of interpretation that systematically represses the political significance of differences of power within a society.

More recently, a historian using anthropological methods has illustrated this tendency of writers within the humanistic disciplines to be enchanted by the forms they study. In the title chapter of *The Great Cat Massacre*, Robert Darnton describes an incident in a Parisian printing shop of the early eighteenth century in which some apprentices, feeling overworked and otherwise mistreated, get their revenge on their employer. Among other things, they are troubled by some cats that have been howling over their bedroom and making it difficult for them to sleep. Their initial response is to imitate this howling for several nights over the master's bedroom. Ordered to get rid of the "cats" bothering the master, but not the favorite of the master's wife, which is called *la grise*, they kill this favorite first, hide it, and then massacre the other cats in the neighborhood, eventually stringing them up on a makeshift gallows. When the owner of the shop and his wife arrive to see what they have done, the workers break into gales of laughter, assuring the wife that they did not kill her favorite. In subsequent days, they reenact this scene among themselves.

Darnton's interpretation of this event is masterly. It combines a historical analysis of class relations and social history, an understanding of folklore, a symbolic and psychological explanation of ceremonies like the charivari, and a scholarly and literary analysis of the textual forms in which this story is available to us. As he concludes,

> The joke worked so well because the workers played so skillfully
> with a repertory of ceremonies and symbols. Cats suited their purposes

perfectly. By smashing the spine of *la grise*, they called the master's wife a witch and a slut, while at the same time making the master into a cuckold and a fool. It was a metonymic insult, delivered by actions, not words, and it struck home because cats occupied a soft spot in the bourgeois way of life. Keeping pets was as alien to the workers as torturing animals was to the bourgeois. Trapped between incompatible sensitivities, the cats had the worst of both worlds.[38]

Beyond explaining its folkloric basis, however, what Darnton does not address is the identification within this joke of women with cats and of female sexuality with witchery. It is clear Darnton's sympathies are with the workers in this story; and his identification with this culture, marked by class and occupation, keeps him from seeing that the relation between class and sexual antagonisms in this joke is not securely bounded by that culture, and in fact may disturb one's drawing of its boundary.

Darnton finds this joke to be in a "splendid Boccaccian style" (*GCM*, 100), but even those who also love to *épater* the dominant classes might find the humor here rather more equivocal. Not so Darnton, who does not use phrases like *a given social order* simply for the purpose of pragmatic specification (*GCM*, 23). He uses them to represent his conviction that social order is imposed upon human nature like a divine institution, a magical consensus, or an ideal framework or structure: "All of us, French and 'Anglo-Saxons,' pedants as well as peasants, operate within cultural constraints, just as we all share conventions of speech" (*GCM*, 6). This assured use of the first person plural and this unquestioning assumption of conventions is as typical of the modern humanist as is its result, a conception of texts in which the possibility of variant readings is either rationalized over cultural differences (as in the case of the master's viewpoint) or else passed over entirely (as in the case of the woman's). Rather than recognizing the political differences always involved in interpretation and thus critically regarding our conceptions of culture, social order, and linguistic conventions, he takes these latter as a means of erasing the differences. In this way, he produces for us a form of discourse unruffled by conflict. No wonder he finds in this eighteenth-century text an innocence and transcendence missing from the modern world. As he writes, in a comment that recalls the work of Douglas as well as some of the sillier comments made by Bakhtin and others about carnival: "By seeing the way a joke worked in the horseplay of a printing shop two centuries ago, we may be able to recapture that missing element — laughter, sheer laughter, the thigh-slapping, rib-cracking Rabelaisian kind, rather than the Voltairian smirk with which we are familiar" (*GCM*, 101).[39]

To avoid these kinds of problems in analyzing the joke's relation to its audience, I might further revise my definition to say a joke is "a text in a context that allows someone to take it as an occasion of humor — that is, as conveying a nonserious or playful meaning, usually inspiring smiles or laughter.'' In this way (I do not pretend to a complete definition) I would shift the emphasis from the joke as a formal object to the social situation of its reception. At the same time I could avoid the problem of a coercive universality, as only ''someone'' need identify the joke as such.

Nevertheless, this definition is perhaps even more coercive than my previous, less sophisticated approaches. For this version implies that ''someone,'' an individual or individuals, may grasp a joke in isolation from a more general field of social relations. It implies that we act as separate individuals in deciding on differences of genre, context, and other forms of power in which meaning is produced. In other words, it still implies that a formal definition of a joke is not political. It obscures the consideration that a joke is an effect contingent upon forces that may be identified with individuals but are never entirely coincident with them. Therefore, it fails to account for the fact that the joke about vaginas I quoted earlier might not be a joke at all (might be an assault, or simply an example,[40] or a compliment, and so on), depending on how it is told or read. It fails to account for the fact that a bit of behavior, an image, or any other kind of text may be a joke *and* a threat *and* an assault. Moreover, it ignores the fact that people may be compelled to ''take a joke,'' or to consider a text as a joke, when they do not want to. Such events occur, even though we are told by a psychoanalytic critic, Norman Holland, that culture ''does not pressure us so much as it either confines us or broadens us'' and that culture physically coerces us ''only'' by denying ''some individuals some choices.''[41] In descriptions like this, culture again appears as a game: no courts, no prisons, no police states but in words.

To resist the authority of the humanist concept of culture, one must insist on a definition of jokes and all other signifying practices according to their historical articulation. Analyzed in this way, the meaning of a particular text is theoretically unlimited, since political perspectives are as various as are imaginable subjectivities. There is no proper context for understanding a text, no such thing as a work ''in its own time,'' because this singular ''context'' or ''time'' papers over political differences and possibilities. Simply because a text has found meaning in a particular society, we need not imagine ourselves to be restricted by that society in making sense of it. However, if we are not aware of the historical dimension of any act of interpretation—if we imagine any interpretation has a transcendent or objective authority—we are repressing political differences and the possibility of political change. If we adopt the attitude of neutrality, we are producing deviancy in order to produce our identities. Only through an insistence on the politics of rhetoric can one resist this tendency to turn cultural understanding into cultural idealism.

If we are to avoid the trap of neutrality, the appearance of a genre like the joke must be analyzed politically as a construction of meaning, which, like any such construction, bespeaks specific organizations of power. Then we can still analyze jokes even though "the joke," closely regarded, dissolves into a heterogeneous play of differences (wit, humor, comedy, satire, puns, insults, threats, promises, courts of law . . .). We can become critics if we regard history as rhetoric and thus refuse to put history into a rhetorical prison. Rather than acting as if there are no police states but in words, we can act with an understanding of the materiality of signifying practices, including those involving language.

This is not to say that in a text we are faced with an incomprehensible chaos of meaning. The range of meaning in a text is always severely limited by the politics put into play by a particular approach. In other words, it is limited by the rhetorical authority called upon in a particular instance of interpretation. For this reason, texts can never be perfectly translated between contexts even though they have no proper context and can always be displaced from one context to another. (The famous untranslatibility of jokes and other kinds of texts, such as poems, is not an argument for an objective theory of the text; it is an argument against an idealist treatment of such concepts as form, genre, structure, and reception.) Within the articulation of any reading, there is always an objective limitation to a text's power of meaning. An example is the limitation, in the present analysis of the joke about the Texan and the Harvard man, that this joke cannot be regarded as an innocent bit of play.

This latter is no small consideration. It would be as wrong to say there is no such thing as an innocent joke as it would be to say all jokes are fraught with political significance. I cannot read this joke for my purposes here without it being something other than the "same" words were when I first told them, say, to a friend over the phone. However, to analyze this consideration in terms of the politics of reading is not to say it is foolish to speak of a story being "just a joke" or to believe a particular telling of a joke is "innocent." It only means that innocence, like any other quality, is a political relation. *Political* does not mean guilty; it means mobile, subject to change, open to possibility, open to other powers of meaning.

III

A new joke acts almost like an event of universal interest; it is passed from one person to another like the news of the latest victory.[42]

As it remains one of the more provocative studies of jokes and interpretation, Freud's *Jokes and Their Relation to the Unconscious* is a useful text for exploring the question of the politics of reading. Certainly it would be easy to analyze the politics of Freud's interpretation of jokes. These days, that is, one might analyze the politics in which certain differences of education, class, and gender are assumed to be universal and universally correlated with differences of behavior.

After all, it is for this reason that Freud can worry over the formal definition of a joke, its different types, its difference from the jest, and so on, like the veriest philosopher: because he takes his reading to be universal. More simply still, one might consider his examples of jokes with special reference, say, to the role of women in them and to Freud's comments on that role. A male scientist who never says a word about objectification while commenting more than once about a joke in which women are alternatively umbrellas and taxicabs, wives and whores, is not really guarding his universal flanks from a political analysis.

To say this kind of analysis would be easy is not to say it is unnecessary or unimportant. Nor is it to say the reading undertaken here would be harder or, to use another term that might be Freudian, more valuable. My reading is, perhaps, only a little more unlikely. It is more useful to the work at hand because it turns away from a conventional consideration of Freud's politics to concentrate on a particular instance of Freud's reading—which is political anyway, according to my argument. However, the politics of Freud's reading and Freud's politics as they are conventionally understood are not precisely the same. If the latter involve certain positions—religious skepticism, political liberalism, and so on— the former involve the more general question of how Freud assumes the position.

In any case, consider the strange career of one joke, the "Home-Roulard,"[43] in *Jokes and Their Relation to the Unconscious*. Freud returns to it several times, as he does to a number of other jokes in this study, but the Home-Roulard's movements through the text are particularly intriguing. Like Trabb's boy in Dickens's *Great Expectations*, this character, the Home-Roulard, seems to possess a significance disproportionate to its minor role in the text. It is a bad joke, Freud tells us, and yet—he takes care to add in a footnote—"As soon as we take into consideration the peculiar pleasure derived from jokes, we find that the 'bad' jokes are by no means bad as jokes—that is, unsuitable for pleasure." (So John Stuart Mill noted that bad jokes "do affect people's minds."[44]) Therefore, Freud concludes, "it would be unjust to exclude examples like the 'Home-Roulard' from the discussion of the nature of jokes" (*JRU*, 121 n).

This character first makes its appearance when Freud is trying to describe a major division in types of jokes. As he glancingly acknowledges, this division echoes the distinction in idealist aesthetics between pure art, or art proper, and forms of representation that do not have about them the definitive quality of disinterested playfulness. The reader needs to know that *anziehend* may mean both "attractive" and "the act of dressing" and that "Home-Rule" was a topic of some note in late nineteenth-century Austria. Consider:

> From the point of view of throwing theoretical light on the nature of
> jokes, innocent [*harmlosen*] jokes are bound to be of more value to us
> than tendentious ones, and empty [*gehaltlosen*] jokes of more value than
> thoughtful [*tiefsinnigen*] ones. Innocent and empty jokes are likely to

get the problem of jokes before us in its purest form, since with them we avoid the danger of being confused by their purpose or having our judgement misled by their good sense. On the basis of such material our perception can make a new advance [*kann unsere Erkenntnis einen neuen Fortschritt machen*].

I will select the most innocent possible example of a verbal joke:

"A girl to whom a visitor was announced while she was at her toilet complained: 'Oh, what a shame that one mayn't let oneself be seen just when one's at one's most *anziehend!*' " (Kleinpaul, 1890.)

Since, however, doubts arise in me after all as to whether I have a right to describe this joke as being non-tendentious, I will replace it by another one which is extremely simple and should really not be open to that objection.

At the end of a meal in a house to which I had been invited as a guest, a pudding of the kind known as 'Roulard' was served. It requires some skill on the part of the cook to make it; so one of the guests asked; "Made in the house?" To which the host replied: "Yes, indeed. A home-*roulard.*" (*JRU*, 94)

Freud has some difficulty in figuring out where he should begin to illustrate innocence, and one may well face a similar difficulty in understanding this passage. First of all, though, consider the way a pudding displaces a girl *en déshabillé*. On the surface of it, the pudding may indeed seem more innocent than the girl. Why, though, should Freud retain in his argument the false beginning (if it is that) of this not-so-innocent joke about the girl?

The translation of the Standard Edition of Freud's works offers one possible interpretation, one that might even be called a Freudian analysis if it seemed intentional. It translates *einen neuen Fortschritt* as "fresh advances." In this suggestive translation, Freud is making a fresh advance, a sexual move, in the guise of innocence. He is mimicking the role of the girl in the joke, a role that demonstrates the complicity of innocence and its other, even as he tries to make a distinction between these qualities. Thus, if we follow this translation, in the very style of his writing Freud becomes the subject of his own analysis. This flustered style is equivalent to the flustered girl, and Freud includes and then rejects the joke about the girl because he must both admit and deny his implication in his own theory.

Bad jokes, we know, often make people groan rather than laugh. Indeed, this is how they may be identified as bad jokes, as Freud remarks. This reading may seem like a bad joke, a groaner, if it suggests that an element of subjectivity appears in Freud's scientific analysis with embarrassing obviousness or with crude desire, as in Freud's description of "smut."

This is not to say such a reading is wrong. After all, it does seem necessary to explain the entrance of this style of spontaneity ("Since, however, doubts arise in me after all'') into this piece of writing, which had some revisions made for its second edition and in any case is hardly a work that generally shows signs of hasty composition. Even without the translation of the Standard Edition, one might have found Freud's vacillation over this joke rather suggestive. Why is there this *naïvité* or *faux naïvité* in Freud's presentation (Freud also writes of the *naïve* and *faux naïve* in *Jokes*)? Why this displacement of one joke by another at this point in the text? For even if one accepts the Freudian interpretation of Freud's verbal behavior here, it is not enough merely to point to the guilty inno- cence of the pen with which he tries to distinguish aesthetic purity in jokes. Pre- sumably, one wants to explain in more detail the significance of this style.

One could elaborate further the analysis of this passage by adding another reading that now, these days, also seems relatively obvious. If it is not a bad joke, it may be a cliché that will create little or no effect (Freud also writes of clichés in *Jokes*). This cliché arises if one argues that the pudding displacing the girl is only superficially more innocent, with no content or purpose to disturb our judg- ment.

In commenting on this second joke after his initial presentation of it, Freud writes that the "single word," *Home-Roulard*, "has transported us, with the economy of a long détour in thought, from the circle of ideas of the kitchen to the remote one of politics" (*JRU*, 123). It is this movement that he identifies as the source of this joke's innocent pleasure. However, in an age in which "the per- sonal is political" has become a feminist slogan, interpreting this innocence does not take much doing. In this interpretation, *home* is a pun on *homme*. We see that the kitchen and the pudding—and, for that matter, the girl incommoded by her visitor—are remote from politics only within a patriarchal and capitalist defini- tion of politics. Within that definition, the Home-Roulard *is* a joke and arguably works according to Freud's reading of it. However, this definition is itself polit- ical and, within Freud's terminology, tendentious. Freud classifies tendentious jokes as either being obscene, aggressive, cynical, or skeptical; and it does not take a genius to see how the political situation implicated in this joke—the oppo- sition of the categories of the domestic and the political—affects the definition of the obscene, implies an aggression toward women, and is cynical toward the domestic authority seemingly given to women. (I leave the question of the skep- tical aside for the moment, for reasons that will become apparent.)

Again, I do not emphasize the ease of this reading because I consider it trivial. I do so because, again, one could say Freud has anticipated it. He has given this political reading of the pudding as he has given the Freudian reading of the flus- tered girl's displacement by it. Thus it is that we find him, after he has labored for some pages over the distinction between innocent and tendentious jokes, pointing out in the next section of his study that "strictly speaking only jests are non- tendentious," or serving only to produce pleasure. He writes that all jokes, prop- erly speaking, promote their thought by "setting themselves up against an inhibiting and restricting power," which is that of "the critical judgement" (*JRU*, 132, 133). One can extrapolate from this passage a political analysis of the sort I made earlier; and in fact Freud cites the play of schoolchildren, university students, scientists, drunken men, and artists as belonging to a "rebellion against the compulsion of logic and reality [that] is deep-going and long-lasting" (*JRU*, 126). Moreover, his study includes references to the mockery of oppressive institutional forms and procedures, including those of language.

Still, there remains the problem of explaining this improvisational style, which is extremely improvident in a study that identifies itself as a scientific work. What is the significance of this waste of energy, this construction of the unforeseen, this narrative turn? Freud says an interest in vision is typically a displacement of an interest in touch: If we accept for the moment this narrative sequence, what is Freud touching on at these points in his writing where his vision clears, where he surprises himself with his revisions?

This is not a question of finding fault with Freud's writing. It is not even a question of finding fault with his logic—as one could, of course, in any number of places in this text. The question is one of style rather than one of logic or truth. However, this question of style may be extremely important if one wants an understanding of the Home-Roulard, the displaced girl, and the problems of defining reading and politics I have taken these to represent. Freud even argues that jokes are entirely a matter of style. Whatever else a paraphrase and an analysis may be, Freud notes, and whatever value they may have, they are no longer jokes: they do not make us laugh. So in the end, if we follow the Home-Roulard far enough, this all may have something to do with logic and truth.

This Home-Roulard is not merely a bad joke, within Freud's estimation, one in which "the only existing link between the two disparate ideas is the one word" (*JRU*, 120–21 n), and not only a bad joke that finally is found to be tendentious rather than innocent. It is also a joke that suffers from being topical. Of "the moment of topicality [*das Moment der Aktualität*]," Freud says, "There are jokes which are completely independent of this condition, and in a monograph on jokes we are obliged to make almost exclusive use of examples of this kind." However, as he goes on to explain, the unfortunate Home-Roulard is not among these.

> For instance, the joke made by my friendly host when he called a
> pudding that was being served a "Home-Roulard" . . . does not seem
> to me to-day nearly so good as it did at the time, when "Home Rule"
> provided a standing head-line in the political columns of our daily
> papers. In attempting to estimate the merits of this joke I now attribute
> them to the fact that a single word has transported us, with the economy
> of a long détour in thought, from the circle of ideas of the kitchen to
> the remote one of politics. But at the time my account would have had
> to be different, and I should have said that this word transported us

from the circle of ideas of the kitchen to that of politics, which was remote from it but was certain of our lively interest because we were constantly concerned with it.

Freud comments, "The vital force of topical jokes is not their own; it is borrowed, by the method of allusion, from those other interests, the expiry of which determines the fate of the joke as well." The moment of topicality, he continues, is "indeed an ephemeral but especially rich source of pleasure joined to the sources of the joke itself [*Das Moment der Aktualität, welches als eine vergängliche Lustquelle zwar, aber als besonders ergiebige zu den eigenen des Witzes hinzutritt*]" (*JRU*, 122–24).

The independent joke, one might say, is another version of the innocent joke. Therefore, it is destined to be contradicted. Just as the innocent joke proves not to be innocent, so will the independent joke prove to be dependent on topical allusion. Given a different viewpoint, it will be destined to take part in a narrative (let us make a small joke) of disallusionment. Is this reading of Freud's improvisatory style also authorized by Freud?

On the one hand, every joke is said to call for "a public of its own" in such a way that "laughing at the same jokes" becomes "evidence of far-reaching psychical conformity" (*JRU*, 151). In this description all jokes would seem to be topical, related to a limited community. On the other hand, we have been told allusion is a special although common condition: "Allusion is perhaps the commonest and most easily manageable method of joking and is at the ground [*zu Grunde*] of the majority of short-lived jokes that we are accustomed to inserting into our conversation and that cannot endure a detachment from this mother-earth and independent preservation [*die wir in unsere Unterhaltung einzuflechten gewöhnt sind, und welche eine Ablösung von diesen Mutterboden und selbständige Konservierung nicht vertragen*]" (*JRU*, 79–80).

So again a contradiction appears, and again the question of narrative direction arises. This is the question of whether the detour Freud analyzes in the moment of topicality ever brings us back home: whether it really is controlled by an "economy." For this detour is as much a factor in the presentation of Freud's analysis as it is in the jokes under his analysis. In discussing the relation of repression to tendentious jokes, Freud may say, "Instead of setting out the long détour by which I reached an understanding of this situation, I will try to put forward [*darzustellen*] a short synthetic exposition of it" (*JRU*, 135). But this putting forward or representation is itself a detour. It implies an original ground from which the exposition is detached, just as Freud's analysis in its moments of unforeseen revision creates such an effect of detachment, and just as his analysis regenerates innocence (in the form of the jest) even as it conflates the innocent joke and the tendentious joke, the lady and the pudding.

Again, then, it would be easy to add to the Freudian and the feminist readings of the Home-Roulard. One could give a Derridean reading that points to a series of complexly overlapping terms—*pudding/girl, purity/impurity, innocence/tendentiousness, pleasure/seriousness, jest/joke, economy/detour*, and so on—and describes in this series a rhetorical logic that echoes not only idealist aesthetics but also all of Western metaphysics. As if to suggest this reading just as it suggested the Freudian analysis, the Standard Edition translates the passage on "the method of allusion" in the following terms: "The factor of topicality is a source of pleasure, ephemeral it is true but particularly abundant, which supplements the sources inherent in the joke itself." Moreover, the editors' notes giving historical references and explaining problems of translation serve practically, one might say, to deconstruct Freud's notion of universality. (Unless one reads it as it appears in the passage I have taken as my epigraph: "A new joke acts *almost* like an event of universal interest" [my italics].)

In the narrative turn of Freud's analysis, then, one would see the logic of the supplement: the addition, revision, or reclassification of textual elements that marks at once an excess and a lack of meaning in the text or, again in Freud's terms, at once a deepness and an emptiness of meaning. Freud classifies allusion as a kind of "indirect representation [*indirekte Darstellung*]" (*JRU*, 80), and in this reading the notions of direct and indirect representation would also join in the logic of the pudding and the girl.

Again, to say such a reading is easy—now, today—is neither to discredit it nor to applaud it. Nor would I wish this series of false starts in my own analysis to suggest that these different types of reading, like the different types of jokes in Freud's representation, can be described as if this representation makes no difference: as if these types of reading exist as enchanting forms that can be detached from social circumstances in which they touch on matters as trivial and profound as teaching and tenure, hiring and publication, knowledge and nonsense and power.

Following the detour that I have taken to be Freud's text, turning roundabout these readings I have imagined to be formally distinguishable from each other, my argument is that language is neither illusion (as it appears in certain readings of idealist metaphysics, Marxist dialectics, and Freudian heremenutics) nor a groundless allusion (as it appears in certain readings of Derridean deconstruction). It is better described as a joke. "A joke," I quote, alluding to the moment of topicality I have imagined throughout this analysis and have, in a sense, turned into a narrative that raises certain questions about reading. Or: "literary theory," I say again, quoting myself, "is a joke."

What sense does it make to say such a thing? To so twist the meaning of a word like *language* as to equate it with a joke, or to so twist the meaning of *a joke?* (But then, to react this way, we would have to know what language is, seriously speaking—we would have to have a metaphor that is not a catechresis, a metaphor that would be a proper definition . . .)

I am arguing that it makes no sense to ask whether this description is serious or not—whether it is *just*—or whether it is just a joke. In analyzing a topical joke about the names of two brothers, one of whom was insulted by the joke, Freud says of the insult, "I cannot say whether it was justified. But jokes do not as a rule enquire into that" (*JRU*, 21). My argument is that it is not in jokes but rather in the historical articulation of jokes that the concern with justice appears. Justice has no meaning unless one considers terms like *joking, seriousness*, and *language* as forms of discourse or, in other words, as terms constructed of and through political differences.

Freud said "it would be unjust to exclude examples like 'Home-Roulard' from the discussion of the nature of jokes." Why? What, then, is justice? Just us, runs the joke: the community, or culture, implicated in the ability to make sense of any joke or of any theory. This culture is not the same as the public Freud speaks of in *Jokes and Their Relation to the Unconscious*, those who can appreciate the joke as such, who can properly appreciate it. Nor is it the same as the public that can interpret the joke by Freudian or other means. The culture I am describing is not and can never be entirely present: independent, universal, innocent, neutral, transcendent, or anything of that sort. It is rather the imaginary law that has to exist, that is read into being, so a joke can have meaning. This culture is heterogeneous and always only imaginary. It is subject to irreducible political differences. For this reason it cannot be defined as a hermeneutic circle, which for all its indeterminacy remains an idealizing form. This culture can be recognized only in terms of the issue of rhetorical authority. To view texts socially and historically in this way is to see the truth, logic, and cultural context they address as issues of politics, not of "the world." Instead of chasing the tail of their favored idealization of totality, critics taking this approach would challenge the rhetorical effects taken to represent totality.[45]

This sense of culture detours questions of identity and diversity, propriety and illegitimacy, and reality and nonsense. ("Reality is for those who can't face up to drugs" says a contemporary joke that echoes Freud's linking of students, scientists, artists, and drunkards.) Culture in this sense is the imaginary power of authority contested within and between different readings, within and between different signifying practices of all sorts. Its definition is not decided by analytic insight or by narrative discovery but rather by the struggle over justice, the contest over meaning, that is social life. It is in this social life, this history to which my writing is appealing, that it is just to identify language as a joke: as a struggle over meaning that demands an interminable analysis.

Let us return, then, to Freud's discussion of the "special position" of the skeptical joke, which now may be said to name the transformation of girls into puddings and kitchens into politics and other such nonsense:

To the classes of tendentious jokes that we have considered so far—
    exposing or obscene jokes,
    aggressive (hostile) jokes,
    cynical (critical, blasphemous) jokes—
I should like to add another, the fourth and rarest, the nature of which can be
illustrated by a good example:

"Two Jews met in a railway carriage at a station in Galicia. 'Where are you
going?' asked one. 'To Cracow', was the answer. 'What a liar you are!' broke out
the other. 'If you say you're going to Cracow, you want me to believe you're going to Lemberg. But I know that in fact you're going to Cracow. So why are you
lying to me?' "

This excellent story, which gives an impression of oversubtlety, evidently
works by the technique of absurdity. The second Jew is reproached for lying because he says he is going to Cracow, which is in fact his destination! But the
powerful technical method of absurdity is here linked with another technique,
representation by the opposite, for, according to the uncontradicted assertion of
the first Jew, the second is lying when he tells the truth and is telling the truth by
means of a lie. But the more serious substance of the joke is the question about
the conditions of truth [*die Frage nach den Bedingungen der Wahrheit*]. The
joke, once again, is pointing to a problem and is making use of the uncertainty of
one of our commonest concepts. Is it the truth if we describe things as they are
without troubling to consider how our hearer will understand what we say? Or is
this only jesuitical truth, and does not genuine truth consist in taking the hearer
into account and giving him a faithful picture of our own knowledge? I think that
jokes of this kind are sufficiently different from the rest to be given a special
position. What they are attacking is not a person or an institution but the certainty
of our knowledge itself, one of our speculative possessions. The appropriate
name for them would therefore be "sceptical" jokes. (*JRU*, 115)

In reading this joke, in which philosophers might recognize an example of the
dizzy Gricean runaround of communication, do we laugh, with Freud, at the fact
that the remote circle of politics is brought into the kitchen—or do we laugh (also
with Freud?) at the very notion of this distance, this difference? Do we laugh,
with Freud, at the girl whose word gives her away—or do we laugh (again with
Freud?) at this distance, this difference, between the attractive and the clothed?
"Freud" is another name for this joke, this language, this theory, in which the
approach to a destination is always a detour of subjectivity through society; in
which truth is always a pleonasm, "genuine truth," a trope; in which there always remain other possibilities for laughter, for a new victory; in which the conditions of truth are always only possible.

IV

*Excessive laughter typically occurs in an older population and
is often associated with senile and presenile dementia. It was
originally described in patients with tertiary syphilis who
manifested a characteristic style of self-directed humor known
as "Witzelsucht," in which complex parodies were made of
one's own actions or words. Excessive laughter can always be
differentiated from natural laughter by its lack of social context
and because other listeners or participants never share the
patient's sense of humor or enjoyment.*

—Duchowny, "Pathological Disorders of Laughter"[46]

"It's just a joke" and "I'm only joking" are common expressions in English.
They are models, perhaps, for phrases generally associated with horror films:
"It's just a movie" or "It's only a movie." And of course there are still other
variations: "I'm just teasing," "I was only kidding," "That's mere rhetoric,"
"That's just a lot of talk," and so on.

At first glance, an expression like "It's just a joke" probably seems comforting. It does not appear as an idea but as a reassuring interjection or sympathetic
noise. Just as the appropriate response to a friend's sad story may be the simple
punctuation of vocables like "oh," "ah," "wow," "shit," or "geez," so may
"It's just a joke" seem an expression that comes to us as naturally as the gesture
of reaching to touch someone disturbed by a monster, cinematic or otherwise.[47]
It seems an innocent expression, the kind of thing a sociologist or ethnographer
might analyze to show how people order their social relations through the most
commonplace as well as the most complex conversation.

Even if we try to analyze them in terms of ideas, phrases like "It's just a joke"
may seem to evoke a soothing innocence. In this commonplace reading, such
phrases tell us that we should not take a joke "too seriously." They suggest that
the joke is play, pure and simple. In this commonsensical analysis, we hear the
voice of Kant speaking to us from the crowd. We are told we should not be disturbed in any way by a joke because it does not speak beyond itself. If an event
is just a joke or a person only joking, this figure is innocent of meaning. "I didn't
mean anything by it," we say. Or "It doesn't matter," we may say, "I was only
kidding." The joke is treated as if it does not signify. It is treated as representational play rather than responsible meaning.

However, phrases of this order may be given a different reading. In this
second reading, the very need to assert innocence in such a defensive way suggests that meaning is not so easily discarded. In using these expressions to distinguish play from the socially responsible practice of meaning, we paradoxically
suggest that this distinction is bogus. It appears bogus because it cannot go with-

out saying. It cannot automatically illuminate our lives with moments, frames, and territories of innocence. It must depend for its light on an agreement won from other people, and it must flicker and die out when such agreement is not forthcoming.

Even as they serve to exculpate the joke as an object or joking as an activity, expressions like "It's just a joke" suggest that meaning never has anything to do with objects or activities in themselves. They may even be said to call into question the concept of an object or activity "in itself." Critically regarded, such expressions tell us that the difference between "natural laughter" and "excessive laughter"cannot always be determined by physicians, psychologists, aestheticians, sociologists, anthropologists, or anyone else. They remind us of the disturbing similarity between laughter and suffering: the similarity between expressions of pleasure and pain that is exploited, for instance, in *Looking for Mr. Goodbar* when the character played by Dianne Keaton is murdered and her strobe-lit face appears to mimic its earlier appearance in scenes of ecstasy. We are reminded that social context and proper behavior cannot be established with neutrality except in relation to the politics of established institutions, such as medicine, the discipline of sociolinguistics, or the practice of misogyny in motion pictures.

The situation of laughter is that of language, which appears with self-evident propriety only when we assume a mastery of its forms that the materiality of language, when closely analyzed, rejects. This materiality, to which we must always return if we are to resist passively receiving and reproducing culture, is not simply the physical text in question. It is that text as a social object, the object of historically specific practices through which it is institutionalized; read or ignored; distributed, censored, or quoted; made part of this tradition or that; and, in short, constituted as an object. The materiality that repels formal propriety is not the limit to reading or to reason, as pathology might be suggested to be the boundary to normality or nonsense the border to sense, so that we simply know our limits when we come up against it. Rather, this materiality is history as the subject of discourse. To put it another way, it is the historicity of all subjectivity, the implication of transgression in all the limits of our knowledge, or of unconsciousness in consciousness. From this perspective, we can describe this materiality in terms of the way a word at which we stare may come to lose its sense, take on the abstract and fragmented quality that letters and figures may have in dreams, and thus lead us to see that meaning does not exist outside of the social relations in which it is implicated in conflicts of perception, feeling, action, identity . . .

In their very form expressions like "It's just a joke" imply that meaning is a power and that we struggle over this power in relationships with others. So a phrase like "It's just a joke" carries its own negative within it. To say a story is "just a joke" is to say as well that it is not just a joke, that it may be other than a joke. This phrase may indeed convey innocence, but only by evoking a world in which this quality is contingent upon communicative agreements that can never be entirely taken for granted. We may be reminded of the way another phrase, "You're kidding," often is used ironically to mean "You're not kidding" but even so remains uncertain as an illocutionary form, on the boundary between a question and an assertion.

It might seem that Freud's entire analysis in *Jokes and Their Relation to the Unconscious* is directed against the commonplace reading of expressions like "It's just a joke." Is not his entire analysis devoted to showing how behaviors commonly thought to be innocent of meaning—jokes, parapraxes, dreams, neurotic symptoms, and so on—are actually extraordinarily dense with meaning? And yet, as we can see in the case of the Home-Roulard, innocence persists in putting itself forward in Freud's writing. In ways unaccountable within any unified reading of this theory, his work appears structured by a relation between innocence and its other resembling the relation in phrases like "It's just a joke" and in jokes like the story about the Texan and the Harvard man. His writing seems to put forward this paradoxical relation even in its portrayal of the changes played upon the intentions of the haughty ego by the bumptious Unconscious or id, as these characters lead him to develop a grammar radically divided against itself and thus readily appropriated in contradictory ways by Marxists, feminists, and other varieties of readers.

From this perspective, Freud's writing on jokes appears to recapitulate the problematic nature of phrases like "It's just a joke." In thinking of this struggle over meaning, then, it is interesting to see that at one point in his study Freud says "the passionate movements of a modern conductor seem comic to any unmusical person who does not know how to understand their necessity [*die ihre Notwendigkeit nicht zu verstehen weiss*]" (*JRU*, 190). It seems as if this confrontation, this troublesome difference between cultural authority and uncultured nature, in fact may be the whole story of his analysis, and a story at least as importantly represented in this marginal moment as in his elaborate descriptions of psychical mechanisms.

This situation is not peculiar to Freud's work, either. For instance, Enid Welsford has noted how "it is curious to remark that there is a constantly recurrent tendency to bring buffoons and learned men into connection with one another."[48] Similarly, "we laugh at fools," wrote Hazlitt, "and at those who pretend to be wise."[49] Or, as Kant wrote in a discussion of jokes,

One laughs at the simplicity of the nature that does not understand
dissembling, and yet one also enjoys the simplicity of the nature that
crosses up that art. One waits for the common manner of the remark
that is affected and carefully planned to have a beautiful appearance;

and behold! it is the unspoiled innocent nature that one did not expect to find, and that the man displaying it did not mean to uncover.[50]

As these writers and innumerable others who have dealt with the subject of comedy attest, a great deal of humor turns on the relation between the cultured and the uncultured, with each side taking its turn in being the butt of the joke.

Kant is a particularly interesting complement to Freud. Analyzing jokes in the *Critique of Judgment*, he writes,

> In everything that is supposed to excite a lively convulsive laugh there must be something absurd (in which the Understanding, therefore, can have no satisfaction). *Laughter is an emotion from the sudden transformation of a tense expectation into nothing.* Precisely this transformation, which is certainly not enjoyable for the understanding, yet indirectly pleases it very forcefully for a moment. Therefore its cause must be in the influence of the representation on the body and in the interaction of this on the mind. It is not, indeed, that the representation is objectively an object of pleasure (for how could a delusive expectation give pleasure?), but simply that it brings about an equilibrium of the vital powers of the body through a mere play of representations.

He then discusses some examples, the following among them:

> When the heir of a rich relative wants to arrange a properly ceremonial funeral, but he complains he cannot properly succeed, "because" (says he) "the more money I give my mourners to look sad, the happier they look," we laugh loudly; and the reason is that an expectation is suddenly transformed into nothing. One must note well that it must not be transformed into the positive opposite of an expected object—for that is still something and can often be afflicting—but into nothing.[51]

As with Freud, it does not take much doing to see specific political attitudes in what Kant regards as "nothing" or as a "mere play of representation." In this instance, rejected from the Understanding are the possibility that pleasure and grief might not be categorically opposed emotions; the possibility of irrational gratification; the possibility of a culturally significant relation between money and the transcendence of death; and thus, in general, the possibilities Freud analyzed as the basis of his revolutionary work.

Of course, Kant's example is not worth considering here as a curiosity or error in relation to Freud's work. It is valuable for the irony that appears when one considers how Freud's work does, in effect, criticize Kant's and yet remains as unconscious of the politics of its rhetoric as is the *Critique of Judgment*. Moreover, Freud's is not the only modern work that remains marked by the idealist aesthetics represented by Kant. From writers like J. Huizinga and Roger Callois right through to the editor of a recent anthology of sociolinguistic essays on speech play,[52] one finds idealist definitions of play, joking, and art still being reproduced—even when a writer carefully notes, as in the last instance, that play is culturally relative. Even writers who explicitly distinguish their ideas from Kant's, such as Jurij Lotman, still may end up with definitions of jokes that are idealized because they fail to recognize the possibility of disputed definitions.[53] As with Kant and Freud, one finds that the claims of innocence in these works repress the significance of the contest over meaning in social life.

When stated so broadly this idea is banal, like the slogan: Everything is political. In this book the word *political* is bound to seem tiresomely iterated. However, as Derrida suggests, this is a banality "that experience shows us we must unceasingly recall."[54]

In an essay, "Cultural Anthropology and Psychiatry," Edward Sapir took note of this circularity in the dialectic of the wise fool:

It is very doubtful if the normalities of any primitive society that lies open to inspection are nearer the hypothetical responses of an archaic type of man, untroubled by a burdensome historical past, than the normalities of a modern Chinese or Scotchman. In specific instances one may even wonder whether they are not tangibly less so. It would be more than a joke to turn the tables and to suggest that the psychoanalysis of an over-ritualized Pueblo Indian or Toda might denude him sufficiently to set him "regressing" to the psychologically primitive status of an American professor's child or a professor himself.[55]

Still, even while noting that this circularity is "more than a joke" or less than innocent play, Sapir stopped short of appreciating its political implications for the disciplines of anthropology and psychiatry. It is ironic that Bronislaw Malinowski was able to face these implications more squarely precisely because he was a less flexible, less literary thinker:

The African is becoming an anthropologist who turns our own weapons against us. He is studying European aims, pretenses, and all the real and imaginary acts of injustice. Such an anthropology is no doubt mutilated and misguided, full of counter-prejudices, and charged with bitter hostility. It is often blind in its intransigence and sweeping in its wholesale indictment. But it cannot be ignored by the man of science; and it would be better if the practical man did not treat it as a joke or as an insignificant and minor excrescence.[56]

In being more than a joke, Malinowski realized, this dialectic of the wise fool could be a threat to the knowledge and institutions of his society. While he was never shy about putting it to political use, he rejected the idea that the interpretation practiced within his discipline was inherently political; but still he saw that the potential for reversing the relation between the cultured and the uncultured was no joke.

The challenge jokes pose to interpretation may be seen even in the way "culture" has come to be marked by subtly contradictory meanings in the contemporary parlance of the humanities. In its broader sense, *culture* is the term opposed to *nature*. In this sense, it summarizes all that is distinctively human. In its more limited sense, it refers to differentiated groupings of people (the culture of Americans, of Navahos, of the working classes, and so on). Thus, if anthropologists from outer space were to grapple with this word, they might see it as a kind of joke. Culture, the word for all that is human, is also the word that draws the boundaries separating humans from each other. This marvelous "fatality of language" (to borrow Hazlitt's phrase for wit[57]) perfectly illustrates the humanist denial of politics and the inevitable disturbance of language by this denial.

As it has come to appear within the contemporary humanities, the grammar of this word, *culture*, represents the attempt to absorb difference into identity. This denial of political differences leads contemporary intellectuals toward idealist formulations of the mechanism of the joke just as it led writers such as Kant, Hazlitt, and Freud toward such formulations. Within this denial of politics, the confrontation between the cultured man and the fool that appears like a compulsion in jokes and their analysis is defused. Looking beyond disturbances of language, resisting the struggle over meaning evident in phrases like "It's just a joke," intellectuals *culture* jokes. They turn into meaningful forms these works that pose the question of meaning and cultural form. They invent a dialectic of the wise man and the fool contained, circulated, by the joke. Although some writers, like Bergson and Meredith, may emphasize the role of laughter as a means of social control, whereas others, like Baudelaire and Schopenhauer, will see it as a way of going beyond social boundaries, they remain confined by this opposition insofar as they fail to see that it can be understood only in terms of struggles over inequities of power. Otherwise, it becomes a safe, cultured, and harmoniously, tragically, or ironically balanced opposition. It only makes sense that Bergson should write of social control for most of his essay on laughter and yet, in the last section, devote some space to the consideration of laughter as a relaxation of thought, social conventions, and the like. As long as one takes an idealist view of language, this apparent opposition is really a reproduction of sense, a reassuring circularity, an affirmation of the unified identity of interpretation.

What, then, do phrases like "It's just a joke" mean? In the first place the joke is just a text to which we only respond. This first place is always imaginary. It is historically secondary to institutions of communication; but then these institutions can be described only provisionally because they are conceivable only on the basis of history, in which people never meet under conditions of perfect equality.

Thus, like a joke, Freud's text is "only a text." It is only possibly any particular form of meaning or any form of meaning at all. Like a joke, Freud's text produces meaning through the struggle over the definition of signifying forms — a struggle that conveys the sense people make of history in their desires to preserve, alter, or revolt against the terms in which it appears to them. In this struggle preserving the form of a text may be, paradoxically, a most conservative or most radical gesture, depending on the history at stake in a particular reading. Hence the irony that figures like Derrida and Jacques Lacan may claim to be more faithful to the texts of Freud than others and may appear revolutionary, at least for a while, in this faithfulness. A term like *orthodox revolutionary* may seem like a joke, but to say it is a joke is not to say it is without meaning.

V

First child: We have a new baby in our house.
Second child: Boy or girl?
First child: I don't know. They haven't put any clothes on it
*   yet.*

—Old joke

Like common parlance and the language of contemporary disciplines of interpretation, Freud's analysis remains enchanted by the opposition between innocence and meaning. To an extent this enchantment is inevitable and even unremarkable. Significance does not come from this opposition but rather from the rhetorical order in which it finds a part to play, an order never read once and for all because the political differences it represents will take on different meanings within different schemes of interpretation.

This is not to say there is no way of choosing among different interpretations. What is important is the use such an analysis may have in changing the ways our lives are determined by the unconscious reproduction of signifying forms such as boys and girls, homes, politics, innocence, Harvard men, fools, and the Unconscious.

The importance of considering this reproduction may appear more clearly through an analysis of another work that has proven very influential in the humanities and human sciences in the twentieth century, although it is much briefer than *Jokes and Their Relation to the Unconscious*: A. R. Radcliffe-Brown's article, "On Joking Relationships."[58] No anthropologist who has followed Radcliffe-Brown in studying the structure of kinship relationships has been able to ignore this work, and most in fact pay ritual obeisance to it even if they set out to modify it. It is a fitting test, then, for further exploring the denial of politics and the consequences of this denial in the contemporary definition of culture.

Radcliffe-Brown's basic definition of joking relationships is simple enough: they are relationships of "permitted disrespect." Questions certainly may be raised about the breadth of this definition,[59] but of greater concern here than the formal constitution of his object of study is the scheme of analysis to which he subjects it. Joking, he argues, is a feature of relationships that involve both conjunction and disjunction, such as conflicting allegiances within a kinship system. This joking is a way "of organising a definite and stable system of social behaviour in which conjunctive and disjunctive components . . . are maintained and combined." It is not the only way, as Radcliffe-Brown describes it. Ironically, its role is comparable to that which may be played by elaborate formality. "The alternative to a relation of extreme mutual respect and restraint is the joking relationship, one, that is, of mutual disrespect and licence."[60] This comparison goes so far that those who do not adhere to the formal behavior of joking may appear as uncultured rubes. Thus, Radcliffe-Brown quotes another anthropologist, Ruth Landes, on a society in which cross-cousin joking is expected: "cross cousins who do not joke in this way are considered boorish, as not playing the social game."

What is significant about this analysis is the way the anthropologist identifies with the imaginary law of the cultural boundary. Believing he has discerned this law in the specific form of the joking relationship, he places himself within it, uncritically accepting its control. In this way apparent contraries (joking transgression of the law and the formal institution of law) are made identical. Boors, as defined by the social game, are just that. There is no identifying with these figures, with the way they might identify themselves and the significance of their behavior, or with the historical significance this behavior might acquire. Nor does there appear any possibility that culture might be something other than a harmonious organization ratified by the automatic application of the category of deviancy to behaviors that violate its imaginary ideal. Within this analysis, a culture is just a culture to which one only responds. It preserves itself, absorbing all differences within its identity, which is untouched by historical differences. Allowing for certain limited displacements, *culture* acts here in the same way as *context* in Searle's work, *convention* in Culler's, and *community* in Fish's.

A widely cited article published almost a quarter of a century after Radcliffe-Brown's may help to illustrate how the denial of politics takes form within this scheme of understanding. In "Mossi Joking," Peter Hammond attempts to reformulate and refine the tradition of interpretation begun by Radcliffe-Brown. He does so by analyzing the structure of joking and arguing that it "may serve as an adjustive mechanism by providing for the concurrent maintenance of communication, control, and the culturally harmless catharsis of potentially disruptive emotions." (If it did not take us away from the subject at hand, we might pause here to wonder how many ideas are born and shaped by alliteration and similar devices that are "merely" rhetorical, merely matters of style, but in which the materiality of language yet seems to wink at reason.) This language of systematic neutrality rules over an article that says, for instance, as if in passing,

> Because of its relation to the pivotal institution of marriage, sibling-in-law joking is perhaps the most frequently used adjustive mechanism in Mossi social structure. The potential for marital conflict is high. This appears to be due to the combined factors of a sexually differentiated enculturative experience that results in marked dissimilarities in adult male and female personality; to an age difference between husbands and wives of at least ten years; to the classic stresses of polygyny; to the subordinate status of Mossi women, particularly of junior wives within their husband's patriclan; and to the possible dissatisfaction of a woman's parents, particularly her mother, at the loss of their daughter's services or at the inadequacy of bride-wealth payments.[61]

Culture is composed of differences as radical as these, and yet culture is conceived always to remain itself, a coherent and homogenous mechanism. It is conceived as a law to which all the subjects under this analysis belong equally, no matter what the disparities may be in their experience, social position, gender, or economic role. The text of culture, like the text of the joke, is the same text for all. Political differences and contradictions literally cannot appear within this conception of culture, just as multiple and conflicting readings of jokes cannot appear.

But then we need not leave Radcliffe-Brown's original work to see the consequences of this conception of culture spelled out. In a footnote to that article, he mentions a court case in which a man, he believes, "may have committed a breach of etiquette" in joking inappropriately. As Radcliffe-Brown sees it, the man was punished in a "hardly satisfactory way" by a magistrate, presumably a colonial official. "A little knowledge of anthropology," he writes, "would have enabled the magistrate, by putting the appropriate questions to the witnesses, to have obtained a fuller understanding of the case and all that was involved in it."

Even if we do not question the appropriateness of an anthropologist's desire to put the knowledge of his discipline, or even a little bit of it, at the service of colonial law — and this is a big *if* — there still remains the matter of satisfaction in this little drama. With what kind of satisfaction is Radcliffe-Brown concerned here, and whose satisfaction is this? Questions such as these, which are the questions of all politics, the questions of *desire*, simply cannot appear within this conception of culture. They have always already been answered by the anthropologist's identification with this imaginary law. Thus, one may note that the anthropologist does not question the guilt of the man. His only concerns are the manner by which he is judged and the mode of his punishment: the characteristic concerns, the *procedural* concerns, of the humanist intellectual. For Radcliffe-

Brown as for Kant, history is not at issue in jokes. The only issue is that of their proper or appropriate interpretation.

What distinguishes Radcliffe-Brown's work within the history of the human sciences is that the questions constituting interpretation are identified with this law of culture that still maintains an imaginary authority over the discipline of anthropology and, in fact, through a series of limited displacements, over many areas of our contemporary disciplines of interpretation. The case was somewhat different for Kant—broadly speaking, one could call this difference "reason"—whereas for Freud culture had not yet been systematized in its narrower sense, so that he still could conceive of it within the nineteenth-century concept of an evolutionary "civilization." For Radcliffe-Brown, however, the dialectic of the wise fool appears in the relation between variable social forms and individual deviancy that is the story, in short, of the contemporary humanities and human sciences.

If the joke, or any text, is to be conceived without a disabling underwriting of authority, critical theory must comprehend the struggle over meaning represented by a phrase like "It's just a joke." Intellectuals who analyze jokes are wont to comment in passing that studies such as theirs often seem to deal with simple jokes, dull jokes, or jokes, like those of Freud's study, that do not weather time and translation very well; but comprehending that one can respond to a joke by saying "That's not funny" and even by denying that it is a joke must be a rigorous condition of any theory of linguistic form. Popular language here often speaks with more perspicuity than intellectual theory. When we speak of a person who "can take a joke" or of the problem of "getting" or "not getting" a joke, we at least make clear the violence and the struggle involved in joking.

Stated so baldly, this description is mere academic melodrama. When presented within a historical analysis, however, the melodrama typical of contemporary critical theory at least has a chance to become the more subtly detailed language of politics and desire. After all, what text could be more intriguing than those differences over the meaning of cat-killing described by Darnton? In struggles over the definition of jokes, as in the intellectual history echoing in the joke about the Texan and the Harvard man, one may see history appear as conflicting conditions of meaning: conditions as limited and tiresome, or as stunningly illuminated by desire, as our political apprehension allows them to be. Rather than seeing history as an ideally constituted field of knowledge, we may see it as a question of knowledge: the question of change. The fact that the theories, procedures, and information enmeshed in this question are historical variables does not compromise the continuing urgency of this question.

Jokes, then, are special forms of discourse but also examples of the basic condition of any form of discourse: that it is always only possible. As the analysis of jokes may indicate, a text is always contingent on, alluding to, projected toward, appropriated by a political situation that can always be challenged. Like every form of discourse, a joke is a way of reading; and reading is a signifying practice implicated within a conception of culture that may be fought.

The meaning of jokes is always produced by a certain interpretive purpose, even if that purpose is to produce "innocence," "purposelessness," "nonsense," and similar phenomena. This situation of interpretation cannot be formally specified as a universal relation among such figures as speaker, audience, and text because it is always more and less than any such organization. On the one hand, as a political object, an object of desire, the text will always exceed such formalities, bearing the possibility of other and differing readings. On the other hand, as it will always be limited in specific ways, depending on the reading of the moment, the text always falls short of such a formal organization. As previously noted, the difficulty of translating jokes, poetry, or other kinds of texts does not speak to their formal objectivity but to the general consideration that reading is always translation.

Reading is always rereading. A text is not an objective thing but rather the object constituted by the conditions of meaning within a particular discourse. A text is always only the effect of a reading. This consideration does not mean a text is unreal or anything one may wish it to be, as theorists of textual objectivity fear. On the contrary, it means a text is always as real as the forces of politics but, like these forces, historically real: open to change.

There is no text that is not an occasion of power, which is manifested according to distinctions, categories, relationships, procedures, and forms that require a political interpretation, since any formal systematization of them would repress the differences at play in their articulation. However, this is not to say there is no point to formal analysis. It is only to say that any signifying form, like the joke, is as mobile and as open to change as we are able to make it through the critical analysis of rhetorical authority. For authority is always imaginary, but the power of authority is always real.

VI

The gravest Book that ever was written, may be made ridiculous, by applying the Sayings of it to a foolish purpose, for a Jest may be obtruded upon any thing.
— Archbishop Tillotson[62]

Here's a night pities neither wise men nor fools.
—Fool to Lear (3. 2. 12–13)[63]

In criticizing the failure to recognize the politics of interpretation, I began this essay with a text that is a bit of contemporary ephemera, the joke about the Texan and the Harvard man. Perhaps, then, I may imagine a certain balance here by closing with a consideration of a more traditional text that involves an "all-licensed Fool" (1. 4. 206), wise men, authority, hierarchies, struggles over language and politics, and—within a certain reading—all the issues discussed to this point. And since the all-licensed Fool is so important in this reading, it should be noted right from the start that "license" at the time when *King Lear* was written referred, in part, to the requirement that writings be given permission to be published. This requirement included regulations as to the number, location, and activities of printing presses. Performances, including common speech, were also involved in these regulations. To say the Fool is all-licensed is then still to suggest he is licensed, or bound to certain controlling powers that are not those of human nature or universal truth but rather those of a specific form of society.

From the very beginning of *King Lear*, the issues of rhetoric and authority are foregrounded. As a play that begins with the issue of defining and allocating value, *King Lear* also begins with a concern for establishing proper language or a proper way of apprehending language. Particularly interesting in this regard is the scene in which Goneril and Regan verbally whittle Lear's retinue down to nothing (2. 4). This scene is especially dramatic and dramatically disturbing in its consequences because it reduces Lear to language. He is not reduced by his daughters to an ordinary man or to mere nature, as he complains with his sovereign capacity for hyperbole. Instead, his authority is subjected to the license of language that he put up for grabs in the first scene in the play. In this way a mythical ancient England is symbolically introduced into "the general hypertrophy of rhetorical consciousness" that Frank Whigham has described as characterizing the courtly life of Shakespeare's time.[64]

Of course, in this first scene Lear did not realize he was dispensing with his authority. Intending only to evoke a proper language, he never intended to cede authority to discourse. However, in the ceremony he staged with his daughters, in which truth was made to appear as an issue of verbal competition, Lear dramatically awakened language. Without changing his own position of authority, he made it appear that this authority had never really been his. He made it seem as if it had always been an issue of language, a creation of the politics of discourse, rather than the self-evident property of his existence as a man, a father, and a sovereign. In short, he made authority appear as a matter of performance rather than essence.

Lear made it physically possible for Goneril and Regan to mistreat him, but more important, he made it rhetorically appropriate for them to appropriate this power and mock the authority he once held. As language in this scene is awakened to itself—to its license—one might even say the ceremony staged by Lear creates the characters of Goneril and Regan. As the Fool says, they are Lear's "parings" (1. 4. 193).[65] Hence the irony that Goneril and Regan rationalize the way they plan to treat Lear by figuring that his foolish treatment of Cordelia suggests he may treat them as foolishly if he is not forestalled. In giving language its license in this first scene, Lear licenses his own destruction.

This is not to say this opening scene inaugurates all the tragic events of the play, as if authority was authority, pure and simple, before Lear in his dotage made a mistake in judgment and exposed himself to attack. On the contrary, if it shows nothing else, this scene shows that authority cannot be simply distinguished from land, wealth, patriarchal position, and political rule. In fact, one way of describing Lear's error is to say he imagines authority is properly separable from the forms of power through which it is asserted. As a result, he cannot appreciate the profoundly measured significance of Cordelia's pledge—"I love your Majesty/ According to my bond, no more nor less" (1. 1. 94–5)—and cannot anticipate the conclusion logically drawn from his actions by Goneril and Regan. (If Lear should "carry authority with such disposition as he bears," Goneril tells Regan, "this last surrender of his will but offend us" [1. 1. 307–9].) Moreover, the problem of defining authority becomes even more vexed as the play goes on to show this problem entering into relations between youth and their elders; differences between male and female power; questions of how one can distinguish among natural, supernatural, and social influences; discussions of the relative legitimacy of positions given by birth and gained by merit; and a host of other topics that crisscross each other and so give us an impression of the way reality was mapped in Jacobean England.

This opening scene does lead to political conflict, but it does so because Lear makes an ineffectual attempt to repress political differences within his ceremonious evocation of an idealized discourse of love that seems not to make reference to such realities. As Lear might say, this opening scene does not create dissension and violent disruption out of nothing. Conflicts already exist, at least potentially, as Lear recognizes in his attempt to divide his kingdom without antagonizing anyone. One reason these conflicts break into the disturbing actions of the play is that Lear is unwilling to accept that he cannot establish a discourse of authority—more specifically, of courtly love—unmarked by these conflicts. Although Lear deliberately, ceremoniously, calls it into being, he immediately forgets that this discourse of love is discursive performance rather than the essential truth at which he is aiming. He confuses his authority over language with the authority of language, and as a result he is offended by Cordelia's response even though it is a reply measured out in terms of his own artifice. Thus, it is not authority that appears irreducible in this play but rather the difficulty of articulating the relation between authority and power. Lear's authority is not at first inviolate and then abused or betrayed; it is at first an effective power and then, when he loses himself in language, a disruptive absence in the struggle over power in the play. Authority as anything other than a trope of power is what is put into question.

Given this context, Lear's later comment on authority is striking but, typically, a rather obtuse oversimplification: "behold the great image of authority: a dog's obeyed in office" (4. 6. 160–61). Whatever Lear was before its opening scene, the play does not give us grounds to infer that his authority was ever a simple and indubitable property. At best it may have appeared as forms of discourse protected from competition by custom: the discourse of mastery and service, the discourse of courtly love, the discourse of nature, and so on. Although it may have appeared self-evident in this state, authority could not have been self-sustaining. It must have depended on the relations instituted among land, wealth, patronage, armies, and the other forms of power in Lear's world. Even if we imagine a state prior to that which appears in the opening scene of the play, a mythical prehistory to this mythical history, we cannot logically conclude that authority in this state would have appeared essentially different from the way it appears in the play, subject to the disguises, forgeries, acting, lies, and physical violence that flourish among those who would strip Lear of authority and those who would return it to him. (It is when he is disguised, one remembers, that Kent tells Lear, "you have that in your countenance which I would fain call master"; and he is still disguised when he seems to respond to an unmediated presence as he goes on to tell Lear that he is referring to "Authority" [1. 4. 28–30].) In this prehistory, the disguises, forgeries, and other disturbances of this play may not have been recognized as such because the elements of this world may not have been called upon to justify themselves before an idealized conception of language; but still, authority in this state could not have been separated from the license of language. It simply appears that this license may have been entirely possessed by the sovereign: that all language then was sovereign language. The play begins with the problem of a break from the formal sovereignty of the past or, in other words, with the problem of historical change as this is conceivable in a society facing the contradictions in the nature of monarchical government.

So as we can gather from the way authority appears as an issue in *King Lear*, this play does not present us with a question of authority that is in any way universal. The question of authority in this play cannot be generalized over all of Jacobean culture, much less over wider areas of literature and history, unless we ignore the political conditions it puts into play. By the same token, as it is represented in opposition to authority, power in this play is not a value in and of itself. It is complicit with the authority it is made to oppose. Simply to speak of power here as if in reference to an aspect of all societies would be to occlude the politics of this play just as surely as referring to authority as an autonomous value occludes its patriarchal, monarchical, landed, courtly specificity. This consideration holds even if we use terms contemporary with Shakespeare, such as *Machiavellian*, to describe the images of power in this play.[66] Such a term is inaccurate unless we note how the definition of authority in this play teams up with the definition of arbitrary "Machiavellian" power to produce a sense of meaning.

The question of authority can extend our understanding of literature and history if we examine it in terms of the politics of rhetoric. If we question the nature of authority in this play instead of assuming that particular statements, characters, and other aspects of the play naturally hold authority over others—if we do not simply comment on the vicissitudes of authority in this play but instead consider the rhetorical conditions that make it possible for authority to be an issue—we can analyze these historical conditions of meaning. We can see authority brought into question in the play. We can consider history as the subject of political struggles instead of assuming that a coherent ideology, theme, worldview, or historical reality governs this play.

We then can see how this play exceeds the dialectic of the wise fool that has so often served to reproduce a reassuring sense of universality for works like this hallowed tragedy as well as for the most trivial of jokes. At the same time we can see how readers can construe this play so variously in terms of Christian or skeptical themes or in terms of ideas of ontology, nature, sexuality, family, and various other topics. They can do so because they assume boundaries are drawn and values marked in an authoritative way in this work. They do not see how the opening scene of the play may be taken as a virtual parable of the impossibility of regarding discourse as a harmonious consensus or totality that one can command from a neutral position. What is this play about if not the indissoluble relation between the exercise of language and the exercise of inequity, conflict, and violence? When Edmund says, "Fine word, 'legitimate' " (1. 2. 18), how can we measure the irony and seriousness to which this comment is bound except in terms of a difference between joking and serious language that is not coherent within this play and that cannot be made coherent unless we repress the differences of power that exist, in effect, even before the beginning of the play?

So look again. What does it take to make sense of language in this play? Generally the characters in *King Lear* appear trapped in a region of action between sycophancy and martyrdom and in a region of speech between wisdom and foolishness. They are trapped in this scheme of representation because it appears necessary and yet impossible to identify immediately with authority. This is the main contradiction of courtly life as it is portrayed in this play: that truth must speak and yet cannot simply speak itself. It must speak in cryptic, equivocal, or contradictory ways. (Hence the dramatic and verbal paradoxes that flourish in this play.[67]) Truth can receive, adapt to, comprehend, and aid—but not initiate—action. In its origin, action, like speech, must be a deviation from authority. When one strives to maintain or reproduce authority, one cannot escape this contradiction. As the Jacobean motto has it, *Qui nescit dissimulare, nescit regnare*.[68]

In this rule, truth, which is identified with the human subject, is dissevered from power, which is identified with social life. Social practices, including language, cannot help but be disturbed by this contradiction, especially when it is made public by an authority that loses its necessary sovereign reserve, ceases to dissimulate, and thus appears as arbitrary power open to competition. As soon as he makes his authority appear to be subject to discourse, Lear makes it a wandering figure that can never completely coincide with any individual or individual statement. Consequently, it can become exceedingly difficult to distinguish wisdom from foolishness and sycophancy from martyrdom in *Lear*'s language and drama. When the king's authority is exposed to language — when language is exposed to the deadly candor of authority — language becomes the motley forms of discourse that must contend with each other in the play. In this problem of rhetoric we see as well the contradiction of competition, which is instituted as a formal ceremony but immediately exceeds its instituted end; and in this entire scheme of representation we see the politics of Shakespeare's representation of history. We see the conditions of meaning, the authority, with which we must identify in order to support any coherent reading of the play, which is to say, any reading that can formally distinguish truth, whether this be described as Christian, tragic, or whatever. From such a perspective, this drama of a loss of sovereignty is yet designed to produce a language of sovereignty and to make this language appear incontestable, since it encompasses the fate of both kings and clowns.

Society longs for authority and is resentful of power: this is the tension that makes possible all the drama of this play, no matter where we may judge truth to be in any particular instance of speech or action. This rule establishes authority and also establishes its contradiction: its utter inaccessability and deadly candor. In considering how this play can make sense of authority, it is vital to note this rule by which history is conceived. As history is viewed from this standpoint within authority and without power, truth cannot be conceived to rebel against society or to initiate action in any way. History is so conceived in this play that one must follow it rather than change or lead it. The grounds of society are beyond society: human beings are more than social animals. For this reason, the controversy in the play over the origins of things in fate, the stars, the gods, and different conceptions of nature does not undercut authority but rather supports it. This controversy supports authority by distancing it from the practices of social life, including discourse. According to this conception of history, it follows from the fact that human action is always a maneuver that society is governed beyond itself, by an authority to which one is bound even in the perversities of madness and rebellion.

The longing for authority and the resentment of power in this scheme of representation ensure that one will not identify with society and yet will never break with society, because the form of historical change is always indirect: a maneuver of truth. In *King Lear*, only stupidity carries immediate conviction; any other qualities must strive for a compromised expression, as in the way one of Gloucester's statements — "So distribution shall undo excess,/ And each man have enough" (4. 1. 72–3)—is made when he is enfeebled, guilt-stricken, blinded, suicidal, and ignorant of the fact that he is being led by his son, who is disguised as a madman. Conversely, the great danger in this situation is that of naming authority. Giving it this immediate form brings it into the presence of the power that is supposed to differ from it and thus exposes authority to mockery while exposing individuals to harm if they call upon authority, as when Kent tries to come, as Lear puts it, "betwixt our sentence and our power" (1. 1. 172). When Lear calls attention to the implication of authority in power by formally trying to separate them—"Only we shall retain/ The name, and all th'addition to a king" (1. 1. 137–38)—both of these consequences ensue.

Still, it is crucial to see that these consequences, the mockery of authority and the evil that befalls those who call upon it, produce authority, insist on authority, even as they show its downfall. Authority is bound to be produced in this way unless we insist on a political criticism that disrupts the sense that can be made of this play so as to analyze its conditions of meaning.

Through the only authority that seems conceivable in this play, society is made moral as well as historical. The proper maneuver is to identify with authority without identifying it: to identify without naming and yet without saying nothing. The only way to move from discourse into truth is by displacing meaning from oneself onto an authority that must be as urgent as it is nameless. This is the formula for a loyalty that always asserts itself and yet always withholds itself, protects itself, from the deadly candor of authority. In other words, it is the formula of a dedicated courtier laboring to transform this politic dedication into the idealized form of conscience. Moreover, it is a formula for the activity of authorship in a situation in which failure awaits anyone who appears too grossly servile before authority even as censorship and criminal prosecution await anyone who does not measure his or her deference finely enough.

All the shifts of language in this play, from the erasing of Lear's retinue to Edgar's creation of an abyss of words to cure Gloucester of his despair, probe for an immediate source of authority: in familial and biological relationships, in nature, in social hierarchy, in the cosmos, and in language itself, among other places. In response, these maneuvers find nothing but further discourse, especially discourse marked by paradox, which makes it appear that truth never has a safely conventional form. As the Fool says of Goneril and Regan to Lear, "They'll have me whipped for speaking true; thou'lt have me whipped for lying; and sometimes I am whipped for holding my peace" (1. 4. 186–88). Even in the opening scene, when Cordelia says nothing because she has paid attention to the conditions of meaning created by Lear and her sisters, this play may be seen as insisting on the impossibility—and the undesirability—of directly naming authority, speaking truth, and fixing meaning. In other words, it may be seen as insisting on the ever-present potential for values to be transvalued.

"The art of our necessities is strange," says Lear, "That can make vile things precious" (3. 2. 70–1). Or "Be Kent unmannerly/ When Lear is mad," Kent tells the king (1. 1. 147– 48). The transvaluations that permeate the language of characters like these are no different in form from those that make Edmund desire to revise his illegitimacy or Goneril and Regan their position in the kingdom. The only difference is that these latter characters, while equally certain that truth governs language from beyond it, do not long for authority in their resentful desire for power. Despite all their underhanded maneuvers—and this is the telling difference between their maneuvers and those of Lear's adherents—they are not circumspect enough to feel themselves trapped between sycophancy and martyrdom. They lack a conscience, which in this play is nothing more or less than one's limitation to this range of action and speech.

It is not simply the fact that they are disloyal or rebellious, then, that marks these characters out. More significant is the fact that they take on these positions without reserving the name of authority. It is because they admit to no confusion about origins, as in Edmund's scorn at Gloucester's astrological sense of fate, that they are marked out as being evil.

In this perspective, again, we can see that this play does not have meaning in terms of the abuse or the loss and regaining of authority. If it does have meaning, it is because the play is about the havoc wreaked when authority asserts its presence, when society faces the deadly candor of authority. As it links the production of a conscience to a confusion over the name of authority, *King Lear* is an elaborate formulation of the sense of tragic necessity produced when one identifies with both authority and power even as one sees them as radically differing from each other. It is the tragedy of strategy with a conscience or, from a slightly different standpoint, of loyalty with guilt. It is the tragedy of a culture that believes in the power of language and so believes in the necessity of producing conscience to divide this power and to maintain the ideal of authority. The play is designed to demonstrate the stupidity of Edgar's last speech—"The weight of this sad time we must obey,/ Speak what we feel, not what we ought to say" (5. 3. 325–36)—and yet to insist on the virtue of this belief that language should be a matter of truth rather than power.

In this play, as in the joke about the Harvard man and the Texan, the problem with using the dialectic of the wise fool as a basis for interpretation is that we immediately generate a theme of truth and error, nature and artifice, naïvité and pretension, good and evil, or the like, as if we were naming dramatic entities that forever reappear throughout history, speaking to us across the centuries, maintaining the continuities of humanity. When we see the politics at stake in the meaning of *King Lear*, we also see the possibility of understanding the play differently. Then the transvaluations of identities suggested by the relation between Lear and the Fool and by all of the paradoxes in this play do not compose a unified text. They compose a struggle over meaning with no center or ultimate ground except what we bring to it in our desires for meaning or, we might say, in our performance. What I have identified as paradox in this play is neither circular (as in the dialectic of the wise fool) nor irreducible as a rhetorical figure. Approached critically, this figure loses its substance and unity, appearing as one practice of reading among others: one way to make sense of rhetorical deformations, differences, and inequities that cannot support a neutral interpretation. History is the struggle over meaning that this approach causes to appear on the composed surface of the text, on the imaginary ground of culture.

Chapter 2
Ethnographia Mundi

I

*Within the boundaries of the tribe the writ of the same culture
runs from end to end.*

—Malinowski[1]

*The bourne, the well from which the twilit norn, the ancient
goddess of fate, draws up the names is at the edge of the poet's
land—or is the edge itself the well?*

—Heidegger[2]

In twentieth-century anthropology, culture breaks with its past. Like someone
doffing an outmoded suit, culture turns away from *Bildung* or spiritual refinement (Cicero's *cultura animi philosophia est*[3]). "Civilization" in the Enlightenment mode, with its styling of European as universal values, is also put aside.
Like the spiritual dress, it is a fashion henceforth to be resurrected only in nos-
talgic, ignorant, or wanton attack on modernity. A similar fate meets culture as
the name for an unreflective sense of national, racial, or folk superiority.

Divesting itself of this history, culture slips into the uniform of a scientific
concept. By the second half of the twentieth-century, culture becomes the boundary of our social life (culture versus nature) and the source of our social differences as well (the culture of the Navahos, of Americans, of the working class,
and so on). Its writ, its boundary, comes to underwrite all human institutions and
activities. As A. L. Kroeber and Clyde Kluckhohn comment in their survey of

49

the history of this concept, "In explanatory importance and in generality of application it is comparable to such categories as gravity in physics, disease in medicine, evolution in biology."[4]

In some respects this modern culture was first formulated in Germany and England in the late nineteenth century and even earlier.[5] The historicism described by Hans-Georg Gadamer as the outcome to the Romantic critique of the Enlightenment falls under this definition, in which culture draws the boundary of understanding around one's own time or around the context proper to any work, event, or person.[6] Yet it was not until the twentieth century that culture became arguably the most powerful discourse within the interpretation of signifying practices of all sorts. During this time it became basic to the newly institutionalized discipline of anthropology and also appeared integral to much of the work being done in other social sciences and in the humanities. Interpretation in fields as diverse as history, sociology, literary criticism, and psychology came to rely on this hermeneutic boundary that was conceived to be universal and yet geographically and temporally relative. To see the power of this modern conception of culture and the difference it makes in the practice of interpretation, we need only look at how many of the course offerings in a modern university ("The History of France, 1750–1848," "The Medieval Church," "Identity and Community," "Colonial American Literature," and so on) insist on a relation between knowledge and the relative boundaries of time and space. One might almost say that the meaning of culture has been shifted from individual, class, or national aggrandizement to professional comportment. Whereas culture in the liberal humanism of the nineteenth century was thought to transcend politics, culture in this more modern conception encompasses politics along with every other aspect of social life. Rather than asserting the superiority of truth to power, it establishes truth by rationalizing forms of power.

Of course, in universities and elsewhere hosts of intellectuals still claim works must transcend their time if they want to be called art, refer to "our world" in a way that shrinks the globe to a few neighborhoods in North America or Western Europe, or analyze what it means to be human solely on the basis of contemporary white middle-class behavior. We know, too, of the Nazi treatment of *das Volk*. The old fashions will be revived at times, even though modern anthropology would preserve them only in the shadows of memory. The traditional meanings of culture (as in "a cultured man," "uncivilized behavior," and so on) continue today to percolate through popular discourse and rigorous scholarly works. "As late as 1950," notes Marvin Harris,

> Radcliffe-Brown's "Introduction" to *African Systems of Kinship and Marriage* included an opening quote from Gobineau advising Europeans who wish their civilizations to spread of the importance of knowing and comprehending those who were to be benefited. This is followed by the

author's wish that "this book will be read not only by anthropologists, but by some of those who are responsible for formulating or carrying out policies of colonial government in the African continent."

Harris also notes the disturbing fact "that the professionalization of anthropology as a discipline coincided with, and was intimately associated with, the rise of raciology."[7] However, he does so in order to separate the concept of culture from the ethnocentric origins and political commitments in which it has been entangled. Similarly, if Malinowski's support of colonialism is mentioned at all, it is generally treated by contemporary anthropologists as a regrettable excrescence on his work (one that can, however, be understood in relation to the culture in which he lived . . .). As far as the discipline of anthropology is concerned, it does not matter that the concept of culture is muddled in everyday discourse, smudged with prejudice and partisan politics here and there, contaminated with local values in this expression or that, and even in scholarly writing subject to major controversies over its definition from the late nineteenth century to the present day. What finally matters is not the mess of words about culture but the way this word, as the boundary of our social life in all its historical forms, is an imaginary law reigning over the institutionalization of the discipline of anthropology in this century.[8] And not only over anthropology: as Richard A. Shweder has pointed out, "Culture theory cuts across disciplines."[9] Culture has power across the entire range of what the French so optimistically call "the human sciences."

The break with the past that constitutes this distinctively modern conception of culture is not incidental to this conception. It is its initiating gesture. It draws a boundary that produces history, in the form of identity and difference, by denying history. This gesture sublimates history into the law of this concept that is destined to prove compelling through all the confusions over its use. The modern concept of culture breaks with the past by denying the politics of its own history, and it continues this gesture in every act of revisionary criticism by which contemporary intellectuals comprehend and refine the work of their predecessors without challenging this locus of discourse. Not to question this initial gesture, this drawing of a boundary, is to accept the status quo. And although we may want to ignore culture, leap beyond it, or else return to a day when an intellectual could appeal to a transcendence that was not conceptual but a matter of faith, taste, or common sense, everyone today must deal with this concept in one way or another.

To analyze this concept through the history of ideas—to analyze it *as* a concept—would be to reproduce it. We would trace a law obscured by shifting clouds of dust stirred up by transient politics, misguided desire, sloppy thinking, and similar contingencies. On the other hand, again, we cannot simply break with this concept, no matter how alluring such a prospect may be to Nietzscheans and practitioners of the avant-garde. We cannot single-handedly scramble above the discourse of human identity and difference that dominates social understanding in the modern world. Despite their history of ideas approach, Kroeber and Kluckhohn do have a point: in the modern world it makes no more sense to say "I don't believe in culture" than to say, with one of the characters in Louis Malle's *Atlantic City*, "I don't believe in gravity." If we analyze culture as a discourse and so find how it embraces concepts extending across the social sciences and the humanities, such as "context," "community," "competence," "convention," and "norm," it becomes clear that critics cannot refuse to participate in this discourse.

This is not to say anyone is condemned simply to reproduce the discourse of culture, which then would be the book within which we live like prisoners of an unchangeable lexicon, grammar, and syntax. Nor am I arguing that all of anthropology has been (to borrow Marshall Sahlins's phrase) "a grand intellectual distraction, bourgeois society scratching its head."[10] Those adopting this discourse have often produced valuable work that takes them beyond this discourse. (Culture is not a fashion that becomes totally useless when outmoded.) In addition, we can expect this work to be crossed with other discourses that may challenge the discourse of culture with which they share quarters. (Culture is a discourse of modern understanding but not *the* discourse.) We can also expect that the discourse of culture will challenge itself. (The premises of culture follow rhetorical paths rather than strictly logical rules.) Furthermore, anthropologists differ greatly among themselves in their definitions of culture, in their conceptions of cultural explanation, in the extent to which they are "hard" or "soft" cultural relativists, and in other respects.[11]

Still, it is important to question the power of culture to produce knowledge in a form that represses the significance of political differences in society. In this form it maintains a peculiarly modern form of idealism that still bears some relation to the themes of the liberal humanism of the nineteenth century. As Lévi-Strauss suggested in describing the education of a native leader in *Tristes Tropiques*, this power is a kind of writing: the drawing of a boundary of identity and difference, *ethnographia mundi*. It is important to read this writing instead of seeing it as the immaterial border of a text, the neutral territory in which interpretation is practiced. Although it may not totally liberate us from culture, this reading of the writing of our reading—this critical reading—may make our conceptions of law and liberation less compelling boundaries to our desires and to the ways we act on those desires.

To pursue this reading, I am not concentrating my attention on the ways culture is transgressed, contradicted, or otherwise questioned in the works that also support it. Although I do touch on this issue at some points, as in my discussion of the work of Clifford Geertz and Sapir, I am concentrating on the discourse of culture as it runs across different texts. I am analyzing the way it appears as a consistent scheme of rhetoric, and thus of politics, even though its various elements do not appear in any work or discipline as a totality. Obviously, then, my first argument is that "one must not respect the whole," as Roland Barthes puts it.[12] The conception of discourse as a totality must be called into question.

II

> Imagine a use of language (a culture) in which there was a
> common name for green and red on the one hand, and yellow
> and blue on the other. Suppose, e.g., that there were two
> castes, one the patrician caste, wearing red and green
> garments, the other, the plebeian, wearing blue and yellow
> garments. Both yellow and blue would always be referred to as
> plebeian colors, green and red as patrician colors. Asked what
> a red patch and a green patch have in common, a man of our
> tribe would not hesitate to say they were both patrician.
>
> —Wittgenstein[13]

The boundary of culture can always move toward greater particularity or greater generality. Its zero points are the individual, on the one hand, and universal history, on the other. One can make a study of the classic type in anthropology, of an isolated African tribe, or one might analyze some modern phenomena in terms of "the age of industrial capitalism." No matter where the boundary is moved, however, one cannot participate in the discourse of culture without accepting the authority of certain figures of speech. These include the cultural boundary, context, and deviancy; but perhaps the most powerful of these figures is the metaphor of totality. It is so powerful because it suggests the condition of all metaphor: the stipulation of context through the displacement of context. As metaphor is a sign of mastery, according to Aristotle, the metaphor of totality may lead us to question the mastery represented by the discourse of culture.

Within this metaphor, one takes a tribe to be an isolated community naturally bounded by geography or some other form of writing (the writing of race, religion, class . . .). One takes it to be something like Durkheim's *conscience collective*, a society that "is always present and always operating,"[14] or something like C. Wright Mills's "total society."[15] Having made the assumption that "within the boundaries of the tribe the writ of the same culture runs from end to end," one then proceeds to analyze its features. When the culture in question is more general, as in the worldview of which Robert Darnton writes, "the common basis of experience in a given social order,"[16] the difference is purely formal. The scope and level of the analysis are changed but not the subject, which is still culture.

As the discourse of culture appears through this metaphor of totality, it represses the reality of political differences and historical change. If differences are noted, sooner or later they are transcended. As in the example I have taken from Wittgenstein's writings, culture is assumed to be uniform across all its differences. Within the discourse of culture, we cannot imagine a member of a tribe who could speak against the identities held in common by the tribe, including his or her own identity as a plebeian or patrician, and make any sense in doing so.[17]

Nor is this example frivolous because it is presented as a hypothetical case, a philosophical illustration. Consider Wittgenstein's key notion of family resemblances in the use of words: the notion that different games, for instance, are all defined as games by virtue of their relation to a common set of features, even though no two games may draw exactly the same features from the set and even though no game represents the complete set. This notion participates in the discourse of culture by repressing from the analysis of meaning recognition of the political differences to which language is subject at every moment of its use. It implies a consensus on the significant features of things such as games — or, say, jokes — that does not exist except as a political phenomenon or, in other words, as a phenomenon of discourse.

Rather than being a mere figure of speech, as the saying goes, Wittgenstein's use of the word *family* is significant. It may be taken to mark the insistent politics of culture, the insistent materiality of signifying practices, in his philosophy. This metaphor is not simply a metaphor, just as jokes are not just jokes, and just as the family is something more than an institution we can take for granted in the analysis of society. (What of the child who rejects or is neglected by the family, the parent who takes off, the families refused recognition, like homosexual couples, or the case of bastards?) Jonathan Lear's wry comment, "It seems to me no accident that Socrates went to jail, and Wittgenstein went to the movies," is very apt. As he adds, "The 'rationality' of a tribe's beliefs and practices is taken by Wittgensteinians to be sacrosanct in part because they ignore the possibility that the tribe may contain natives who are engaged in a reflective examination of their own beliefs and practices."[18]

Obviously, in analyzing the metaphor of totality in this way, I am trying to contribute to critical practices developing in recent years in virtually every discipline with which this study is concerned, including philosophy, law, sociology, Marxist and feminist theory, history, anthropology itself, and literary theory.[19] It is obvious, too, that the approaches taken by writers in these disciplines do not all lead to the same destination, even though their apparent convergence may indicate some common ground in the perception of the situation of intellectuals today. This is a situation characterized by the increasing specialization and fragmentation of studies, by devaluation of the traditional liberal arts, and by a growing emphasis on technology and technocratic reasoning, among other features. Without laboring to define the precise relation of my argument to the arguments made by all the others who have written on this topic, I want to emphasize that we cannot simply dismiss the metaphor of totality by seeing it as a figure of speech we can replace with a more adequate description.

Clifford Geertz, one of the most sophisticated of contemporary anthropologists, describes culture as an "acted document," a "manuscript" that is "foreign, faded, full of ellipses, incoherencies, suspicious emendations, and tendentious commentaries . . . written not in conventionalized graphs of sound but in transient examples of shaped behavior."[20] Yet Geertz will still note without irony that the focus of anthropology is on "natural communities."[21] He accepts this *donnée*, this bottom line of culture, even in a book that includes an essay on "common sense" as a misnomer. Although his work deals with the complexity of comparing and describing foreign cultures, for Geertz culture is always culture. It always expresses itself as a totality, no matter how much it may be rent by conflict. Explicitly dedicated to the interpretation of culture as a hermeneutic circle, his work is meant to mediate between cultures. Like the work of the linguist who sees cultural understanding as leading to "the role of the cultural broker whose function is to bridge the gap and mediate the differences which separate us from each other,"[22] Geertz's work is designed to explain or translate cultures to each other. In the style of modern humanism, the same style that leads Hilary Putnam, the philosopher, to note in a discussion of the relativity of meaning that we "are above all human beings,"[23] Geertz's work is constituted by its rationalized repression of politics.

Geertz has the habit, common among modern humanists, of occasionally making specific remarks about his political attitudes. For instance, he mentions that he prefers Jeffersonian notions of human rights to Leninist notions (*LK*, 221). But because he is committed to the metaphor of totality, he is compelled, as it were, to produce the following footnote to one of his essays:

> Even amidst the massacres of 1965, where probably somewhere between a quarter and three-quarter million Indonesians were killed by other Indonesians, a perverse kind of justice doing persisted. In the area of Java where, thirteen years earlier, I had worked, the army assembled village populations in the district capital square, asked each to indicate who the "Communists" among them were, and then assigned the condemned of one village to the condemners of another, and vice versa, to take home and execute. (*LK*, 230 n)

Geertz's use of "perverse" as an adjective in this passage represents his Jeffersonian conscience, but it also represents the ultimate incoherence of his idea of "justice doing." This incoherence makes it theoretically impossible to distinguish between Jefferson and Lenin and between justice and massacre. (It also makes it impossible to determine whether these pairs of terms are in any ways apposite.) This rhetorical perversity follows inevitably from a discourse of culture committed to interpreting categories like "justice" in the terms through which any given social order dispenses them. Although Geertz justly mocks those who would criticize his work for recognizing cultural relativism, he fails to see that he cannot assume the position of the cultural relativist, the position from which one views culture as a bounded totality, without implicating himself in the relative placement of that boundary line in his work. As his drawing of this boundary reduces the past to the status of anecdote ("the area of Java where, thirteen years earlier, I had worked"), the future to a silence utterly beyond the present, and present political differences to a homogenous ground ("Indonesians . . . killed by other Indonesians"), his work of translation inevitably betrays the values he professes as his own. The problem with cultural relativism is not that it disables the power of judgment, as is often alleged, but that it obscures the ways judgments in fact are made.

The case is similar when Geertz argues for a "nonevaluative" and "technical" criticism of ideologies. In doing so he notes that his own ideological position "is largely the same as that of Aron, Shils, Parsons, and so forth." He does so in order to fend off "the danger of being misinterpreted" as arguing for the nonevaluation of ideologies (*IC*, 200 n). Yet Geertz does not see that this separation of personal politics from professional discourse assumes the possibility of an interpretive neutrality that his own studies of culture contradict.[24] His conception of science enables him to believe he can rise above ideology in his criticism, but this conception is ahistorical. It ignores the ways science is institutionalized in relation to material differences within and among nations. Following Geertz's own reasoning in his studies of culture, we can see his conception of science as a form of ideology. We might recall Raymond Williams's suggestion that as a concept "ideology" is repeating the history of "culture."[25]

It might be objected that Geertz's prominence in his field does not ensure that his work is an exemplary case of anthropology. Similar objections might be raised on behalf of Wittgenstein, Malinowski, and the others names I muster here. But I am not claiming Geertz or the others are exemplary, even though I am trying to create an impressive vista by conjuring with writers whom contemporary intellectuals have judged to be influential. Although I am not doing justice to Geertz, Wittgenstein, and the rest, I am not trying to do them justice. My subject is not these figures, their *oeuvres*, or the various traditions and influences to which their work may be related. My subject is the discourse of culture, and I am analyzing the politics of that discourse. As noted previously, my examples are not individuals or individual works but forms of representation that transgress the boundaries of these works and the disciplines with which they are associated. My subject is a rhetoric that has become integral to interpretive disciplines in the second half of this century, even though it neither comprehends nor is comprehended by these disciplines in their empirical diversity. I am not describing a totality but rather some figures, relations, and procedures that give the effect of a totality that is distinctively modern, the totality of culture. My argument is that we cannot attribute this discourse solely to individual writers and works if we would understand the social grounds of its meaning: understand how the power of culture becomes the truth of culture.

To speak of a culture to which we belong or to which others belong, to describe and understand these cultures, is already to engage in rhetoric that is political. No language of justice, science, or any other field escapes this consideration. Of course, this consideration may be easy to ignore if we think of culture in terms of the classic anthropological model, which is concerned with societies from the past or from areas foreign to the student. However, as Harris shows, this avoidance becomes more tricky if we do not rationalize the history of anthropology as a discipline. It becomes still more difficult if we refuse to take for granted the language of deviancy, maladaptation, pathology, anomaly, nonsensicality, and marginality used historically within the discipline of anthropology as a means of ratifying the identity of cultures. If we are not blinded by the mystique of professionalism, we might also see a form of politics in the usual protocols of anthropological investigation, which direct the fieldworker to participate socially in a culture while refraining from critical activity in regard to its practices except, possibly, in writing, the field of freedom Kant allowed to intellectuals.[26] In any event, it is important to note that the politics of this discourse have little to do with conventionally defined political positions. Lucien Goldmann writes of cultural totality as comfortably as Geertz or, for that matter, William F. Buckley, Jr.[27]

I am not exempt from implication in this discourse. I am no angel, and outside the heavens of religious faith there is no point from which the politics of discourse unfold as a sublime vista of struggle, oppression, alienation, exploitation, rebellion, and utopian promise. We can see the politics of culture only in the act of working to change the textuality we take to be natural: the politics by which we live, breed, and read. Insofar as culture is coterminous with the textuality contemporary intellectuals take to be natural, the criticism of this discourse cannot help but be political. Just as the imposition of the metaphor of totality is a political gesture, so is my insistence on unassimilable differences within history.

This similarity does not mean we may as well choose the one as the other. It means, first of all, that critical theory is indissolubly related to such matters as racism, colonialism, human rights, and massacres, no matter how distanced and complexly mediated the relation may be. Second, it means failure to come to terms with this relation will result at best in critical incoherence and at worst in the willing submission of critical activity to the most vicious forces in our world.

No doubt I must seem melodramatic in thus inflating the polemics of critical activity in what is, after all, a rather rarified example of academic discourse. No matter. The rhetoric will not be wasted if at least it is irritating: if at least it forces a contrast to the infinitely polite idioms, including more sophisticated forms of melodrama, that so often allow vicious practices to be overlooked in the rational discriminations of intellectual professions.

Not that idioms such as the metaphor of totality are always presented with perfect equanimity. Dell Hymes, the sociolinguist, stumbles over this metaphor when he notes that "what counts as a language boundary cannot be defined by any purely linguistic measure."[28] Trying to define a "speech community," the sociolinguistic analogue to "culture," he writes,

> To participate in a speech community is not quite the same as to be a member of it. Here we encounter the limitation of any conception of speech community in terms of knowledge alone, even knowledge of patterns of speaking as well as of grammar, and of course, of any definition in terms of interaction alone. Just the matter of accent may erect a barrier between participation and membership in one case, although be ignored in another. Obviously membership in a community depends upon criteria which in the given case may not even saliently involve language and speaking, as when birthright is considered indelible. The analysis of such criteria is beyond our scope here—in other words, I duck it, except to acknowledge the problem, and to acknowledge the difficulty of the notion of community itself. (*FS*, 50–51)

Although Hymes is exceptional among contemporary intellectuals for making this acknowledgment, what is the status of a scholarly work in which knowledge, whether it be the scholar's or the community member's, must quail before this boundary of the community? This is a recurrent gesture in the discourse of culture, as when Robert A. LeVine writes, "Indeed, without such common understandings (of symbolic forms such as gestures, dress, property, writing, visual and theatrical representations, careers, relationships), what kind of social communication, or community, would be possible?"[29] Marx's response, to turn philosophy to *praxis*, might displace this uneasy question with a different problem; but then even the Marxist tradition is bedeviled by the metaphor of totality or, one might say, by the persistent figure of Hegel.

This issue is even more difficult than Hymes indicates. For even as he shies away from "the notion of community itself," finally contenting himself with a definition he acknowledges to be a tautology ("a community sharing knowledge of rules for the conduct and interpretation of speech" [*FS*, 51]), he does not even begin to question the *language* of community. Seemingly neutral and universal terms like *membership*, *participation*, and *rules*, in and of themselves, constitute the community Hymes describes. Conversely, they rule out the reality of different perspectives on social relations. Hymes does not acknowledge the possibility that membership might be a contested status that cannot be described from a neutral standpoint. It does not appear to cross his mind that there might be something askew in the very idea that the abstract individual "member" is the key element of a speech community. For all its recognition of complexity, his description of the speech community, like LeVine's conception of culture, represents a demand for social consensus. Leaving no way to articulate irreducible conflicts within the community, it also leaves no way to conceive of change except as a startling imposition of the outer world on the soul of the community.

The problem does not end there. Even if we imagine Hymes could draw the boundary of a community with the bland assurance of a *savant*, there would still remain the problem of evaluating significant features in "the conduct and interpretation of speech." How many interactions must we observe to distinguish rules from their violation? How are we to evaluate the relative significance of various rules? How do we know when an interaction has begun and when it has ended?

These are not simply questions about the conditions of empirical knowledge. They are questions about the conception of history involved in any analysis of signifying practices and yet systematically denied in the discourse of culture. It is not sufficient to say, with Gadamer, that "the closed horizon that is supposed to enclose a culture is an abstraction."[30] Nor is it sufficient to conclude, as does Gadamer, that culture must be conceived of in terms of an unfolding temporality. This conception still reconstitutes totality in the form of a unified historical tradition. Like Hymes's abstraction, it still represses the reality of historical struggles over differences of power by sublimating them in the cultural boundary. The same effect occurs in Sahlins's *Culture and Practical Reason*, despite its acute analysis of the contradiction between instrumental and symbolic conceptions of culture in anthropology and Marxism. When he describes his basis for interpretation by saying, in reference to the work of Lucien Sebag, "Meaning is always arbitrary in relation to the physical properties of the object signified; hence the concept refers in the first place to a code of distinctions proper to the culture in question,"[31] his notions of "the first place" and of the "proper," along with his more general notion of the cultural "system," ignore the contested status of meaning in the historical world. Sahlins's more recent work goes beyond such notions to show that in the historical world implicated in the drawing of the cultural boundary—this world that cannot appear as long as we subscribe uncritically to the discourse of culture—we can begin to read the politics of our knowledge.[32]

In an essay first published in 1932, Sapir delved brilliantly into the complexities of this cultural knowledge. With works ranging across the fields of anthropology, linguistics, psychoanalysis, and art, Sapir was far from being naive in his attachment to this word, or mess of words, *culture*. In an earlier essay, he had described it as one of a number of "empty thrones"[33] in the language of modern society. *Culture*, he wrote, is a term that possesses undeniable power and yet lacks a clear definition. So he asked the question: Who or what occupies or should occupy this throne? As he commented in "The Emergence of the Concept of Personality in a Study of Cultures," "Culture is not, as a matter of sober fact, a 'given' at all. It is so only by a polite convention of speech" (*SW*, 596). In the 1932 essay "Cultural Anthropology and Psychiatry," he was able to develop a brilliant critique of the metaphor of totality in the discourse of culture; and yet he remained so bounded by this discourse that his reasoning finally led him into forms of incoherence and expressions of political obsequiousness that are only too characteristic of those who compulsively reproduce this discourse without Sapir's wit, erudition, and style. It is because it presents such a dramatic battle over the possession of the empty throne of culture that "Cultural Anthropology and Psychiatry" remains such a valuable essay. Although it does not exemplify culture as it is written about nowadays or even as it was addressed in 1932, it does engage the discourse of culture in a way that cannot be avoided today if we are to negotiate obstacles that trip up Sapir and legions of less interesting writers.

In this essay, Sapir wants to clarify the cultural boundary. "The concept of culture," he writes, "as it is handled by the cultural anthropologist, is necessarily something of a statistical fiction." It is a fiction because two people who nominally belong to the same culture may be as different "as though one were the representative of Italian culture and the other of Turkish culture." In a neo-Kantian fashion, Sapir says it "is not the concept of culture which is subtly misleading but the metaphysical locus to which culture is generally assigned" (*SW*, 516). The concept of culture can be redeemed from the confusion over its use if we recognize the metaphysics of space as a conceptual fiction:

> We have learned that the individual in isolation from society is a conceptual fiction. We have not had the courage to face the fact that formally organized groups are equally fictitious in the psychological sense, for geographically contiguous groups are merely a first approximation to the infinitely variable groupings of human beings to whom culture in its various aspects is actually to be credited as a matter of realistic psychology. (*SW*, 519)

Just as he argues in "The Unconscious Patterning of Behavior in Society" that "the terms 'social' and 'individual' are contrastive in only a limited sense" (*SW*, 544), so does Sapir in this essay use a comparison between cultural anthropology and psychiatry to free the boundary line of culture from the fixed writings of metaphysical dogma. In their place he would put a pragmatic and tolerant description of space. "Cultural Anthropology and Psychiatry" concludes with a plea that psychiatrists be tolerant toward differences in individual personalities and turn to anthropology for help in learning this tolerance.

At first glance it is difficult to fault this conclusion. Students and intellectuals in modern Western societies are taught, at least officially, to respect the value of tolerance; and in any case a concept admitted to be a fiction becomes a very slippery customer. Although I may find fault with this term or that, this opinion or that, this bit of logic or that in Sapir's analysis, he need only agree with me, switch his perspective to mine within the dialectic of personality and culture, to turn my objection into support for the relation he draws between these terms. There would seem to be no way out.

This is just the point. There would seem to be no way out of the totality of culture as it is conceived to be a methodological fiction instead of a metaphysical locus. For even with this fiction we are returned to the metaphysical space of idealism, in which Sapir may be heard saying, with Terence, *"Nil humane a me alienum puto ergo homo sum."* We are turned away from the historical and political differences repressed in the name of this humanism, in historically specific ways, in Terence's time as in our own.

Borrowing Herbert Marcuse's phrase, we might say repression takes place in Sapir's tolerance of rhetoric: the very tolerance he uses to counter formalism, scientism, metaphysical dogma, and social oppression. Seeing that "the elements of culture that come well within the horizon of consciousness of one individual are entirely absent in another individual's landscape," as he puts it in "The Emergence of the Concept of Personality" (*SW*, 596), Sapir sees that the line of culture can be drawn in an infinite number of ways between the zero points of the individual and universal history.[34] Like Geertz, however, he does not see the theoretical incoherence into which he is led by his belief that culture, properly conceived, can paper over these differences. Consequently, in "Cultural Anthropology and Psychiatry," he is capable of a passage such as the following:

> Still other cultural patterns have neither a generalized nor a specialized potency. They may be termed marginal or referential and while they may figure as conceptually important in the scheme of a cultural theorist, they may actually have little or no psychological importance for the normal human being. . . . Some of this marginal cultural property is held as marginal by the vast majority of participants in the total culture, if we may still speak in terms of a "total culture." Others of these marginal patterns are so only for certain individuals or groups of individuals. . . . Culture, then, varies infinitely, not only as to the manifest content but as to the distribution of psychologic emphases on the elements and implications of this content. According to our scale of treatment, we have to deal with the cultures of groups and the cultures of individuals. (*SW*, 518)

Sapir must make his own analysis of culture an affair of marginal potency and abnormal psychology in the same essay in which he urges psychiatrists to draw on its power of tolerance and humanistic understanding. He must question the category of totality in the same sentence that describes a marginality and in the same paragraph that describes a normality that are inconceivable without this category. He must translate the questionable "total culture" into a more reassuring term, *scale of treatment*, in the same sentence that resuscitates culture in a totalized, although relative, form.

Sapir is led into this incoherence because he is one of the most brilliant participants in the discourse of culture. Incoherence of this kind may not seem so apparent in mediocre works in the humanities and social sciences. Their progression from sentence to sentence moves so compulsively within the discourse of culture that their language does not seem to be on display, available for view qua language. Sapir, though, realizes he must struggle to reach a language of neutrality. In this essay, it seems as if he is fighting an impulse to recognize how completely his conception of interpretation and the knowledge arising from it are implicated in political attitudes, conscious or unconscious. Thus, he writes a tentative plea for tolerance as the conclusion to an essay that casually, consistent with his "logic," refers to "the useful tyranny of the normal in a given society" (*SW*, 514). Surely he means these words to be neutral or purely descriptive, and just as surely they defeat this intention. They show how interpretation is bound to be political. They show how the terms of culture are bound to be implicated in the terms of historical struggles that allow no room for neutrality in their description.

It only makes sense that Sapir should conclude another essay, "The Unconscious Patterning of Behavior in Society," with a plea for repression of a kind that also appears in his other writings:

> Complete analysis and the conscious control that comes with a complete analysis are at best but the medicine of society, not its food. We must never allow ourselves to substitute the starveling calories of knowledge for the meat and bread of historical experience. This historic experience may be theoretically knowable, but it dare never be fully known in the conduct of daily life. (*SW*, 559)[35]

This plea represents perfectly the way the modern discourse of culture institutes history through the denial of history. As Sapir testifies, what "dare never be fully known" in this discourse is historical experience. This must be made unconscious "meat and bread" rather than knowledge that can be mastered. The mere thought that this experience might become fully known threatens to be a cure that kills us.

Knowledge does not pose this threat because Sapir is actually a latter-day Cassandra who can foresee the consequences of complete consciousness. Even if we did not have centuries of theologians, philosophers, mystics, poets, and such types, whose works offer rather convincing evidence that this kind of knowledge is at the very least rather difficult to conceive, Sapir's own writing shows that he believes statistically normal human beings to be in no danger of suffering from an overdose of consciousness. Historical experience poses this threat in the passage only because it must pose it if Sapir is to be rescued from the more immediate danger of recognizing that consciousness does not entail mastery. His Romantic call for a limitation of knowledge allows him to assume that knowledge may be systematically distinguished from the unconscious "conduct of daily life" even as his own work may be seen as challenging this idealist conception of knowledge. This contradiction arises from his attempt to maintain a ground of interpretive neutrality, which appears here as the realm of historical experience that he does not want to subject to analysis. In this way the passage submits criticism to "the tyranny of the normal."

As this essay may indicate, turning a geographical or metaphysical boundary into a fictional one is no way out of the totality of culture. In Jacques Derrida's words, "This geometry is only metaphorical, it will be said. Certainly. But metaphor is never innocent. It orients research and fixes results. When the spatial model is hit upon, when it functions, critical reflection rests within it. In fact, and even if criticism does not admit this to be so." I take this quotation out of context, since Derrida is referring to the structuralism of Jean Rousset, not to Sapir or the discourse of culture. Or is he?

> As concerns qualities, forces and values, and also as concerns nondivine works read by finite minds, this confidence in mathematical-spatial *representation* seems to be (on the scale of an entire civilization, for we are no longer dealing with the question of Rousset's language, but with the totality of our language and its credence) *analogous* to the confidence placed by Canaque artists in the level representation of depth. A confidence that the structural ethnographer analyzes, moreover, with more prudence and less abandon than formerly.[36]

In the absence of Sapir's, or Hegel's, terrifying figure of total consciousness, Derrida's meaning is, as usual, difficult to grasp with confidence. But, of course, this confidence is one of the objects of his critique, as this passage illustrates. In any case, his writing may serve as a useful context to Sapir's at this point if it emphasizes, first of all, that a rhetorical figure is always political ("It orients research and fixes results"). Second, it may be valuable if it suggests a relation between the understanding of totality and the understanding of context.

Like the metaphor of totality, context does not provide a neutral representation of the world. Nevertheless, whether one takes it to be only a representation of the world—a fiction—or some kind of reflection, context is as unavoidable within the discourse of culture as is the metaphor of totality. It is the other side of the boundary of totality that yet is included within the totality, determining its meaning. It is a figure within the text of culture or another name for culture. It is the figure that must suffer the obscure destiny of being an alien so that we may know where we stand and may feel at home there: here. As Heidegger puts it, "We live in a neighborhood, and yet we would be baffled if we had to say in what that neighborhood consists. But this perplexity is merely a particular case, though perhaps an exceptionally good one, of the old encompassing perplexity in which all our thinking and saying finds itself always and everywhere."[37]

III

> *It is only in normal cases that the use of a word is clearly prescribed; we know, are in no doubt, what to say in this or that case. The more abnormal the case, the more doubtful it becomes what we are to say. And if things were quite different from what they actually are—if there were for instance no characteristic expression of pain, of fear, of joy; if rule became exception and exception rule; or if both became phenomena of roughly equal frequency—this would make our normal language games lose their point.*
>
> —Wittgenstein[38]

Like *boundary* and *totality* and the other words over which I am lingering, context plays a prominent role in the practice of interpretation among contemporary intellectuals. Obviously, I devote this attention to it because I want to call into question the practices involved at the present time in criticism, theory, and university teaching. This is not to say I take context to be an especially privileged figure. To come to terms with context and the other figures I am shoving onto center stage is not to master the discourse of culture. At best, it is to analyze the significance of this discourse in some of its most general elements, relations, and movements. This analysis merely touches on a multitude of figures involved in this discourse while entirely passing by a crowd of others, even though they are no less important than the players I feature because they best suit my purposes. For instance, in addition to its relation to the cultural boundary and totality, context is associated in the discourse of culture with identity, integrity, normality, competence, appropriateness, and similar terms; and so by contrast, it is related as well to figures like the alien, deviancy, abnormality, extraterritoriality, childishness, and vulgarity. But the fact that this analysis cannot come near to a complete consideration of such terms does not mean it is necessarily a useless or botched piece of work. It only means that in this respect it is like any critical analysis and that readers should be alert to the contexts it cannot contain, cannot even name.

In "Signature Event Context," Derrida pursues this line of thought. He argues that every sign, "linguistic or nonlinguistic, spoken or written (in the usual sense of this opposition), as a small or large unity, can be *cited*, put between quotation marks; thereby it can break with every given context and engender infinitely new contexts in an absolutely nonsaturable fashion."[39] Although he notes that he "will not conclude from this that there is no relative specificity of the effects of consciousness, of the effects of speech (in opposition to writing in the traditional sense), that there is no effect of the performative, no effect of ordinary language, no effect of presence and of speech acts" (*MP*, 327), he does conclude that these effects cannot be structurally connected to any ultimate origin, whether intentional or conventional. He argues that "there are only contexts without any center of absolute anchoring" and adds that "this iterability of the mark is not an accident or anomaly, but is that (normal/abnormal) without which a mark could no longer even have a so-called 'normal' functioning" (*MP*, 320–21).

The argument is intricate, rigorous (to borrow one of Derrida's favorite words), and challenging. Its major weakness—and perhaps the major weakness of Derrida's work in general—is in its articulation of the "relative specificity" of the effects of presence, speech, and so on. While Derrida notes, in passing, that he will not deny these effects, neither does he explore them outside of philosophical discourse. Even when his writings deal with texts most philosophers would not classify as philosophy, he reads them in terms of philosophical issues. Therefore, one might criticize the *topicality* of Derrida's work: the audiences it does and does not address, the issues it does and does not raise, the constructions of society to which it does or does not lend itself.[40]

To this end, we might begin by examining the significance of a declaration such as that in "The Ends of Man": "Any questioning of humanism that does not first catch up with the archaeological radicalism of the questions sketched by Heidegger, and does not make use of the information he provides . . . remains historically regional, parodic, and peripheral, juridically secondary and dependent, whatever interest and necessity it might retain as such" (*MP*, 128). For what is this but the dogmatic specification of a curriculum, a professorial laying down of the law? Similarly, one might ask for whom, for what privilege, a "rigorous" reading can posit a "general" structure of communication rather than a "relatively specific" effect (*MP*, 327)? Who or what must we be to find access to this generality?

It is on this basis, more or less, that Michel Foucault has criticized Derrida's work. While this kind of criticism does not necessarily invalidate Derrida's deconstruction of context as a bounded relation, it might call attention to the historically specific ways context may be binding though not bounded, powerful though rationally incomprehensible, effectual though logically incoherent. In other words, it might call attention to the fact that any formulation of context, like any critique of context, is always implicated in the historical realities of society. Even though this implication is seen never to be fixed, bounded, or absolutely anchored if it is viewed by someone committed to the general or transhistorical case, those unable to view things from this height may be caught within contextual boundaries as certainly as if they were set in concrete (as they may be, as in the case of prisons). Anyone who is out to deconstruct humanism should know that communication, like humanity, is never a general case or "possibility."

In analyzing the role of context in the discourse of culture, then, it may be useful to move from Derrida's philosophical criticism to the work of a writer interested in the relative specificity of contextual boundaries. In its traditional distinction between speech and writing, as in other respects, this work may be said to be comprehended within Derrida's critique. However, in a reading that is politically flexible rather than philosophically rigorous, this work may allow us to get at an understanding of context that goes beyond Derrida's because it stops short of the generalities (philosophy, Western metaphysics, logocentrism, and so on) to which he drives his terms.

Consider, then, Basil Bernstein's *Class, Codes and Control*: a most curious book in this or any context. Whereas Derrida's work, outside of France, appears mostly to have influenced a small group of critical theorists, Bernstein's sociological studies have had a major influence in the theory and practice of education in Great Britain and the United States. In fact, quite an argument has occurred over whether Bernstein was ever the theorist of "deficit" language he was taken to be, or whether much of his influence has resulted from a misunderstanding of his work. (In the introduction to this collection of essays, he regrets and seeks to correct this "misunderstanding.") As a question of what Bernstein really meant in his earlier writings, this argument must be dreary and fruitless. If this uncertainty over the interpretation of his work is related to the conception of language within his work, however, a more interesting perspective may be developed.

As one moves from the first essays in the opening volume of *Class, Codes and Control* to those written later, this volume (*Theoretical Studies Towards a Sociology of Language*) may seem more like a novel than a work of science. It appears to be the narrative of twin characters that first appear under the names of the public code and the formal code, reach maturity under the names of the restricted code and the elaborated code, continue under these names to be refined and altered, and meanwhile, at some points throughout their life, appear totally unlike themselves. (Those who complain that Derrida writes in a deliberately difficult way might do well to read the plain English of Bernstein and other humanists and see if it does not turn on them, when it is read carefully, as much as Derrida's writing does.) If Bernstein's work has this novelistic appearance, it obviously suggests some Derridean questions that might be raised about the human sciences as schemes of representation; but then again, this characterization may seem too unfair to warrant anyone's attention. Let us consider, then, his ideas.

Simply put, the restricted code is associated with the working class and the elaborated code with the middle class, although Bernstein takes pains to note that this association is merely a social happenstance and not a necessary or absolute connection. Whereas the restricted code is "generated by a form of social relationship based upon a range of closely shared identifications self-consciously held by the members,'' the elaborated code ''is generated by a form of social relationship which does not necessarily presuppose such shared, self-consciously held identifications, with the consequence that much less is taken for granted.''[41] The restricted code is associated with a family upbringing in which social roles, personal identity, and linguistic practice are relatively fixed, whereas the elaborated code is associated with a family upbringing in which these are more variable and open to change. In a simplified example of the restricted code, a child asked to interpret a picture that involves a man throwing a ball might say, ''He threw that ball over there,'' while a child who speaks in an elaborated code might say, ''The man in the blue shirt threw the ball into the yard next to him.'' Relatively speaking, the restricted code is dependent on context and traditional, the elaborated code independent of context and open to innovation.

Bernstein will claim that the two codes are completely equal as far as the sociologist is concerned: ''Clearly one code is not better than another; each possesses its own aesthetic, its own possibilities.'' But he admits that society ''may place different values on the orders of experience elicited, maintained and progressively strengthened through the different coding systems.'' Moreover, he argues that if a child is to be successful in school, ''it becomes critical for him to possess, or at least to be oriented towards, an elaborated code'' (*CCC*, 135–36). In addition to this pressure from social values and educational practices, there is the pressure of Bernstein's own faith in the rationality he associates, at least at times, with the elaborated code. This code, he writes, ''will facilitate the verbal transmission and elaboration of the individual's unique experience'' (*CCC*, 128). Through it, the concept of self will be differentiated, whereas ''there is no problem of self, because the problem is not relevant'' in restricted code (*CCC*, 132). Social control in the environment of the elaborated code ''will be based upon linguistically elaborated meanings rather than upon power'' (*CCC*, 155). Similarly, it may be said that education ''is in itself not making children middle class'' (*CCC*, 199). Although ''the value system of the middle class penetrates the very texture of the learning context itself,'' the elaborated code on which schooling is based ''does not entail any specific value system'' (*CCC*, 186). We need to distinguish between ''the principles and operations, that [it] is our task as teachers to transmit and develop in the children, and the contexts we create in order to do this'' (*CCC*, 199).

So the adventures of the main characters in this book result from the action of context, an action that is rhetorically meaningful and yet violent and illogical. Bernstein writes of ''cultural discontinuity based upon two radically different systems of communication'' (*CCC*, 144). He sees different cultures and different systems of communication as bounded totalities, in principle equal to each other, that just happen to have met in the context of society and schoolroom. Thus, he will note that the speech models of the elaborated code ''are incumbents of specialized social positions located in the system of social stratification'' although "in principle this is not necessary" (*CCC*, 130). The historical realities of society have only an anecdotal, or contextual, relation to culture. Like the elaborated code, culture is conceived to be essentially independent of social context even though this culture, like the elaborated code, may be found, empirically speaking, in a certain characteristic structuring of power. Different codes, like different cultures, are regarded neutrally and independently, as equals, even though these codes and cultures are always discovered within specific social relations that give certain codes and cultures power over others. And this power is so strong that at times it invades Bernstein's neutrality, leading him to idealize the elaborated code, as we have seen, despite his protests to the contrary and despite his avowed aim of reforming education so that it will be more sensitive and responsive to the children of the restricted code.

Hence the great irony in the career of the restricted and elaborated codes: that the elaborated code in which they are described has proven to be just as dependent on context as the restricted code is supposed to be and yet also independent of context in a way that escapes the "universalistic" meaning, "in principle available to all" (*CCC*, 176), that Bernstein identifies with the elaborated code.

On the one hand, Bernstein's claim that he was misunderstood by those who read him to say working-class children have a deprived and inferior language shows how absolutely fixed to a specific context his words must be.[42] If he is telling the truth about his intentions when he wrote these essays (assuming it makes any sense to pose a qualification such as this), his intentions were betrayed as they were moved from their mental context to the context found in the elaborated code of his writing or when they were moved from this context to the context of their reading; the betrayal is certain, although its precise site is moot. And whether he is telling the truth or trying to rationalize his earlier work in claiming to have been misunderstood, the need to create a context, an introduction, to try to establish his true meaning still shows the elaborated code to be a prisoner of contexts.

On the other hand, this dependence on context is also an independence of context that is not universalistic but irrational. It is an independence of context because there is no finite number of contexts on which his words have proven or can be proven to be dependent. Instead, there are the revisions, alterations, and inconsistencies in his presentation of his characters; his ironic account of his intentions; the context in which educational officials must have read his work in order to use it to implement various programs aimed at compensating for the cultural disadvantages certain children were presumed to have; and the contexts drawn by various critics of Bernstein, like William Labov, and supporters of Bernstein, like M. A. K. Halliday and Mary Douglas, and readers somewhere in the middle, like David Silverman and Brian Torode — not to mention the present context and contexts yet to come. In all of these, radical discontinuities of culture and communication appear that cannot be reduced, or elevated, to an overriding context. These discontinuities cut across the rule of context and thus may lead us to recognize how misleading it is to build any sociological analysis on a concept of equality that expresses morality by repressing political realities. These contexts are explicable only through the kind of political analysis that sociolinguistics in general, and Bernstein's work in particular,[43] represses within the concept of culture.

Again it might seem that I am not doing justice here. After all, idealist conceptions of knowledge are questioned throughout this volume, and in its concluding essay Bernstein directly takes up the subject of power in an argument he introduces as follows:

> Educational knowledge is a major regulator of the structure of experience. From this point of view, one can ask "How are forms of experience, identity and relation evoked, maintained and changed by the formal transmission of educational knowledge and sensitivities?" Formal educational knowledge can be considered to be realized through three message systems: curriculum, pedagogy and evaluation. . . . The term "educational knowledge code" . . . refers to the underlying principles which shape curriculum, pedagogy and evaluation. It will be argued that the form this code takes depends upon social principles which regulate the classification and framing of knowledge made public in educational institutions. Both Durkheim and Marx have shown us that the structure of society's classifications and frames reveals both the distribution of power and the principles of social control. (*CCC*, 202–203)

It is significant, however, that the restricted and elaborated codes appear in this chapter only through a glancing allusion. It is also significant that Bernstein introduces the chapter with the comment, "The reader may consider that this paper is out of place in a book concerned with language and socialization." For what this essay makes apparent are precisely those irreconcilable discontinuities that I have described in this volume: in this space of culture. Here, the power Bernstein says does not exist in the elaborated code is said to pervade knowledge in any form. The society and educational institutions that had been only contexts to forms of language are here intrinsic to them. The class relations that "in principle" had nothing to do with the restricted and elaborated codes here act directly on them.

In these contradictions we confront the rhetoric of context, the space that is beyond culture or another name for culture, the alien that bestows identity, the extrinsic that proves intrinsic. The differences between this essay and the rest of the volume, like the ways Bernstein differs from himself even within the rest of the volume, must appear within sociology as faults. They represent either a failure in Bernstein's writing and thinking, a failure in history (as when authors introduce collections of essays with apologies for the way "any collection of pieces written over a period of years must show certain inconsistencies and changes"), or a failure in my sympathy as a reader. Sociologically, such differences must be exiled from reason, made an inessential context to the thought Bernstein was pursuing or ought to have been pursuing. Within a political analysis of Bernstein's writing, however, these differences appear as the characteristic (il)logic, the rhetorical movement, of the discourse of culture, which continues even in this last chapter. (For instance, in the language of *forms, systems, principles, classifications*, and *frames*, which suggests society is a homogenous and bounded space that can be grasped in its totality through rational analysis.)

These differences are the consequence of a discourse that begins its history with a gesture that represses history. More specifically, they represent the movement of the boundary between text and context that determines meaning. This movement can never be fixed theoretically but will always be fixed historically in practices such as reading, writing, teaching, and formulating public policy. It may be unjust that Bernstein's writings were read as demeaning lower-class language and were used to support programs based on this reading, but there is no such thing as a just reading. We never just read. Justice takes on meaning in social life, in which meaning is always contested. Whatever else it is, reading is always a political act, whether or not we recognize it as such.

This is one reason it is doubtful that Noam Chomsky's analysis of linguistic competence can be useful for the analysis of performance. These investigations could be transferred to the differences of performance only by linking a conception of semantic competence with a conception of pragmatic competence that includes the possibility of political contestation and thus exceeds the boundaries of lexical, grammatical, and syntactical propriety. To use the kind of biological analogy Chomsky favors, it is as impossible to generalize from his conception of competence to performance as it is to extrapolate the writing of Shakespeare's plays from a scientific knowledge of the muscles of the human hand.

Of course, to recognize the politics of reading or other social practices like writing and teaching is not to exempt ourselves from appropriation, misinterpretation, betrayal, and abuse. Still, this recognition may help to make us critical toward the institutionalization of meaning in our lives and thus may make us better able to contest that institutionalization. When culture appears as discourse and not as a community of human beings in a fixed context, whether real or heuristic, it becomes possible to act in a very different way among the people one is studying and among the other people studying them. When we see the workings of power where we had seen nothing but meaning, principle, difference, or context, it becomes possible to challenge the ways power is organized.

In itself, theoretical recognition is a poor enough thing. But to work to alter the terms of our lives, we first have to recognize that these terms are political and therefore open to change. For the sociologist or sociolinguist, this recognition may be inconceivable ("Being 'appropriate to the situation,' " according to Halliday, "is not some optional extra in language; it is an essential element in the ability to mean"[44]). But conserving the meaning of a discipline should not be the aim of critical analysis.[45]

In relation to Derrida's critique of context, this consideration of Bernstein's work may illustrate how imperative it is to act on the politics at work in the determination and alteration of context. Bernstein struggles over communication in a way that is naive, crude, and provincial in comparison to Derrida's writing. However, his work may show that sophisticated professors and rubes, like middle-class and working-class children, appear as such only within historical relations that are as real and as moving as they are fundamentally resistant to rational resolution. Derrida's work is likely to give the impression that the appropriate response to the dilemmas of context, perhaps the only response, is to pursue an interminable analysis of the boundary line: the mark, the trace, and so on. Through its very "faults," Bernstein's work may lead us to recognize that analysis is always a political practice and will be misguided if it looks for its constitution in theory that is conceived to differ from the binding immediacies of social and historical involvement. Derrida's brilliant and relentless writing is likely to appear much more useful to the critic of authority than Bernstein's, but it may need to be put in the context of work like Bernstein's if it is not itself to become an authority that leads intellectuals into utterly submissive political attitudes in the very writing and teaching they feel to be bold, uncompromising, and iconoclastic.

In variations and alterations of context or in any other form, differences of power are instituted in relation to specific human beings, even though no ideal boundary can be drawn around this situation.[46] In respect to context as in all other respects, the discourse of culture forms an imaginary law; but this is not to say that this law is without power. Laws are instituted and given power through the discourse of culture in institutions ranging from families and schools to governments. The imaginary nature of such law may appear to those privileged to be exempt from them and also to those who face their sanctions without such privilege. In any case, in the absence of historical change these laws remain real even for those who may believe they see through them, whereas for many they are simply as real as real can be.

Ironically, "the many" are always "the exceptions" that governments, like Wittgenstein's philosophy, submit to their "rule." The normal cases of which Wittgenstein writes, like normal cases in society, are not a majority discovered through an innocent empiricism. The metaphor of totality ignores the sanctions by which normality is invented and maintained. This metaphor displaces the organizations of power that exclude certain differences from meaning and so make it possible to identify the totality as such. It is only in the form of symbols (of territory, propriety, normality, and the like) that culture exists as a totality of signifying practices; and these symbols master no one but those disposed to imagine them as the fulfillment of desire.

Normal cases are produced through social institutions and through the idealization of those institutions in philosophy and other forms of ideology. We do not find the normal and the deviant as people open a box and find the pieces to a puzzle. We create these close relatives of text and context in the discourse of culture, and an analysis of their role in this discourse may help to further illustrate the political implications of this language game.

IV

> *There is no document of civilization which is not at the same time a document of barbarism. And just as such a document is not free of barbarism, barbarism taints also the manner in which it was transmitted from one owner to another.*
> —Benjamin[47]

Within the discourse of culture, the boundary of culture must run through itself as well as around itself. In order to be itself, culture must separate the normal majority from deviant minorities. This majority need not be an empirical proportion of a population. It may be a model judged to be normative even though it is incessantly violated. Whatever perspective we introduce into the concept of culture, the fact remains that it must identify categories of deviancy in order to have any definition at all. In this identification, it must deny meaning to the members of these categories and thus must condemn them to a kind of internal exile. As individuals or as members of groups, particular deviants may gain an approved status and so cease to be stigmatized; but the category of deviancy remains. Culture always establishes normal members of the community, conventions, rules, traditions, and the like through the repression of difference. To adapt a phrase from Borges: culture is an abuse of statistics.[48]

There is a radical difference between deviancy as it is instituted within the discourse of culture and deviancy as defined, say, in traditional Catholic morality. Although some of the types that fall under these categories might seem the same, generally speaking, they really are not so. They are subject to very different rhetorical powers. The discourse of culture does not care, as the Catholic church does, for the state of a homosexual's soul and the chance of redemption this person might have. Like the institutional practices and theories developed around them, such questions have no existence within the discourse of culture. Culture's homosexual is not the church's homosexual. Its deviants do not exist in relation to natural, rational, or divine law. They exist only in relation to the paradoxical law of the cultural boundary, which can maintain the difference between the exterior and the interior of culture only by violating this difference. Since culture is conceived to be a bounded totality, any appearance or behavior that cannot be rationalized into this form of totality must appear deviant. It must seem an intrusion of the exterior into the interior or vice-versa, a sign of immigration or emigration.[49] Thus arises the peculiar power of the discourse of culture: the power to institute normality without appealing to any laws (moral, religious, and so on) except the law of its own constitution.

The most distinctive aspect of this power is that it cannot be recognized by those who are governed by it. Whatever might recognize it is outside it or alien to it, deviant. Culture is power as tautology and thus power as unconsciousness. Insofar as it is committed to the discourse of culture, interpretation must produce unconsciousness in order to have a subject. This is the first function of interpretation within the modern discourse of culture: *secretly* to condescend.

The irony is that a discourse conceived to recognize differences, not stigmatize them as deviancy from an ethnocentric perspective, can do so only by reproducing deviancy as a universal phenomenon. A marvelous instance of this situation crops up in Lévi-Strauss's *The Savage Mind*, as he quotes approvingly an article that rejects an ethnocentric view of normality in one sentence in order to produce the cultural institution of normality and deviancy two sentences later:

> A Hawaiian's oneness with the living aspect of native phenomena, with spirit and God and with other persons as souls, is not correctly described by the word rapport, and certainly not by such words as sympathy, empathy, abnormal, supernormal or neurotic, mystical or magical. It is not "extra-sensory," for it is partly of-the-senses and not-of-the-senses. It is just a part of natural consciousness for the normal Hawaiian.[50]

Hence the significance of the fondness in anthropology for "primitive" cultures into which the fieldworker enters as a student, like the fondness in psychology for the study of "development" in children. The character of the initiate required by these narratives almost inevitably assumes an identification with a cultural totality. The same purpose can be served, as in the branch of philosophy represented by Wittgenstein's work, by appealing almost always to examples and illustrations on a personal scale of relations. This appeal makes differences of power and conflicts over these differences disappear into trivial matters of irony. In the field of linguistics, Labov has noted a version of this tendency in the way researchers rely on thought experiments "in which they put themselves in the position of an imaginary child grappling with fictional data from an imaginary mother," and he has suggested that recent psycholinguistic experiments are limited because the test situation is restricted by the same model.[51] As Anthony Giddens says, contemporary theorists often seem to treat the individuals they study as "cultural dopes."[52]

In anthropology, the very category of the "native" represents the critical assumptions of totality, homogeneity, consensus, and unconsciousness. One basis for these assumptions is the type of society anthropologists traditionally have studied, which is tribal, relatively stable, often preliterate, and limited to simple preindustrial technology. There is no question that such societies do not provide the conditions for the highly differentiated individualism characteristic of modern Western life. However, the category of the native goes beyond this consideration in assuming that for all practical purposes these societies are monolithic. It represents a myth of cultural identity as cultural reality. Through this category culture in general is identified with the dominant culture of a society. In repressing other manifestations of culture as deviancy, this category also idealizes the dominant culture, which it assumes is coherent despite the differences of power that enter into it. This category of the native does not escape theoretical problems in "primitive" cultures, then, any more than it does in more modern sites of investigation.[53]

We cannot avoid these problems by saying there are always "borderline cases," as some ordinary language philosophers like to say. According to this argument, deviancy is in the nature of linguistic reality, as it were. Types are admitted to be idealizations that in reality are composed of resemblances shading off into aberrant types, monstrosities, and utter darkness. Although there is some point to it, this argument begs the question of how types are instituted, maintained, and reproduced. In other words, it begs the question of history and historical change and thus the questions of desire and politics. As a matter of historical fact and in any current social situation, people do not all face the same odds of being termed deviant or normal. The scope of these categories and the ways individuals are marked within them vary according to procedures that cannot be explained except historically and politically. To explain them formally is to rationalize inequities or, in other words, to culture power.

Of course, the problem of defining the normal has not gone unnoticed by anthropologists and other students of social practices. For instance, when Clyde Kluckhohn describes the process of "Studying the Acquisition of Culture," he believes he has a method to avoid mistakes in generalizations or in statements of typicality because he uses sample groups selected to represent age, sex, group, and economic differentials. What he ignores is the problem of the typicality of such a quantitative approach. This approach assumes these differentials are of equal significance and can be isolated from other differences with no loss of meaning. It further assumes that these differentials can be selected out of a society without any concern for the structures and procedures by which power operates in that society. History is assumed to play no part in the existence of these differentials, while it also is taken for granted that culture is integral and so will yield its totality to such a cross-sectional study. In short, this method still demands the existence of a statistical margin that will have significance only as deviancy, if it is recognized at all. Although Kluckhohn shows more awareness of the problem of cultural generalization than many anthropologists, his best insight into method may be parenthetical, which is to say marginal and deviant: "One can . . . record nearly everything (so far as one's unconscious blindspots will allow!) bearing on certain selected universes of behavior."[54]

In work as sophisticated as Lévi-Strauss's, deviancy is not usually produced and dismissed as obviously as in the quotation about Hawaiians. The case is much more complicated in his famous analysis of women as objects of exchange. In this case, the discourse of culture works by identifying with a patriarchal power. It identifies the natural woman as the interchangeable woman and thus denies any meaning to the "woman" who does not fit this definition. Women, Lévi-Strauss writes, "are naturally interchangeable (from the point of view of their anatomical structure and the physiological functions)." A man, he writes, "can satisfy himself by means of some foods" or some women "and go without others in so far as any women or any foods are equally suitable to achieve the ends of procreation or subsistence." Women, he writes, unlike natural species, "are identical"; "the social will" makes them different (*SM*, 125–27).

In this description of women as exchange objects, Lévi-Strauss's anthropology or rationalist psychology ("ethnology is first of all psychology" [*SM*, 131]) depends on a fantasy of women prior to nature. He reads *women* as *woman*. The fantasy is a kind of surrealist *decoupage*: woman as physiological function and anatomical structure, organic woman undifferentiated before the ends of man. The true reciprocity among totemic groups, he writes, "results from the articulation of two processes: the natural one which comes about by means of women, who procreate both men and women, and the cultural one which men bring about by characterizing these women socially when nature has brought them into existence" (*SM*, 125). To put it simply, in order for Lévi-Strauss's analysis of exchange to work, he must identify women with the power of nature and men with the power of culture. Women who are not identical before the sexual desires of men, women for whom giving birth is not simply a biological function, cannot be recognized within culture. This analysis does not make for an anthropology that penetrates to transcendental structures of thought in the human mind. It is anthropology that idealizes institutional power as mind, historical existence as universal structure, and patriarchal authority as human nature.[55]

Many anthropological studies deal directly with the category of deviancy rather than simply causing it to vanish from view, as Lévi-Strauss does in this instance. However, because they cannot recognize that this category is not institutionalized by particular cultures but by the discourse of culture, their analysis of deviancy appears unconscious of its politics and represents this unconsciousness in the subjects under analysis. Even Victor Turner falls into this situation, despite his argument that "sociocultural systems depend not only for their meaning but also for their existence upon the participation of *conscious* human agents and upon men's relations with one another.'' When he describes the ''liminoid'' figures that he says anthropologists should study, figures involved in creating change because their activity is disengaged ''from direct functional action in the minds and behavior of society's members,'' he lists ''poets, philosophers, dramatists, novelists, painters, and the like.''[56] Thus, in discovering consciousness and the activity of social change, all he discovers is idealist aesthetics. Similarly, when Douglas tries to imagine a force that disrupts the discourse of culture as totality, boundary, context, and so on—a force, as she puts it, that ''pulls the sociological imagination off course''[57]—her romantic list of deviants includes radical artists, madmen, religious mystics, and clowns. Neither writer can comprehend the possibility of ''normal'' people rebelling in their lives or the political nature of unromantic deviants like women or different kinds of criminals, much less the ''creativity'' of political practices in general. Like creativity that does not reinforce their conception of culture, figures that do not reassure these intellectuals are driven into unconsciousness.

So when someone like Stanley Diamond lashes out at his profession and yet remains basically uncritical toward the discourse of culture, it is only to be expected that the results should be as politically dangerous as the work of those he opposes. In his idealization of primitive cultures, he apologizes for the deviant category of witches by saying, ''Indeed, further studies of the type of people who are considered witches, within a given primitive society and cross-culturally, should be illuminating, for example, in terms of the conception of the witch as an inordinately narcissistic person, a bad mother or an unfulfilled woman.''[58] This account contributes to the glowing praise of patriarchy throughout his work, and yet even it pales before a neo-Sadeian apologia like the following:

> But let us remember, to adopt an extreme example, that even ritualized cannibalism or the torture of the self or others, recognizes and directly confronts the concrete humanity of the subject . . . it should be noted that in no instance is the purpose of primitive torture the conversion of the victim to the torturer's point of view; ideological imperatives are not the issue.(*ISP*, 154)

Given analyses like these, there is little comfort to be had in Diamond's criticism of American actions in Vietnam, of Fascism, and of similar atrocities. Diamond can see that ''the anthropologist is himself a victim'' of the anthropological practice of treating human subjects as objects, and that ''his power of decision is a fiction, embedded as it is in the exploitative foundations of civilization'' (*ISP*, 93). However, to the extent that he remains within the discourse of culture, he reproduces the very sorts of exploitation against which he rails. We may be reminded of Jean Baudrillard's analysis of slavery and of women under patriarchy and of the way he further resembles Diamond in his idealization of spontanaiety, immediacy, and the spoken word.[59]

When deviancy appears as a category in fields other than philosophy and anthropology, such as psychology, sociology, and literary theory, the way it is treated remains an accurate gauge of the politics involved in these disciplines. It is interesting in this respect that writers in the American social sciences in particular often invoke Marxism as a deviant margin to their analysis. So LeVine, for instance, describes the pressure for normality much as Holland does:

> If one adopts the long-term historical view, one sees every advantageous innovation as an incipient coercion or at least as coercive pressure to conform to a future norm. But the view of the individual involved is often quite different; he responds not to a coercive pressure for survival but to a novel opportunity for personal expression that his environment had not previously offered. A Marxist might say that only the long-term historical view is correct and that the individual is simply short-sighted, but this argument denies the psychological reality in which individuals actually function.

That the view of Marxism in this passage might come from a comic book is beside the point, for its function is simply to repress political analysis. As in so much work that tries to relate psychology to culture, what appears here is Sapir's dialectic without Sapir's restless and discomfiting intelligence. Predictably, LeVine comes to a conclusion that idealizes the most banal ideologies of capitalism as if they have been discovered through neutral psychological analysis:

> Another model of optimal adaptive fit between the distribution of genotypic personality dispositions [defined as the structure fixed within the individual as opposed to the behavioral phenomena of personality] and institutional norms is one in which the norms permit enough latitude for each individual to develop his own adaptive solution through trial-and-error and selective propagation. This model is the explicit ideal of American graduate education, at least at the dissertation level, for it is believed that original scholarship cannot be institutionally formulated in detail but must be worked out by each student in terms of his own interests and capacities, within the broad constraints of scholarly standards. Such a model of optimal adaptive fit is widely applicable. . . . The criteria of success in economic and political competition (where competition is itself institutionalized) are broad enough to allow a variety of adaptive solutions developed by individuals to meet their own needs and the demands of their ecological niche.[60]

This work deserves to be quoted at such length only because its clumsy rhetorical procedures are so broadly compelling. Just consider Talcott Parsons, probably the most influential American sociologist in this century. In an essay on the concept of culture, he, too, raises the specter of the Left. In reply to "what might be called the dissident schools of social theory in modern society," he argues that "a great diversity of observers" has decided that American society is characterized by a "relatively justified inequality."[61] Statistics establish justice according to a relative norm: with such elegant brevity Parsons calls forth the discourse of culture. And he, too, draws on the example of the university. A university, he writes, "is primarily concerned with cognitive rationality and the imperatives of cognitive validity and significance," even though, as an ongoing social organization, it has to "handle property interests" and maintain "internal structures of authority" ("CSSR," 44). The negligibly "broad constraints of scholarly standards" that LeVine notes in graduate education here are the inessential or deviant relations between the knowledge produced within a university and its socioeconomic character as an institution. It is only to be expected that Parsons, too, should comfortably recognize normality and deviance as the basis of all cultural understanding:

> the meaning of cultural patterns seen in the context of their relation to action is *always* in some degree and respect normative. . . . There is, that is to say, always some range of variation from "correct" or otherwise acceptable action in relation to a cultural pattern or complex of patterns and varying modes or degrees of "incorrect" or unacceptable modes of action.

He goes on to instance behavioral codes, language, marriage relationships, and norms of "cognitive validity and significance" ("CSSR," 36).

The treatment of the category of deviancy by writers such as Parsons is revealing, but the point of these comparisons is not to pick a quarrel with these writers' ideas. That is a matter for a history-of-ideas approach to the concept of culture. The important point here is that these ideas are all developed within the discourse of culture. Particular interpretations of normality and deviancy are not at issue but rather the way writers seem constrained to reproduce these categories in one form or another and thus are bound to repress the realities of political differences within categories that appear to have nothing to do with power.

Although the point may be banal, it still is necessary to remember that normality and deviancy are not really two categories. They may be distinguished in terms of differences of power or, more usually, in terms of statistical differences, but such differences are incidental to the two categories. They belong to the methodology of description and measurement, not to the categories as such. Within the discourse of culture, the deviant is merely the shadow of the norm. In this respect, the *normal*, like *text* and *context* and various other terms involved in this discourse, appears as another name for *culture*. It is for this reason that redundant phrases and tautologous definitions, such as Halliday's "relevant context of situation"[62] and Ward Goodenough's definition of culture as "whatever it is one has to know or believe in order to operate in a manner acceptable to its members,"[63] play such an important part in the discourse of culture. They represent the gesture of drawing the boundary: the violent repression of history and the repetitive violence of that history being turned into unconsciousness.

These examples of specific writings are important for showing how statements within the discourse of culture will be inevitably and specifically political. However, a critical analysis of the politics involved here is bound to fall short of its goal unless it is also turned against the reproduction of these categories in any form. Otherwise, we quarrel with a particular definition of femininity instead of challenging the entire institution of gender. We persuade the American Medical Association, say, to recognize homosexuality as a legitimate form of sexuality and yet allow the legitimation of forms of sexuality by the medical profession to go without question. We criticize particular writings about culture or particular terms within these writings while allowing the discourse within which this rhetoric is generated to reproduce itself as a relation between our unconsciousness and our secret condescension to this unconsciousness.

In the absence of a greater social challenge, we allow this discourse to be reproduced as irony. This is the dominant trope in the elite art and criticism of modern Western nations because it represents the relative nature of the boundary drawn to institute the modern discourse of culture. The discourse of culture is ironic because it marks the discovery of the world as a whole, the world beyond ethnocentrism. It is no accident that the dominance of this discourse corresponds to a time when Western nations are receding from the political imperialism of the nineteenth century while expanding their power according to practices (economic, communicative, cognitive, and so on) represented as being institutionally neutral.

It might seem a long distance from such considerations to particular writings in fields such as anthropology and sociology, much less to a field like literary theory. And, indeed, the relation between the West and the Third World and its implication in the discourse of culture are beyond my ability to pursue except in the broadest of gestures. Nevertheless, it is within the scope of this argument to insist that politics of global significance belong directly and immediately to all the practices of the human sciences, no matter how far removed these may seem to be from such concerns. Because I am drawing on a great range of contexts to develop an argument that theory in individual disciplines is political in its every aspect, it might appear that I am trying to exaggerate trivial aspects of disciplines like literary studies into their entire character. If so, this perception is testimony only to how trivial we have made ourselves: to how much of ourselves we have abdicated to the unconscious functioning of institutions.

To be sure, there does not seem to be even a trivial political significance when someone like Umberto Eco argues that "the text is nothing else but the semantic-pragmatic production of its own Model Reader." However, he can make this argument only by generating a class of deviant readers, as critics traditionally have in trying to tame literature or the reading of literature. And just as political considerations have always been integral to these attempts at whipping literature into shape—as in the worry in the eighteenth and early nineteenth centuries that servants might idle away their time or inflame their baser passions by touching inappropriate literature—so are they involved in Eco's semiotic argument. In this case the politics are narrowed to matters of professional discipline and legitimacy, but Eco's attitude toward these matters is also an attitude toward society at large.

Eco maintains his model of interpretation by comparing a certain reading of Kafka to the product of a narcotic euphoria: an illegitimate product, an illusion. It is not really a "reading" that would disturb his theory but a species of intoxication, an uncontrolled and irresponsible effect of the body. It is deviant according to the same imagery critics traditionally have used to dismiss the perceptions of working-class and poor readers, political agitators, and in general, those who were unconventional in ways unacceptable to the dominant culture. Moreover, the reading Eco dismisses from the realm of meaning—a reading of Kafka's *Trial* "as a trivial criminal novel"[64]—suggests the community between "high" and "low" art that Eco's theory is designed to bar from perception, just as if he were proclaiming the fine old tradition of humanism. Only the power of political repression can prove to us that the banality of reading *The Trial* as an existentialist parable, say, makes any more sense than its reading as a trivial criminal novel. (The latter reading, indeed, seems very suggestive. Imagine what would happen if one took this novel literally, as it were, refusing its usual psychological characterization, and thus seeing significance in its triviality rather than in profundity of one sort or another. This triviality then might show how strange it is that newspaper accounts of crimes, say, are written as they are and not as Kafka wrote.)

The similarities between Eco's treatment of deviancy and its treatment within a long-standing literary and philosophical tradition are a significant indication of the politics at work in his theory, but the difference between this theory and humanist tradition should not be forgotten. In the eighteenth and nineteenth centuries or at earlier times, certain readings would be classified as deviant because these readings or their consequences were perceived as threats to social order, moral integrity, beauty, or similar entities. In Eco's theory, these political considerations appear only in the choice of imagery or examples. In this form, they become "unconscious." They appear in this way because deviancy within the modern discourse of culture does not belong to any argument or state of things. Deviancy is the category automatically produced by drawing the cultural boundary, the "model," and therefore it neither requires nor accepts any argument. It is made to be without meaning by the exigencies of a discourse, not by individual statements. Perhaps the best image for the deviant as it is produced in the discourse of culture is the *desaparecido*, the figure so removed from social relations of all sorts that it appears only through the denial of any recognition of its existence. The legitimacy that cultural relativism or pluralism may grant particular deviants does not change the fact that the discourse of culture remains as a mode of understanding and thus as a way of producing legitimacy and deviancy.

This image of the *desaparecido* may seem extreme. But extreme measures are required for understanding how anyone who has spent any time teaching has not learned how students will produce readings that are wildly euphoric (to use Eco's image) even though these students have already been subjected to considerable disciplinary authority in their earlier schooling. Culture is not, as Julia Kristeva has described it, "the general text" of which texts are part "and which is, in turn, part of them."[65] Although culture is a discourse that produces a specific conception of general and particular texts, which I have been analyzing here, texts appear interrelated within culture only to those who have subscribed to this discourse. To put it simply, culture allows people like Eco to ignore the rhetorical authority they exercise as writers and teachers and thus disappears the organizations of power from which this authority is drawn.

An emphasis on the relativity of the cultural boundary makes it possible for us to read a culture without seeing the political and historical nature of its phenomena and without seeing the implication of the observer in the same politics and history. In Melville J. Herskovits's anthropological formulation, the interpreter accepts "the validity of every set of norms for the people who have them, and the values these represent."[66] Similarly, in Putnam's philosophical formulation, the interpreter accepts "the interest-relativity of explanation."[67] This emphasis makes it rhetorically possible to preserve an underlying humanism: a faith in a universal human nature that drones on through all the differences like a prolonged bass note, making them perceptible and meaningful to each other, or that pulses through them, or that somehow blooms from them as a harvest of "potential" or "richness." Thus, in a formulation Derrida's work has accustomed critics to see, Kluckhohn argues that the "traits of a zoological species are not the less objective or in a sense 'universal' because of the occasional birth of 'sports' or 'monstrosities.' " In the example Kluckhohn uses in another passage, "In spite of loose talk (based upon an uncritical acceptance of an immature theory of cultural relativity) to the effect that the symptoms of mental disorder are completely relative to culture, the fact of the matter is that all cultures define as abnormal individuals who are permanently inaccessible to communication or who consistently fail to maintain some degree of control over their impulse life."[68]

Despite its evident power, the coherence of this emphasis on cultural relativity cannot withstand critical analysis. In the first place, ethnocentrism appears as a political and historical reality that is not dissolved by cultural relativity but indissolubly allied with it. Logical incoherence is a result of this situation,[69] but this is significant only in relation to a larger political result. The fact that the interpreter assumes the position of one who is able to accept the integrity and difference of other cultures—indeed, even to recognize "other cultures" as such—implies a specific state of sociohistorical circumstances and thus a specific political standpoint toward the world. As Foucault says, one "cannot speak of anything at any time."[70] The assumption of this position is not a possibility for everyone at every time in the history of the world. It is inconceivable apart from conditions virtually nonexistent before the twentieth century and relevant only to a miniscule number of people even within this century. In Derrida's words,

> Now, ethnology—like any science—comes about within the element of discourse. And it is primarily a European science employing traditional concepts, however much it may struggle against them. Consequently, whether he wants to or not—and this does not depend on a decision on his part—the ethnologist accepts into his discourse the premises of ethnocentrism at the very moment when he denounces them. This necessity is irreducible; it is not a historical contingency.[71]

Or, as Diamond puts it, in one of his better moments, "Relativism is the bad faith of the conquerer, who has become secure enough to become a tourist."[72]

As the quotations from Kluckhohn indicate, the universal aspects of human nature discovered by anthropology and the other human sciences are always produced through the exclusion of "sports," "monstrosities," or other deviants. These aspects are universal only within the modern discourse of culture. Although it plays a rhetorical role similar to terms like the *proper* or the *moral* or the *true*, it is not equivalent to them. It is not a transparent translation of their meaning, and its appearance in discourse does not simply reproduce their rhetorical role. The *normal* is involved in signifying practices (such as those that define the human sciences in relation to the natural sciences; the formal separation of knowledge from nationality, race, class, and religion; the statistical view of humanity; and modern political forms) in which there appears a binding relation between rhetorical and historical realities.

The idea that we can rise above this criticism by reaching a mature level of abstraction (as opposed to "an immature theory of cultural relativity") is also incoherent. Kluckhohn's argument about abnormality is a relatively simple case in this regard. In order to see the problem with his cross-cultural abstractions of communication and impulse control, we have only to look to the way Russian security forces, legal institutions, and psychiatrists cooperate to treat what the West calls "dissidence" as "insanity." For description to rise above context, as Kluckhohn would have it, it must paper over such differences in the institutionalization of power in different societies. Otherwise, it is verifiably untrue that there are "symptoms of mental disorder" universally recognized as such. Nor can we avoid this criticism by arguing that every culture always has a category of the abnormal, whatever differences there may be in the practices by which it is designated and treated. Then we simply are indulging in the kind of mythological syncretism that produces history as the history of ideas, which is the modern form of the universal histories of the Renaissance. To say "mental disorders" are recognized in all cultures, including within this category phenomena variously conceived to be constituted by divinity, genius, ill humors, psychological trauma, and neurochemical imbalance, is to be enchanted by language to the point of historical hallucination. In its continual discovery of the same within differences, this approach simply reproduces across all cultures a form of identity that is compelling only to the institutionalization of a particular kind of intellectual. Intellectuals in this way multiply their specular images, listen in amazement to the echoes of their own voices, and believe their narcissistic projections are all there is to perceive in the world, or in culture, or in language—whatever the ironic resting place may be. The only necessity described by this approach is the necessity of an intellectual discipline to those who uncritically adopt it.[73]

In this regard, Lévi-Strauss, again, may appear more complex. In *The Savage Mind*, he writes, "I believe the ultimate goal of the human sciences to be not to constitute, but to dissolve man." He relates this enterprise to those "which are incumbent on the exact natural sciences: the reintegration of culture in nature and finally of life within the whole of its physico-chemical conditions." In a footnote, he adds a comment referring to *The Elementary Structures of Kinship*: "The opposition between nature and culture to which I attached much importance at one time . . . now seems to be of primarily methodological importance" (*SM*, 247). But this argument is again a fantasy of nature before man, a nature not articulated by culture. Just as he regards "woman," a socially constituted being, as a universal entity of organs and functions, Lévi-Strauss now regards empiricism, a socially constituted form of knowledge, as an ideal rationality.

In his more valuable moments Lévi-Strauss sees "man" as a creature that produces and is produced by the meanings articulated in myth, arts, tools, books, and, in general, culture, which names a social relation to material conditions. When he forgets himself, as it were, dreaming of a nature before man, repressing the consciousness that analysis is always implicated in historical conditions and therefore can never attain to a neutral instrumentality, his writing about culture becomes a distorted commentary on the sociohistorical conditions of this writing as a disciplinary activity. We cannot put this difference between nature and culture within the brackets of methodology and so have done with it. Instead, we must continually criticize, work on, its irrational necessity. Just as we cannot always say anything, we cannot not say something simply by putting a particular word out of bounds.

In the field of literary theory as in anthropology, when the relativity of the cultural boundary is called on to protect the terms of normality from criticism, this protection proves to be incoherent. Stanley Fish's argument is a case in point:

> the category [of the normal] as it appears in [my] argument is not
> transcendental but institutional; and while no institution is so universally
> in force and so perdurable that the meanings it enables will be normal

for ever, some institutions or forms of life are so widely lived in that for a great many people the meanings they enable seem "naturally" available and it takes a special effort to see that they are the products of circumstances.[74]

As I noted in the preceding chapter, the first problem with this approach is that, despite its qualifications, it universalizes "the institution" and, within the institution, "the normal." The consequence is the repression of political and historical differences within a show of neutral rationality. This show is represented by Fish's easeful style and by his sociological lexicon (viz., "products of circumstances"). The opposition between vague phrases like "a great many people" and "a special effort" marks the inevitable but distorted admission within this discourse of its unjustifiable political status. "A great many people" are the subjects that must be made unconscious of their culture in order for the discourse of culture to be produced. And the "special effort" of analytic insight represents the attempt to repress from analysis a consciousness of its own conditions of possibility, including the condition of secret condescension toward its subjects. Just as E. D. Hirsch, Fish's opposite number, proves arguments by what he takes to be an incontestable appeal to the "sensible man,"[75] so does Fish appeal to the normal man. The difference between the "sensible" and the "normal" is negligible when we consider their rhetorical function and political implications; and, indeed, Hirsch and Fish are opposite numbers only to those who identify uncritically with the discourse of culture. Within a critical approach, their "objectivist" and "subjectivist" positions are bound to each other by predictable rhetorical transformations within this field of discourse.

V

He went up to the traveller, again pulled out the small leather case, leafed through it, finally found the paper he wanted, and showed it to the traveller. "Read," he said. "I can't," said the traveller. "I already said I can't read these papers." . . . Now the officer began to spell out the inscription, and then he read out the words. "It means 'Be just!' " he said; "now you certainly can read it." The traveller bowed so deeply over the paper that the officer withdrew it for fear that he would touch it; then the traveller said nothing more, but it was clear he still had not been able to read. "It means 'Be just!' " said the officer again. "It may be," said the traveller. "I believe it is written there."

—Kafka[76]

Some of the incoherence in the concept of culture arises from the manifold uses of this term, which can only aspire to the ideal of scientific discipline. However, we cannot clarify our language on this point and so come to an adequate definition. Nor can this term be refined through the distinction between culture and society, popular among some anthropologists and sociologists, that identifies society with the living persons in a formally isolated community and culture with the practices, beliefs, meanings, and other features of social life that transcend the lives of these specific persons as an ongoing inheritance or tradition. In the first case, we cannot agree on a proper definition of culture because such a definition would represent the very politics of culture, the politics of propriety, it was meant to exclude. In the second, the distinction between culture and society falls apart once we realize that terms like *persons, communities,* and *culture* are not universals but terms constituted within societies and meaningless apart from their appearance in discourse, which is always social and historical.

The problem is not in the language of culture. "Culture" has not simply fallen short of "science" like a long-jumper who misses the mark but may gather his or her forces and try again. The problem is in the failure to understand that culture is a linguistic creation, not a field of study or work to which language is applied after the fact. The delineation of culture in any sense can proceed only by way of rhetorical figures, relations, and procedures, such as drawing the ethnographic boundary, establishing contextual rules to evaluate information within and across cultures, and defining deviancy. This rhetoric has meaning only to those who have subscribed to a certain discourse. Such subscription involves material relations and formations such as geographical placement, distributions of power, technologies of production and control, and institutionalized social practices. These cannot be comprehended within the human sciences because their recognition would disrupt the apparatus of rationality on which the ideologies of these disciplines depend. This apparatus includes elements such as the neutral observer, freedom of discussion, and the distinction between discourse and force. No matter how scientific the discourse of culture becomes, then, the definition of culture must remain political, and in fact most profoundly political in the attempt to give it the character of scientific regularity.[77]

It is history, not reason, that decides the issue of definition. This is not to say that a transcendent agent named *history* leads meaning in a tango across space and time. *History,* here, is not a term that simply substitutes for *culture,* thereby correcting the analysis performed ineptly under the name of culture. *History* signifies the absence of transcendent authority under any name: idealism, pragmatism, community or culture, text, or whatever. It signifies the political constitution of all meaning: the materiality of all rhetoric and the rhetoricity of all signifying practices.

The problem of defining culture does not call for a refinement of this concept or for the invention of a new and better one. It calls for political work. More specifically, it calls for intellectuals to criticize their implication in the discourse of culture and so to resist the authority of this discourse. Despite all the differences in the use of this word, *culture*, the discourse of culture is powerfully institutionalized across the disciplines within the contemporary social sciences and humanities and so acts on our lives, whether or not we assent to it. Insofar as texts are constituted and interpreted within this discourse, it is against this discourse that we must struggle if we are not satisfied with the ways textuality, reading, and writing have been institutionalized.

In the simplest terms, what needs to be understood is that the culture in terms of which we understand textuality is not one imposed on our nature, as the saying goes, but one with which we identify ourselves, consciously or unconsciously. After all, what is the culture to which Shakespeare's texts belong: the culture of Renaissance England, of art, of Western metaphysics, of Elizabethan and Jacobean theater, of courtly society in the late sixteenth and early seventeenth centuries, of patriarchy, of the Unconscious, of monarchical politics, of desire, of certain metaphors? We can read Shakespeare in terms of these or other cultural fields (and of course the choice need not be singular). In any event, the identification of the culture at issue, the portrayal of that culture, and the meaning drawn from the relation between text and culture will be political acts that project the existence of a community.

Community in this sense is always imaginary. It is never entirely present to itself. It is neither an empirical community nor an ideal community but rather a community of desire. It is the community that would have to exist if our experience of reading were to have meaning, were to be culturally recognized, in its every aspect. This community would be the totality that culture always demands and yet contradicts. It is always imaginary, an impossible concatenation of the rhetorical movements through which we articulate our relation to the words of a text; and yet the real force of such imaginary identifications is manifested in the way our lives, in every aspect our language gives to them (reading, eating, work and play, and so on), witness to the organizations of power in society. Community is not innocent because it is imaginary.

Culture understood as discourse is not an authority but a will to power. It is an appeal to understanding rather than the ground to which one appeals for understanding. It is a contested social desire rather than a coherent frame to the production of ideologies. To analyze culture as this *lack* of interpretive authority is to make reading, which is always a political exercise, a deliberate interrogation of its own political nature. One views authority as a matter of identification rather than a matter of truth, objective or subjective nature, understanding, context, or some other conception more or less deliberately taken from the traditions of philosophical idealism.

This is not to say that authority is simply a psychological matter. Although it always remains imaginary, the cultural authority with which we identify is constructed of social relations; and therefore its psychology will always involve material forms of power that are historical variables.

If we view culture as discourse in this way, interpretive authorities are seen always to stand in material relationships to each other. These relations may include disjunction, conflict, partial allegiance, and all the other rhetorical figures, relations, and procedures of discourse. (As Wittgenstein writes, "The civil status of a contradiction, or its status in civil life: there is the philosophical problem."[78]) For example, statutory and constitutional codes of law may form an interpretive authority but only in relation to their empowerment, whether by the courts, political rhetoric, pedagogical practices, or other means. In their turn, these forms of empowerment stand in complex relations to each other or, more exactly, are always being constituted by these relations. In this situation and others, the only transcendent authority that stands over individuals is the totality they imagine in their interpretation of a given text.

The task of criticism is not to identify this imaginary totality and replace it with a real totality of social relations, for there is no real totality. There certainly are binding relations, the points at which authority becomes a compelling force acting on individuals. However, there is no coherent logic, inevitability, or rationality directing these relations, even though they will show, for instance, the inequalities in the distribution of power within a society. To think otherwise is to idealize society or the state or history and thus to identify, consciously or not, with the dominant powers within the inequitable situation in which one finds oneself. The task of criticism is to insist on the imaginary nature of totality, to show the lack of authority in discourse, and thus, by analyzing the historical nature of desire, to turn it away from institutionalized powers and make it available for social change.

In this way, understanding culture as a discourse may lead us to understand that authority is never real, no matter how binding it may appear in an interpretive situation. It is always the effect of an identification with an imaginary community: with an imaginary totality of relations. Therefore, it is always open to a future in which, and a desire by which, it can be changed. This is not to deny that authority may forcefully inscribe its way of reading on individuals, becoming an indubitable and all-encompassing reality for people subjected to sufficient power, as in Kafka's penal colony, Pinochet's Chile, or any number of other places. The effect of this critical analysis is a refusal to see any boundary of complete coherence and totality even in the extremes of suffering and death. It makes the task of criticism include a commitment to those who have been the victims of oppression in the past along with its commitment to greater social equality in the present and the future. It refuses to cede even the body, even death, to authority.

History, in the old saw, keeps the past alive. Criticism should go beyond remembering the past, recovering it in ever more detail and completeness. Through an identification with those who, throughout history, have suffered to make authority seem real, the task of criticism should be to change the past. As Freud may have argued, criticism should be able to destroy the authority the past may hold over desire.

This language may appear inappropriate. It may seem either euphoric or, perhaps, moralistic, mechanical, bombastic, sentimental, empty—something like that. But then one insight of this criticism is that there are no privileged rhetorical forms. When Marxist critics imply that there are such forms, as when Rosalind Coward and John Ellis compare Brecht's play *The Mother* to Pudovkin's 1926 film of the same Gorky story—"The effect is emotional and strong, but transitory; Brecht's is exemplary and moving"[79]—their position is as dogmatic as the position of elitism in which critics on the right place themselves. The same conclusion applies to the way avant-garde writers are apotheosized by critics like Kristeva.

There is no form above politics and no form especially correct politically, although American moralists and the government of the U.S.S.R. would argue otherwise. If language viewed from any perspective (style, theme, plot, and so on) appears unequivocally coherent and transparent to meaning, this appearance simply represents the surface of unconsciousness in the identification through which we are reading the text in question. Critical activity needs to remain mobile, open to and engaged in conflicting readings, so that the authority of the text may be kept in question. If the result is a criticism that sometimes breaks with the protocols of particular disciplines, genres, or other sorts of rhetorical forms, these breaks do not represent liberation, as some theorists of the avant-garde would have it; but they need not represent a failure, a fall from cultural grammaticality. Instead, they bring into relief the political differences always crossing texts in the acts of reading and writing.

As previously noted, in regarding culture as discourse, the first consideration to be kept in mind is that this "logic" does not have a rational or systematic form. This is the first consideration not from any immanent necessity, but because the fields of explanation with which I am concerned here—anthropology, history, sociology, literary theory, and so on—have striven for organization in this form. On the other hand, culture is not simply a text of arbitrary differences, as one might imagine a text to be if it could appear before or beyond the binding relations of social life. (This is the text of structural linguistics and, at times, the text with which Derrida appears to identify his method.) Instead, while this discourse appears as a mobile and formally unpredictable text, it is composed of rhetorical figures, relations, and procedures that establish a historical domain of signification.

We can isolate these elements of discourse, identify them formally, and draw relationships among them that will make them appear coherent, transcendentally ordered, and possessed of a rich interiority of significance. To do so, however, is to transform a discourse of culture into culture pure and simple. This process of transformation is very much the business of anthropology, history, literary theory, and other disciplines, since all disciplines tend to thematize their interest in their institutional forms as a discovery of cultural form. In this way they obscure the absence of authority in culture, which is to say, its lack of authoritative definition, its heterogeneity, and, most important of all, its historical status as a discourse people have made and can unmake through changes in their social relations.

Insofar as these disciplines conceive of knowledge only as rationality or systematicity, they cannot comprehend the imaginary nature of the cultural boundary and thus of all community and identity. They cannot comprehend how power exists in this imaginary form and yet touches us materially, oppresses us, inflicts pain. Consequently, they cannot comprehend how this imaginary form—this culture, this text—may be opened to change as we act critically on the constitution of knowledge within our social practices.

A homely example of this situation, and yet one that is not entirely trivial, may be suggested by the authority of a literary critic. If it takes more than an arbitrary fiat to distinguish among the brands of critical activity in the marketplace today, there is no demonstrable hierarchy of truth in this field. There is only a demonstrable hierarchy of prestige, which comes through recognition, which in turn is an effect of place, circumstance, and historical moment as these conditions happen to winnow out the power of success. To say so is not to assert that all tastes in critical opinion are equal but, on the contrary, to disabuse us of the idealist notion of equality enshrined in the traditional academic belief in meritocracy (and, incidentally, in the belief in tradition itself). It is to assert that literary criticism has a history, as does the interpretation of law or any other subject. Furthermore, we may contribute to this history in an alienated way (by assuming there is no history but only the rule of law) or more consciously (by trying to decide what a critical reading should be instead of trying to decide what a correct reading is). Instead of looking for identities prescribed to individuals by psychology, ontology, or history, we may question the process of identification and change the imaginary authorities with which we identify by working for change in our social life. We may struggle for critical values instead of stumbling over them as we do when culture is taken as a rock one can kick and thus refute all deviants: all those who lack a coherent identity.

In discovering laws, structures, conventions, norms, and similar realities in the object of their analysis, disciplines discover the imaginary necessities of their own institutionalization within society.[80] As Francis Sparshott has noted in the case of E. D. Hirsch's literary theory, "Hirsch's insistence on the priority of authorial meaning rests on the necessity of establishing one meaning for a text, a necessity that obtains nowhere outside the examination hall and its purlieus."[81] (And, it should be added, not even in these places except as they are governed by pedagogical practices neither necessary nor universal in our educational institutions.) If compared to the work of his opponent in this respect, the work of Fish again appears more like Hirsch's than unlike it. Fish simply makes theoretically explicit the uncritical identification with the functioning of an institution that Hirsch puts into his Arnoldian terror of a "chaotic democracy of 'readings,' "[82] which he believes must result if authorial intention is abandoned as the basis for judging the difference between the normal and the deviant in the activity of inter- pretation. Hence Fish's "no sweat" approach to differences of critical approach and opinion.

Tzvetan Todorov, when writing of "the impossibility of escaping verisimili- tude" in *The Poetics of Prose*, illustrates perfectly this institutional compulsion that results from the failure of critical reflection. "The murder-mystery writer," he tells us, "is not alone in suffering this fate" of being subjected to verisimili- tude:

> All of us do, and all the time. From the very first we find ourselves in a situation less favorable than his: he can contest the laws of verisimilitude, and even make antiverisimilitude his law. Though we may discover the laws and conventions of this life around us, it is not within our power to change them—we shall always be obliged to obey them, though such obedience is twice as difficult after this discovery. It comes as a bitter surprise when we realize that our life is governed by the same laws we discovered in our morning paper and that we cannot change them. To know that justice obeys the laws of verisimilitude, not of truth, will keep no one from being sentenced.[83]

Let us make the charitable assumption that Todorov is not writing about partic- ular "laws and conventions" of social life but rather about the difference between laws of truth, which are available to us only in the form of nostalgia, fantasy, and desire, and laws of verisimilitude, which are the only laws present to us, governing us, and which present themselves as being arbitrary. Even if we make this assumption that the author is not simply identifying with the dominant authorities of society, what sense can there be in saying that it is not in our power to change the laws of verisimilitude?

To make sense of this passage, assume that Todorov is not suggesting that there are universal laws of verisimilitude. He is suggesting only that every soci- ety is governed by laws that have the power of truth even though they are founded in social convention and not in any ultimate ground of reality. This passage then would seem to say that there is no way for us not to be in a society, a statement that is at once tautologous (for what are "we" if not a social collectivity?) and insupportable (since "our life" is not a coherent and homogenous whole that can be accurately described as being "governed by the same laws" even within a single society). Moreover, it would seem that this statement is designed to dis- tinguish between fiction, which is associated with creativity, and "the life around us," which is associated with writing that is uncreative and with laws, conventions, fate, and bitterness. This passage then narrates a fall from the freedom of consciousness to the subjection of social life that contradicts its implication that social life in any case is prior to consciousness or, in other words, that truth is a function of verisimilitude.

Such is the incoherence that may result when intellectuals project their institutional compulsions as textual or cultural laws. In this case, the compulsions are characteristic of literary studies even after structuralism. For instance, there is the idealization of art in distinction from life, which serves to maintain the intellectual's authority in canonizing and interpreting texts, among other purposes. (We see how culture is, in part, a recurrent *romantic* gesture.) There is also the valuing of reflection, which is difficult and associated with profound emotion, over physical activity, which is associated with unconsciousness and servility. As it serves to distinguish knowledge from action and truth from social reality, among other things, this aspect of the passage also makes the institution of literature appear detached from society and innocent of any social responsibility.

We could carry this analysis further. For instance, we could consider the assumptions we would have to make in order to support the idea that justice follows laws of verisimilitude. (Surely no one but an absent-minded professor would believe that justice follows a code available in the newspapers.) However, the important point here is that the formulation of cultural laws within our disciplines of interpretation can be seen to represent, and in very specific forms, the sociohistorical positions and political identifications of those who present them.

Of course, there are as many ways of reading as there are imaginable subjectivities. We could read this passage as something of an excursus, the script of a fit of melancholy, perhaps. In that case, if we noticed the incoherence I have analyzed, it might appear to be nothing more than a sign of the disorientation that overcame this writer as he was stabbed by a memory or an irruption of anger that he worked into the appearance of a rational argument. Similarly, when Lévi-Strauss describes man as a player at a card game who "must accept the cards" he is given and who must follow "systems" of interpretation, "rules of the game or rules of tactics" (*SM*, 95), we might ignore the issue of cultural law and instead read this passage as an instance of the mythological habit of thought, by which all human beings (we might argue) develop figures of speech to give a seeming order to their cosmos. Or, as a last example, when Malinowski describes the "legitimate subject matter" of culture — "the establishment of general laws, and of concepts which embody such laws"[84] — we might gloss his words in terms of the spirit of science, its struggles to establish itself, its victories and tragedies, its unquenchable desire, and so on. There are innumerable other possibilities, and I cannot dismiss their value or even assume it is less than the value of the present reading without doing violence to my own analysis.

It is not beside the point to raise the possibility of other readings that may not come close to touching on the concerns of the present analysis. It still is very much to the point, though, to analyze how the discourse of culture shuts down this kind of possibility in accordance with historically specific political measures.

How Lévi-Strauss, for instance, allows for complexity and variation in the game and yet does not recognize that we are not all interchangeable players . . . that some people may be players while others are cards and still others are rules, limits, wagers . . . that a situation in which there is "a connection between the male and the consumer and the female and the thing consumed" (*SM*, 100) cannot be described adequately as a game.

How the desire for scientific law, in Malinowski's case, does not simply derive "inspiration" from the "practical problems" of "colonial policy, missionary work," and the like, but instead is intrinsically allied to the elaboration of such practices.

How the language of cultural law (convention, norm, context . . .) must always produce elisions, *desaparecidos*, forms of repression . . . which must be read if we are not to be, in our reading as in every aspect of our lives, textual functions, figures compulsively reproducing and reproduced . . . the banal oppressor, the tiresome victim . . .

VI

*The duty of the anthropologist is to be a fair and true
interpreter of the Native. . . . He ought to be able to make
clear to traders, missionaries, and exploiters what the Natives
really need and where they suffer most under the pressure of
European interference.*

—Malinowski[85]

*George Bailey, an American who had worked for the right-
wing Springer press group in West Germany, became the head
of Radio Liberty, which broadcasts solely to the Soviet
Union. . . .*

*One of Mr. Bailey's first innovations was to remove the
American supervisors who had traditionally watched over the
copy broadcast to the Soviet Union. "It has to be a Uzbek who
has to decide what Uzbeks want to hear and not a sunburned
American from Iowa," Mr. Bailey said.*

—The New York Times *(10 June 1984)*[86]

The one, perhaps, is quaint, recalling Carlyle's impassioned meditations on the working classes and, more recently, Charlie Marlow's brooding over the face of the jungle. It may be quaint, that is, if it is dated enough so it is not embarrassing and distant enough (how literary, now, the White Man's Burden, Stanley and Livingstone, Tarzan) so we cannot be angry—how can we be angry at history? *Dated, distant, literary, history*—this assortment of words may begin to describe a conception of culture, which is to say, a text that makes a certain kind of sense.

The other, perhaps, is invisible, an anonymous prose (this could be so many newspapers speaking) even if the byline (James M. Markham) and the date of its publication are known. It may seem neutral (with the unremarkable exception of *right wing*), informational, factual, straightforward, transparent—if we believe news can ever not be literary, if we are not Soviet leaders or American leftists, if none of us is "a sunburned American from Iowa." *Anonymous, neutral, informational, straightforward*: these words, too, may begin to describe a conception of text and culture.

But just how different are these conceptions? What is the difference between an anthropologist speaking for Natives and a Uzbek speaking for Uzbeks? The former may be taken to represent a liberal paternalism that has become outmoded and the latter an enlightened approach to cultural relativism. However, these passages can be differentiated in this way only if one fails to recognize the imperative of the modern discourse of culture: *secretly* to condescend.

Historically, there is no such thing as a Uzbek talking to Uzbeks, a Native to Natives. This relation exists only within the tautologous definitions by which political differences and conflicts are repressed within the discourse of culture. What speaks here is not identity but Radio Liberty, the Reagan administration, sunburned Americans from Iowa, stupid and cynical political maneuvers . . .

In both passages, what speaks is the discourse of culture. To say so is not to do away with their differences but to recognize that both passages, through all their differences, can make sense only in terms of this discourse that draws a boundary around the real needs of Natives and the real desires of Uzbeks and thus implies certain relations between figures like text and context, the normal and the deviant, and identity and community. Whereas the differences between the work of Bailey and Malinowski are bound to appear vast if placed in other perspectives, as my initial description indicated, it is urgent that we be able to recognize this convergence in their colloquially American and professorially Victorian styles. Otherwise, we may mistake the renovation of discourse for the renovation of political acts and attitudes when, in fact, we are witnessing a more dazzling projection of imaginary authority.

Scholars, teachers, and writers in the contemporary world do not all sit down and elaborate a theory of culture before they begin to read a text. Most rely on an ad hoc concept of culture, what amounts to a "sense" of the conventions, values, traditions, rules, and other elements involved in the meaning of the text, whether this be a written document, a dance, a painting, a social ritual, or whatever. The fact that this concept so commonly is taken for granted, however, does not mean that our disciplines of interpretation could reform themselves if only more people would examine and refine their premises. No doubt scholars of a theoretical bent will continue to debate how culture should be defined and analyzed, but this debate will remain fundamentally misguided unless the concept of culture is recognized as the product of a massive discourse. It is not an object we are free to fiddle with to make it a better tool, model, or representation. On the contrary, to a very great extent the discourse in which it appears determines our conceptions of tools, models, and representations, among many other things. Political practice rather than conceptual refinement is called for in this situation.

We do not need a more rigorous interrogation of this concept in order to discipline our studies more strictly, to establish clearer rules of legitimacy and illegitimacy in our fields, and to build a hierarchy of values better than those currently in play. Such an approach can lead only to the kind of improvement Mr. Bailey may be said to represent over Professor Malinowski. We need a more rigorous interrogation so we can make our studies more open, calling into question not only their disciplines, rules, and values, but all the conditions and practices that have established these forms and changed them over time. Because the discourse of culture is so thoroughly involved in the constitution of these fields of knowledge at the present time, its interrogation is necessary if we are to confront the concept of history itself: if we are to conceive of history as the articulation of difference and possibility in human life and not as an expression of identity and necessity imposed on that life.

Through the critique of the discourse of culture, it is possible to conceive a freedom that is neither ideal nor utopian but material, provisional, topical, strategic. In this sense freedom is not a state of being to be understood, to be made conscious, but rather a way to live. Such a freedom is bound to appear unsatisfying to those enchanted by the traditions of philosophical idealism (a community that includes those who believe in revolutionary spontanaiety along with political conservatives and reactionaries), but perhaps the strongest opponent to such a conception among intellectuals is not among these characters. Its strongest opponent is probably the professionalism that has made desire an embarrassment if it appears as a struggle for social change—in other words, as politics—instead of appearing as the subject of a discipline such as psychoanalysis, anthropology, or literary theory. In the United States, "the sixties" are currently the time to which this embarrassment is assigned (although those who were students at the time might be surprised at how many professors now long for the lively students of those days), whereas almost every aspect of academic life now leads the student and the professor to "focus" themselves. They are led to specialize (an imperative that now includes the specialized focus on a "core curriculum") and to conceive of knowledge solely as technique, theory, or information. Under these conditions, knowledge becomes an imaginary law rather than the activity of interpretation. It becomes a social *donnée* rather than a social practice open to change.

Perhaps it should be emphasized again that this analysis of law as an imaginary phenomenon does not deny its material reality within the conditions of our lives. Rather, this analysis insists on the absence of authority to which criticism must always return if it is not to yield to the metaphysics of truth, nature, universality, necessity—in the present instance, "culture"—that give power the appearance of being something other than a social creation open to social change. The lack of any ideal authority, any ultimate determination of significance, any transcendental signified, does not mean that laws in the human sciences or anywhere else are "only" ideological and so may be irritably brushed off like so much lint from a coat. It means that power does not exist in a substantial or totalized form.

Power has the form of a rhetoric with which one must struggle in proximate, discontinuous, heterogeneous ways. Its resistance to understanding can be countered only in such ways because power does not follow a unified logic or sense. It consists of the articulation of differences according to rhetorical figures, relations, and procedures that vary topically, regionally, and historically without possessing any original or final form. To regard it otherwise is to identify with topically, regionally, and historically specific institutions—such as the state, or humankind, or reason—and thus to add to the power they already have the imaginary excess, the surplus value, by which teleologies, systems, human nature, and the like are made to emerge from historical events. Thus, in recognizing this lack of totality, this absence of authority, critical practice at the same time must insist on the reality of this imaginary authority and on the material truth of rhetoric. Materialism will forever be the shadow of idealism unless it insists on the material reality of signifying practices of all kinds, including texts in the narrower sense of written documents but also behaviors, events, technologies, institutions, and all other forms of social life.

Thus understood, texts exist only as they are called into being, into the realm of signification, by discursive procedures that may be said to be historically contingent. However, they are historically contingent only insofar as idealist conceptions of teleology or necessity are concerned. This is not to say that texts are "merely" contingent or entirely given over to "pure" chance, as if there could be a realm of event that is not always already discourse. It is rather to say that historical change is not governed by universal laws of nature or divinity or reason but rather by politics.

Consider in this respect that familiar kind of text, a written publication. To a certain extent, the uses of a piece of writing intended for publication may be calculated. Someone involved with the text (author, editor, publisher, critic, or the like) may be able to judge successfully its appeal to a certain audience, the degree of interest or controversy it is likely to stimulate, even its likelihood of becoming a "classic" — but never with any finality. Every text finally is bound only by the irreducible multiplicity of interpretations to which it is subjected through time, a multiplicity neither totally random nor totally rational. Just as we cannot say anything at any time, we cannot say anything for all time. The text is bound only by the logic of discourse, which is a matter of rhetorical configurations constituted by historically specific political contests, not a matter of meaning or intention or truth pure and simple.

Every text is bound only by the fate of its historical distribution and treatment, which in turn are determined by material conditions, technologies, various institutions (such as the institutions of legal and economic rights), social relations (including political conflicts that may be limited to individuals or that may cross the borders of entire nations), and, at last, individuals. Of course, individuals play a part in every aspect of this fate. However, it is not within the power of individual prescription or prediction. This fate, again, is not universal — a fate of metaphysics, morality, genius, or transparent meaning — but historical. The heterogeneous play of the relations among individuals in their social existence constitutes this fate. I deliberately use the term *fate* in contrast to hoary expressions of teleological confidence like *the test of time* and in contrast also to the metaphysics of normality. Historical fate suggests neither justice nor dogmatic rule. It suggests the way meaning takes its chances in a world where the rule of law, truth, justice, taste, and similar ideals operates only in specialized, circumscribed, and conflicting domains of social life.

This incalculability of the text is significant in several respects. Most obviously, it fits with common sense, which is not always to be despised. How many anecdotes do we know of "geniuses" who read certain pieces of "trash" and called them "masterpieces," or how many stories of those who passed over "masterpieces" they considered to be "trash"? (With Freud, one could say here that the text is both shit and gold.) Moreover, this incalculability also describes the complex materiality of the text. Within this incalculability, the text is real and has meaning only as it is materialized through its recognition within specific historical circumstances.

For the present argument, most important is the way this recognition of the text's incalculability emphasizes once again that culture, this field of textual meaning within contemporary disciplines of interpretation, is always an imaginary totality. For many intellectuals today, culture is the ideal that disseminates the politics of interpretation in every social situation. This ideal is as incoherent, flawed, glorious, hazy, vicious, desperate, empty, and beautiful as these situations may be, and yet an ideal the discourse of culture may bring us to regard as somehow overreaching this complexity to become a roof of objectivity sheltering our understanding.

In this respect the concept of culture might be compared to the "Reader" addressed in Romantic and post-Romantic literature. "Dear Reader," I might now write, nostalgically, Romantically. "You," I might imagine. But I do not write to "you," to my "Reader." It is your absence I address, or I make you an absence by addressing you in writing (in fact, Derrida argues, by addressing you in any way). I write to an imaginary culture, which is not another name for *you*, an established identity and transparent meaning. It is a name for your absence and for the sociality where your absence might not be, or where you might be without the destructuring possibility of absence: without you being in a world of death. Texts have this imaginary address in their simplest forms, in a note to a friend or in a joke, and in the most complex of forms, such as history. The fate of the text is not the fate of the author's intentions, society's contexts, reason's laws, the reader's imagination, or anything of the sort. It is rather the fate of this imaginary culture, which is another way of describing the future we are making for texts, the history we struggle to make against all reasonable calculations—the address of desire.

We are unable not to say *man* and *woman*, *human being*, *society*, *culture*, and like words, at least as long as we are saying anything at all. In saying these words, we are unable not to wield universals. This sense of the universal with which language structures us may be seen to be deconstructed within the same language, if it is subjected to rigorous examination. Still, no matter how many professors may be examining it for the telltale abysses of reason, the constitution of identities performed through linguistic structuring needs to be examined in terms of historical conditions. "Culture" might be said to name the modern call of the universal—the call to a constitution of identity, knowledge, truth and error, and so on—and yet this name is nothing, is not even a word or the trace of a word, save in its social uses, whose range and logic are a matter of historically specific condtions. As Derrida has argued, universals in language can be neither argued into the terms of rationality nor argued out of discourse. As a reader of Derrida might argue, they can be fought only through activity directed toward historical change. We can begin to understand culture only by resisting cultural givens, substances, essences, facts, fates, appearances, and identities, including the identity of culture itself.

In resisting the universal, this critical activity might be accused of falling into the dialectical trap of stressing the local and thus representing a myth of spontanaiety, of community versus society, of immediacy versus abstraction, and so on. We can resist this dialectic through a recognition that there is no universal form of meaning but only forms of universality constituted through groups of people in societies according to procedures that can be analyzed and changed. The notion of universality appears necessary only to someone who identifies with the imaginary authority of a culture, whether in love, in hate, or in any other attitude, whereas a historical criticism enables us to describe the imaginary nature of this authority. It can show us that we need not oppose the local to the universal by showing us that the terms of this opposition have never been necessary and, in reality, have always been imaginary. A historical criticism is composed of this revisionary activity as long as we do not reify history in place of essence, substance, identity, and the like: as long as we take historical understanding to be a matter of political activity rather than a grasp of a specific, unified, coherent subject. It gives us this power as long as our critical activity reaches to the way knowledge is conceived so that work for social change and opposition to unconscious resistance are made part of its practice of understanding.

An example of this difference in the conception of knowledge might be taken from the issue of curriculum reform in universities, which in many instances are priding themselves on including "women's literature" in the canon. This goal is not bad, but it will prove to be short-sighted and self-defeating to anyone who desires radical social change in the relations between men and women unless it is carried out as part of a critique of canon formation, of the institution of literature and literary studies, of the institution of art and aesthetic value, and also, of course, of the institution of gender differences. Many people in women's studies departments and elsewhere are pursuing these approaches and are producing excellent work in teaching and various forms of social activism as well as in writing. But the liberal humanism that still dominates the social sciences and humanities deals with this kind of historical situation by reformulating the universal (for example, through a concept of "androgyny" or a revised concept of "female identity" or of "humanism"). It is significant also how *easily* many academics are incorporating the feminist challenge into their roles as teachers and scholars. We need only consider the phrase "a neglected masterpiece," which reproduces in miniature a vast array of traditional values even as it seems to challenge their sway through its application to works by women that generally have gone unrecognized. Or consider the idea of "admitting" or "including" or "adding" women into the canon. What is this thing, this canon, that can turn aside from women or swallow them, as it may happen to choose at a particular time?

A canon is a specialized model of culture, and we might recall here the violence in drawing the cultural boundary that institutes cultural relativism. The anthropologist isolates a phenomenon and says this phenomenon has a meaning in this culture that we should respect, however strange, abhorrent, or incoherent it may appear to us. Thus do scientism and liberal humanism embrace. But meaning is never general to society. Meaning is never homogenous across social differences. Therefore, all descriptions of culture and of phenomena understood in relation to culture are political acts involving identifications with certain people, forms of power, and orders of experience to the exclusion of others. The meaning of a clitoridectomy, for instance, is not the same for the girl undergoing it as for those performing it or for men as for women.

This example may seem Gothic or sentimentally exploitative. When in doubt, even relatively unpracticed orators may know enough to call forth a picture of a crying child. And there might be some point in so describing my use of this example. There is no reason to assume that this text should have any more immunity than any other when it comes to rejecting certain readings out of hand. But no matter how we may explain that this example is no more innocent than any other, the fact remains that this practice is widespread in the world today, especially in a number of Third World countries. It also remains a fact that the practice of clitoridectomy is the kind of cultural text many contemporary intellectuals want to analyze neutrally, within its context, and so forth. Malinowski is not a bizarre participant in the discourse of culture when he repeatedly uses clitoridectomy in *The Dynamics of Culture Change* as an example of the kind of practices Europeans have been ethnocentric in criticizing. He compares it to Western circumcision, controversies over forms of baptism, and the like.

Any number of other examples could be entered here. For instance, the meaning of free enterprise in the United States is not the same for blacks or Hispanics as for whites, for the poor working class as for the wealthy, or for women as for men. And, as previously noted, resolving these differences through the creation of a statistical average or normal member of society can never be a neutral act.

Even assuming the immense unlikelihood that all the people involved in a social activity should be, subjectively, involved in the same activity and the same meaning, to assume that culture is general even in this instance is to assume a peculiar and arbitrary concept of time. We have to imagine that the moment can be grasped, recorded, somewhere above us all where meaning holds sway, while there are no differences in how this moment may be viewed in the future, may have been viewed in the past, or might be viewed at this moment but for contingent acts of exclusion, repression, and the like. We have to maintain this peculiar metaphysics of the moment within interpretive disciplines based on the rejection of such metaphysics.

As should be clear, then, the problem of conflicting interpretations is not simply one of "facts" in relation to "values," as much discussion in the theory of the social sciences would have it. After all, it is impossible to exist in society in any way and at the same time be devoid of values. All activities, including those that cultures would specify as "nonactivity," articulate social meaning and so necessarily take on certain inflections of value. We are unable not to participate in social values just as we are unable not to say universals like *man* and *woman*. The problem of conflicting interpretations does not lie in the matter of values but rather in the concept of meaning as a coherent and self-identical aspect of a cultural situation taken to be homogenous. Once observed, any action or phenomenon cannot help but have meaning, though we may object to kingdom come that it was not intended to have meaning—or *that* meaning. But even assuming *that* meaning to be agreed on by every interpreter around the text in question (the incredible situation that Wittgenstein and speech-act theorists take to be normative), this argument would signify only the meaning that prevails for the period of observation. Only a metaphysics of originality—which, again, cannot be supported within our disciplines of interpretation—could come to the rescue here so as to overcome the differences that always come with historical changes on every level from the nation and the world to the minds of individuals, who we know are liable to rework events in their memories, to forget them, or to displace them into different contexts.

This is yet another reason that the principle of cultural relativism should not be taken as an injunction to respect the system of meaning proper to every culture. Instead, this principle should be an injunction to question this boundary of culture. It should lead us to question the strange idea that there ever existed a situation of "ethnocentrism." It should concentrate our attention on the people whose nonexistent, demeaned, isolated, or repressed subjectivity, as this has been established by "culture," has enabled culture to seem to be. Although ethnocentrism generally is discussed as a phenomenon of intolerance toward other cultures, whether from ignorance, fear, pride, imperial desire, or other motives, from a critical and historical viewpoint the problem of ethnocentrism is the assumption that there can be a centered ethnos. This assumption remains in the principle of cultural relativism, the seeming antithesis of ethnocentrism.

This critical thought, this labor of the intellectual, is liable to seem categorically detached from action. Although this conclusion generally is applauded by the liberal intellectual tradition, which values the image of detachment and objectivity that may be associated with this condition, and denigrated by revolutionaries, reactionaries, and commonsensical people, who view this kind of thought as an impedence to or deferral of the achievement of change, we ought to be given pause by the fact that this conclusion is shared by those with seemingly antithetical attitudes.

The problem is not in the nature of critical thought. The problem is not to come up with a new concept of action or of critical thought or of culture. The problem is to recognize the role that *criticism* and *culture* and similar terms have played in creating the effect of a rhetorical ground, to analyze the historical forms taken by their activity, and by this means to bring within the realm of choices the action, the thought, the culture all around us that have not been recognized as such because they did not fit the imaginary laws to which we have subscribed. Rather than identifying with one culture or with the identity-in-difference of cultural relativism, we can resist the unconscious compulsion of the discourse of culture by working to identify the differences between the imaginary law of culture and the life that escapes it. For example, the fact that the middle-class culture of nineteenth-century England may seem to have commanded gender through an exhaustively elaborated constitution of differences in law, art, literature, and other institutions does not mean that men and women and boys and girls were ever, in fact, totally commanded by this conception of gender.

We can analyze the rhetoric that seems to ground discourse so as to show its frayed edges, its contradictions, its blank spots, its weaknesses. We can use this analysis to dissolve the imaginary authority that culture or history might otherwise hold over us. With this critical understanding of history, we can increase our ability to recognize and change the ways gender or related matters are instituted today. This criticism would not labor to restore or revise an identity (of culture, of history, of truth, of the universal, of masculinity and femininity, and so on). It would be concerned to produce difference: to make a change.

VII

> Language is not a neutral medium that passes freely and easily into the private property of the speaker's intentions; it is populated—overpopulated—with the intentions of others. Expropriating it, forcing it to submit to one's own intentions and accents, is a difficult and complicated process.
>
> —Bakhtin[87]

As I have mentioned, to insist on difference, on a heterogeneous conception of culture, is a gesture of growing popularity. As the recent surge of interest in Bakhtin's analysis of polyglossia and heteroglossia indicates, something is afoot among intellectuals that recommends caution in the imagery of their explanations. This caution appears even in the work of some of the writers I have criticized. Eco uses the image of the encyclopedia to represent his argument that structured knowledge "cannot be recognized and organized as a global system" because "it provides only 'local' and transitory systems of knowledge, which can be contradicted by alternative and equally 'local' cultural organizations."[88] Hymes has noted how "the historical origin of standard languages and linguistic study as instruments of cultural hegemony . . . is unwittingly reinforced by the contemporary methodological canon of defining linguistic theory as concerned only with an ideal speaker-hearer in a perfectly homogenous community, free from all limitations of actual use."[89] Turner has written that "the culture of any society at any moment is more like the debris, or 'fall-out,' of past ideological systems than it is itself a system, a coherent whole."[90] And Kristeva has written a great deal in this regard, identifying semiotic activity and poetic language with "a *heterogeneousness* to meaning and signification" that is "detected genetically in the first echolalias of infants as rhythms and intonations anterior to the first phonemes, morphemes, lexemes, and sentences."[91]

As Frederic Jameson has noted, however, we should be wary of the glamor of concepts like heterogeneity, which may become "a mirage of immanence" or the basis of a new formalism.[92] An insistence on heterogeneity may represent cultural relativism in another form (as in Hymes's and Eco's work). Or it may represent a quasi-religious mysticism that is equally repressive toward political differences (as in Turner's and Kristeva's). Or heterogeneity may become an image of totality despite itself, as it were.[93] So it may appear at some points in Foucault's writings on power, Derrida's on *différance*, and Barthes's on *écriture* and desire. Even Jameson, who gives us this caution about fashionable language, appears to assume points of origin in the development of genres where they are relatively homogenous and fixed institutionally, like utterances in speech-act theory; and he holds to an image of history that is avowedly utopian, in the tradition of the Frankfurt School, and thus, perforce, totalizing. For all his complex analysis of language, Bakhtin, too, still appears to treat language as if words *hold* meanings and thus are contextually fixed forms, however multiple and provisional their meanings may be. Analyzing the work of interpretation is indeed "a difficult and complicated process," and of course I do not expect my own work to escape difficulties.

Still, through an analysis of the discourse of culture, it is possible at least to summarize this difficulty and complexity as the issue of politics. Within the discourse of culture, this issue is supposed to appear only as the object of an analysis that is itself neutral, whether this neutrality is defined strictly by science or philosophy, more loosely circumscribed by the principle of cultural relativity or liberal humanism, or as is most often the case, made something of a hodge-podge of definitions. In any case, I am arguing that the challenge to interpretation today is to recognize its implication in politics, to analyze the social relations through which political differences appear and the social changes through which they have been or may yet be changed, and thus to change history through an identification with the people, the knowledge, the culture—the life—that imagination has made subject to its laws.

In this peroratory form the challenge is likely to appear hyperbolic. To change history: the phrase of a penny-ante demagogue. But then also, read topically, strategically, against the drawing of the cultural boundary (somewhat as Pierre Menard may lead us to read *Don Quixote*), it is a phrase that opens demagoguery to a criticism that may prevent it from gaining the power of law.

Chapter 3
Paranomasia, Culture, and the Power of Meaning

I

*We notice . . . that children, who, as we know, are in the habit
of still treating words as things, tend to expect words that are
the same or similar to have the same meaning behind them—
which is a source of many mistakes that are laughed at by
grown-up people.*

—Freud[1]

Imagine a first reading of *Great Expectations*. In this reading, *Great Expectations* takes the form of an autobiography, but this form is also an allegory of a nation's transformation. The novel draws its readers forward in time from Pip's childhood in a working-class, preindustrial, rural locale to his maturity as a middle-class professional who has climbed the ladder to a partnership in a commercial firm with a thriving branch in "the East." Inherited money, mysterious and tainted money, has been transformed into earned money, rational wealth. Between this beginning and end Pip's destiny seems up for grabs as he is lured away from virtue by the *ignis fatuus* of gentility, and yet this divagation only makes the ending of his adventure seem all the more necessary. Like all the snakes, Sirens, and seeming dead ends that test the values of characters in literary works, the errancy Pip experiences outlines a road of truth. Mapping this road, we can trace this novel's relation to a fable of history created by the middle classes of Dickens's time. Within this fable, the middle classes shrug off aristocratic foibles as they rise from obscurity to improve civilization and to draw a larger world within its moral (and, incidentally, its social, political, and economic) embrace.[2]

At the end of *Great Expectations*, Pip returns to England from the Eastern branch of the firm in which he has worked for eleven years. Seen in terms of this fable, the narrative develops its evolutionary form while diverting readers from this end, drawing them back into questions about origins. It lures its readers into a wilderness, one might say; or a swamp; or, let us say, a marsh, in which life and death seem to be independent figures only in the moment before one notices the ugliness of symbols of life and the perverse attraction death seems to hold over life:

> On the edge of the river I could faintly make out the only two black
> things in all the prospect that seemed to be standing upright; one of
> these was the beacon by which the sailors steered—like an unhooped
> cask upon a pole—an ugly thing when you were near it; the other a
> gibbet, with some chains hanging to it which had once held a pirate.
> The man was limping on towards this latter, as if he were the pirate
> come to life, and come down, and going back to hook himself up again.
> (*GE*, 6)[3]

The confusion over origins in this novel includes speculations about the trauma that caused Miss Havisham's bizarre withdrawal from the world and time, Pip's attempts as a mature narrator to trace the growth of his boyish mind and emotions, the popular guess that Miss Havisham is the power behind Pip's rise in the world, curiosity over Estella's parentage, uncertainty about the relation between one's social background and the definition or acquirement of gentility, and not the least among these, doubts over the value of life in relation to death. While the origins in question are of different sorts, they all are related to the issue of Pip's own birth, which prepares him to be the focus of their mystery and the sufferer of their resolution.

Pip's birth gives him the indeterminate status frequently found among protagonists of the middle-class novel. Such characters commonly represent a conception of the individual freed from traditional restraints and given the opportunity to rise in the world by luck and pluck. However, in *Great Expectations* as in many other works, once the individual so conceived is given birth, there seems to be a need for a new rule of representation. Within a hierarchical society allowing relatively little social mobility, the index of authority in representation might be called the rule of origins. It seems a new rule must come on the scene when doubt is cast on the traditional value of origins, as it is when a character is orphaned and thus cast out of the traditional order of the family. As J. Hillis Miller has put it, Dickens's heroes and heroines "seek some way out that will make possible the achievement of true selfhood, while not necessitating the extreme of anarchic individualism."[4]

To judge by works like Dickens's, although the rhetoric of the Tory or Conservative could not serve bourgeois liberalism, still individuals flinging off the shackles of social class had to be held back from excessive exuberance in the celebration of their universality. In legal theory and elsewhere, middle-class ideology specified the human subject as an autonomous individual, theoretically equal to any other. Individuals were considered able to shape themselves, to be self-made, to the limits of their capacities. Theoretically, the subject was unfettered by local conditions or accidents of birth. The individual was a natural rather than theological or traditional subject and so was considered universal in this nature. If left unrestrained, however, such an individual might be Trabb's boy, whom Pip describes as having a "habit of happening to be everywhere where he had no business." Such a fellow might even be disappointed if he realized he had helped to save Pip's life. "Not that Trabb's boy was of a malignant nature," our narrator comments, "but that he had too much spare vivacity, and that it was in his constitution to want variety at anybody's expense" (*GE*, 503–4). This liveliness, which G. K. Chesterton called "the *bounce* of Trabb's boy,"[5] could impel one straight to destruction.

Within any middle-class discourse that reflected on itself, there had to arise a rule of irony, as I shall call it, nodding to the Romantic tradition in which irony becomes a kind of master trope distinguishing modern feeling, thought, fable, and life in general. If a rule of irony did not arise, everything might become ironic, subject to endless qualification from different contexts and yet maintaining no identity through these changes, as in the phantasmagoric and hallucinatory moments of this novel. A laudable desire for self-improvement then would turn into a culpable greed, ambition, egoism, or febrile restlessness. It would turn into the likes of Trabb's boy or, say, Josiah Bounderby.

This rule explains Joe's determination, early in the novel, to repress any desire for learning he might have. If he were to be educated, Joe figures, Mrs. Joe would suspect him of wanting to rise like " 'a sort of rebel' " (*GE*, 55). This law also accounts for the fact that Pip defeats Herbert Pocket in a fight but loses this victory through fear (and later through Herbert's refusal to remember it). "I felt," Pip says, "that this pale young gentleman's blood was on my head, and that the Law would avenge it. Without having any definite idea of the penalties I had incurred, it was clear to me that village boys could not go stalking about the country, ravaging the houses of gentlefolks and pitching into the studious youth of England, without laying themselves open to severe punishment" (*GE*, 107).

The contrast in the status of learning in these examples is instructive. Learning may appear a matter of rebellion or, paradoxically, the basis of avenging authority, depending on the grammar of the class relations in which it appears. It is indeed childish, it seems, to assume that the same or similar words have the same meanings behind them. Even more to the point here is the way these examples indicate one aspect of the rule of irony that displaces the rule of origins.

According to this ironic rule, events representing the defeat of traditional assumptions can appear in discourse only if a certain chagrin or surprise keeps
them in check. In this way we see irony as *feeling*.

To be sure, these examples are comic. However, this comic perspective need
not appear skeptical or corrosive toward all serious discourse, as John Forster
indicated when he described Dickens's "leading quality" as that of the humor
through which one discovers "the affinities between the high and the low, the
attractive and the repulsive, the rarest things and things of every day, which bring
us all upon the level of a common humanity."[6] To be separated from one's origins
in the middle-class novel is to be the founding term—or the foundling term—of
a new kind of narrative.

The middle-class novel begins with a simultaneous rejection and reconstitu-
tion of individual identity. The middle-class novel says tradition and traditional
authorities are questionable, if not simply bogus on their faces. It suggests that
identity should be an acquired condition, not an ascribed fate.

This may seem a simple statement. It summarizes with sociohistorical banality a complex of features in the history of the novel, in which, of course, no middle-class novel pure and simple is to be found. However, far-reaching consequences may follow from this simply categorized social change. For example,
the consequence at issue here, the rule of irony, does more than teach a certain
feeling. It actually enables us to see a social identity and national destiny in the
representation of an individual. Hence the oft-noted coincidence between the
popularity of the *Bildungsroman* and the rise to historical prominence of the middle classes.

The rule of irony represents an authority that is teleological rather than genealogical; internal rather than external; productive, innovative, profitable, and universal rather than reproductive, repetitive, conservative, and exclusive. In this
way we see irony as *character*.

For the character of Pip, the far-reaching consequences of this social change
set in early. From the very first page of *Great Expectations* the fact that Pip is an
orphan is made to suggest a problem of representation, a problem of "likeness,"
that arises when origins are called into question. This is the problem of the individual who must represent himself in the world because the authorities behind
him have come to seem less than absolutely compelling. They are struck mute by
his novel condition, or they appear at odds with his progress, and so they are
embarrassing, like Joe when he visits Pip in London, or threatening, like "the
Avenger" Pip hires when he tries to play the role of the gentleman. As these
examples indicate, in this new order it is universal nature contending with arbitrary convention, not hierarchical birth cooperating with social tradition, that is
taken to shape the identity of the individual. In this way we see irony as *ideology*.

The middle-class novel has often been concerned with its legitimacy as a
genre, since it cannot identify itself with the ideology of aristocratic taste. In-

deed, this concern is one of its distinguishing characteristics, since it helps to establish the social relations the novel assumes to exist. Playing out this concern, the protagonists of such novels often are occupied with the problem of establishing legitimate forms of themselves, others, and the world in the absence of any absolute genealogical authority. In such novels, the opposite of mastery is not servility but plagiarism. Compeyson, we may remember, is not only the major villain of *Great Expectations* but also a forger. Pip is a bad actor, an *arriviste* undeserving of his glorious appearance, as far as Trabb's boy is concerned. Jaggers is a man who insists on holding everyone so strictly to legal forms as to pervert those forms, in Pip's view, from their proper significance. In these ways and others, from issues of clothing, handshakes, and table manners to issues of personal, social, and spiritual identity, an anxiety over the proper delineation of form pervades this novel. As John O. Jordan has put it, "Pip's early life as a blacksmith's boy establishes a play on the word 'forge' that runs half-submerged through the entire novel."[7]

Of course, in literature and elsewhere in social life, authority had never been absolute and often had not been at all compelling. This novelistic view of the history of authority is an ideological conception of the nature of social change. Although the opposition between the rule of irony and the rule of origins resembles the distinctions between the worlds of the epic and of the novel described by Georg Lukács and Mikhail Bakhtin, an analysis of the way this opposition is formulated as a feature of the novel calls these distinctions into question. It suggests that these distinctions between worlds confuse literary form with historical experience.[8] By showing irony as an ideological identification, an analysis of this opposition between the rule of irony and the rule of origins may also challenge the contemporary reproduction of Romantic irony in the rhetorical distinction between closed and open forms of irony.[9]

The opposition between the rule of irony and the rule of origins is nowhere to be found in a completely systematic or perfected form, but instead appears as a means of producing discourse that may be more or less complexly elaborated in specific works of literature, including even works opposed to middle-class values in many ways. In other words, this elaboration of the difference between ascribed and achieved authority should not be understood as a historical event or as the reflection of such an event. It should be seen as a rhetorical measure. It is an element of discourse that serves specific and often unconscious political ends according to its historical positioning within discourse.

Still, it should be needless to say that the question of authority is no less real and its consequences no less affecting for being political. Consider in this respect Pip's formal representation of himself in relation to his parents, whose absence seems to make the possibility of representation a matter of unreason:

I give Pirrip as my father's family name, on the authority of his

tombstone and my sister—Mrs. Joe Gargery, who married the
blacksmith. As I never saw my father or my mother, and never saw any
likeness of either of them (for their days were long before the days of
photographs), my first fancies regarding what they were like, were
unreasonably derived from their tombstones. The shape of the letters on
my father's, gave me an odd idea that he was a square, stout, dark man,
with curly black hair. From the character and turn of the inscription,
"Also Georgiana Wife of the Above," I drew a childish conclusion that
my mother was freckled and sickly. (*GE*, 1)

Although this passage, too, is comic, this problem of judging likenesses will
grow at a pace outstripping Pip's development. It will dwarf him at every turn of
his narrative, seeming to frustrate his every attempt to establish an authoritative
representation of his past. With the letters on the tombstones as with other objects
in this novel, judgment is put into question. So Dorothy Van Ghent describes the
"animation of inanimate objects" in this novel, which she sees as suggesting
"both the quaint gaiety of a forbidden life and an aggressiveness that has got out
of control—an aggressiveness that they have borrowed from the human economy
and an irresponsibility native to but glossed and disguised by that economy."[10]

Given the presence of "authorities" like tombstones and Mrs. Joe, we have
good reason to doubt whether an earlier date for the popularization of photogra-
phy really would have mended matters. Perhaps we might say that Pip's problem
is not technical representation but ideological representation. However, this statement would obscure the way this novel dramatizes the complicity of technique
and ideology, especially in Jagger's practice of legal procedure. More carefully
stated, the problem is one of founding the possibility of representation by establishing an opposition between proper and improper representation or, in other
words, between the rule of irony and the rule of origins. In this way, we see irony
as *truth*.

Like the gloomy house in which Miss Havisham appears so like and yet so
unlike the woman she was on the eve of her wedding, or, more precisely, like the
convict who lurks behind the gravestone of his parents, the problem of representation repeatedly yanks Pip out of the progress of historical time and upsets him
into a state of being weltering with the confusions of his childhood condition.
Peter Brooks has described "the paradox that in this most highly plotted of
novels . . . we witness an evident subversion and futilization of the very concept
of plot."[11] The order of representation in this novel often comes unglued, as
when Pip encounters Magwitch and, in coming to this wretch's aid, hears a
creaking stairway call after him accusingly, sees the gates, dykes, and banks of a
marsh trying to accost him, and even speaks out loud to a clerical-looking ox he
takes to be a human authority. As this scene illustrates, this confusing state of
being makes it so impossible to distinguish substantial reality from figures of
speech that language seems to take on a life of its own, as if there were no dif-

ference between the forms of words and things. In an exemplary complication, mistaken by Pip for Magwitch and then mistakenly identified by Pip as the devilish partner whom Magwitch invented and presented to him as real, Compeyson interrupts Pip's attempt to bring food to Magwitch, who subsequently describes to Pip the delusive perceptions that afflict an isolated man on the marshes: perceptions that resemble the confusion in Pip's own senses as well as the chaos the reader may observe in the grammar of Pip's social situation at this moment.

On such occasions language seems to speak independently of human agency. It, too, seems to have a habit of happening to be everywhere where it has no business. As a result, Pip also feels out of place, disjoined from proper intentions and ends. As Barry Westburg has noted, the young Pip's inability to pronounce his given name shows "the alien quality of language as the child encounters it."[12] With language in this state, any assumptions one may have about historical progress are lost to a world of fantastic figures unregulated by the rule of origins or irony. This is the narrative problem that follows immediately on Pip's "first most vivid and broad impression of the identity of things" (*GE*, 2). It is the problem of fixing identities once one becomes conscious that they are creations of language, which is not easily understood or controlled even by the Pip who grows to be the well-educated narrator of this novel.

This problem is especially aggravated in Pip's case by his response to the humiliation Estella inflicts on him. To put it simply, Pip desires to be unlike himself and unlike his guardian, Joe. As the narrative continues and Pip receives his great expectations, the result is mounting bewilderment as to what people are like and how to judge the relation between their appearance in the world and their "likeness" or identity.

For the living as well as the dead in this novel, identity appears to be a thing buried or beyond this life. It appears as a concealed wealth, a lure that draws one into playing punishing and unprofitable games, such as those Pip endures with Estella, or blatantly false theatrical roles, such as those adopted by Miss Havisham's relatives in their display of the greed that they call disinterested affection. In these turns of the narrative, figures that will not be pinned down seem to proliferate by their own power. We need only consider the account of Pip's thievery, his whoppers about what he saw inside Satis House ("Come, Pip," pleads Joe upon his confession that he lied, "if there warn't no weal-cutlets, at least there was dogs? . . . A puppy?" [*GE*, 79]), or his impression at one time that Miss Havisham is a witch, at another that she is a fairy godmother. These proliferating figures assert identity only through its displacement and culminate in Magwitch's displacement of Miss Havisham in the role of Pip's benefactor.

This event forces Pip to confront an ironic likeness between qualities that otherwise would appear to be absolutely contradictory: gentility and vulgarity, respectability and criminality, wealth and poverty, violence and civilization, and so on. If we read like John Forster, we may see this as the likeness Pip was prepared ironically to see within himself the more he was distanced from those humble origins in which, as a boy, he met criminals and acted like a criminal. Through the perception of this likeness, the reader can create an ironic understanding between Pip the narrator and Pip the protagonist. This understanding may be further clarified as the rest of the novel works out the implications of Magwitch's revelation. It will strip away from Pip the wardrobe of figures — "questioner" (*GE*, 14), thief, devil, swine, imp and hound, liar, "common labouring boy" (*GE*, 67), gentleman, heroic knight, and so on — that he tries on in his struggle to represent himself in the world. Readers then can find a coincidence between the identities of narrator and protagonist, an end to the dissemination of irony and an establishment of a grown-up perception and representation of the world.[13] In this way we see irony as *nature*.

True, for a while there is only further confusion and another return to that childhood condition in which words, like Trabb's boy, turn up everywhere but where they are supposed to be. For instance, this is the situation when Pip spends a night at a lodging-house after being warned by Wemmick to stay away from his own apartment:

> When I had lain awake a little while, those extraordinary voices with which silence teems, began to make themselves audible. The closet whispered, the fireplace sighed, the little washing stand ticked, and one guitar-string played occasionally in the chest of drawers. At about the same time, the eyes [of a lantern] on the wall acquired a new expression, and in every one of those staring rounds I saw written, DON'T GO HOME. (*GE*, 427)

Finally, though — if the reading I am imagining makes sense — the voices of silence and the writing of light framed in darkness are wiped out by a consciousness of the universal identity beyond figural displacements bestowed on humanity by the Christian God. The decomposing timelessness of Miss Havisham's house is countered by the symbolism of the final courtroom scene, in which Pip attends Magwitch while the sunshine of divinity is observed to fall equally on the stern judges and the hapless prisoners of the state. In this way we see irony as *transcendence*.

The drama of this identity is further secured in the discovery that Magwitch is Estella's father; in the conversion to common sympathies of Miss Havisham, Pip, and Estella symbolized by their experience of fire, fever, and patriarchal force, respectively; and by the understanding ultimately promised between the blacksmith's boy and the fairy-tale princess of the unawakened heart. ("Promised" even in the first ending to the novel, and even if one prefers a dark reading of the form finally authorized — "promised," that is, according to a measured formula of comedy and tragedy . . . if this reading holds.) Furthermore, the reader may take this final reconciliation as a triumph over the narrative's prehistory: those punishing games, destructive to the institution of marriage and all that stems from it, played out between Miss Havisham and Compeyson, on the one hand, and between Magwitch and Molly, on the other. The two main lines of the plot may thus be seen to be drawn together before the novel's beginning and after its end in the issue of desire perverted, exiled, and finally returned to a proper form of apprehension or, in other words, to an authoritative representation. Similar to this formal development is the revision of destructive forms of education—as received by Pip from Magwitch, Estella from Miss Havisham, and Magwitch from Compeyson—into the education linking Joe and Biddy at the end of the novel.

In this way, in contrast to the expense of origins (which can never be fully recovered, which must always be the irrational subject of representational display and rediscovery), there appears the new order of representation, the rule of irony (in which the rationality of the future asserts itself, in which the calculations of morality pay off). The world of necessity yields to the world of probability, the world of violent trauma to the world of recuperation, the world of arbitrary mastery to the world of justice. In this way we see irony as *history*.

Such, in brief, is the appearance of this novel according to a certain kind of understanding. Although the aspects of this novel that I have isolated are by no means all-inclusive and need not be taken to represent the focus of any particular reader's experience of the text, they do suggest a historical understanding of some of the concepts on which professors and students often rely in addressing this text and other works of nineteenth-century literature. From this perspective, *Great Expectations* is less remarkable for its themes of middle-class liberalism and sentimental Christianity than for the complexity of imagery and incident in its manipulations of identity. Just as Pip and Herbert continually overextend themselves until they are threatened with a catastrophic collapse of their financial house of cards, so are other characters in the novel observed comically and tragically overextending themselves, committing themselves to characters they do not have the resources to maintain, until the Christian deity arrives on the scene to hoot their play off the stage as an act even worse than Mr. Wopsle's role in *Hamlet* or Mr. Pumblechook's role as Pip's "self-constituted . . . patron" (*GE*, 119), in which he is the very emblem of all the middle-class ectypes that spring up in the place of traditional authorities. At the end, Pip has learned how to earn, spend, and save money—and in so doing he has learned how to manage and save his feelings while helping to bring order to his life and to the lives of those around him.

However, before the dramatic mystery of the novel is set on this course, before these concluding scenes that can be taken to form a resolution, a different kind of mystery is instituted. This is the mystery of the desire Pip feels for Estella, and an attention to this desire may allow us to see the order of representation developed in *Great Expectations* in a different way. If my reading to this point has been historical, following the argument that works of art seem autonomous only because we fail to analyze them in terms of the culture out of which they are made, this other view of the novel may clarify the importance of such a reading by showing its political implications. In other words, by showing how this novel may be read as challenging the conception of history that has guided my analysis to this point, I will be able to argue that cultural understanding of art is as inescapable as the questioning of this form of understanding is imperative. The creation of the rule of irony will be seen to describe a form of identification necessary to make sense of Pip and *Great Expectations* and yet also unnecessary to this text, which can also be seen to contradict, silence, evade, and in other ways reject this identification. The opposition between the rule of irony and the rule of origins will be seen to describe an imaginary culture: a culture the text asserts and denies in historically telling ways. Like other tropes, irony then will be seen as a form of identification through which readers consciously and unconsciously appropriate texts. It will not be seen as a formal mode or technical device but as a historical and political practice.

I assume the payoff for my reading to this point is clear. It provides a recognition of discourse as a complex marshalling of rhetorical measures in which every element—whether it figures as identity, opposition, contrast, change, difference, or anything else—is historical. In this way it avoids a facile reduction of literature to life by way of schemes of reasoning that are organicist, mimetic, formalist, or in some other way idealist. It avoids as well a naive conception of genre and recognizes an interplay among concepts such as feeling, character, ideology, truth, nature, transcendence, and history within a rhetoric cutting across conventional schemes of classification. This way of viewing the novel dissolves distinctions between literature and other genres of discourse while recognizing historical distinctions among forms of reality. Therefore, it gives us a basis for discussing *Great Expectations* as an instance of discourse as closely related to Victorian diaries, sermons, children's literature, or parliamentary reports as it is to other novels by Dickens and his contemporaries. At the same time, it gives us a basis for discussing the novel in relation to factories, fashions, eating habits, and other aspects of the material and social life of nineteenth-century England.

This reading will hold as long as *Great Expectations* is seen as corresponding to other cultural productions of its time: as long as it reveals a likeness to these other works that can be taken as a textual identity, the key to middle-class discourse. In other words, as long as it seems possible to identify the conventions of a culture to which this novel may be said to belong, we can read it in this way. We can view the novel as a doubling and redoubling of allegorical identities: a literary form that is also the form of an individual's life appears, in addition, as a portrait of social order, a projection of national destiny, and thus an exemplary instance of middle-class writing. The novel, then, is an extended play on words in which a palindrome, Pip Pirrip, turns and returns to reveal its various meanings, all of which are contained in the seed of the narrator's identity.[14]

However, as I am arguing, it is imperative also to question this way of identifying the text. If we do not assume that the concept of culture is a source of reassuring enlightenment, then the best way to reach a cultural understanding of this novel is by groping after the light that illuminates these allegorical figurations. As Henri Fluchère says, Pip's progress in the novel makes him

> a sort of catalyst for problems posed by the human relations at the heart of a society in which moral, sexual, economic, and social imperatives, even though they belong to a given moment of history, appear almost intemporal. If the history of Pip does indeed take on the fascination of fable and of allegory, the themes, the events, and the characters are like symbols, and the reader, like the narrator whose accomplice he becomes and with whom he blends himself, passes through this forest of subtle entanglements to reach, at the end, the ambiguous threshold of an unexplored domain: the one, we are told, where rediscoveries are not menaced by the shade of an eventual separation.[15]

What, we may ask, makes it possible for this novel to have a cultural identity? By what light can it possibly be read? Grahame Smith says, "we believe in Pip's particular reality and so we can believe in his representative force,"[16] but what makes it possible in the first place to compare the shape of Pip's life to a middle-class sense of history? Or to ask a still more fundamental question: what makes it possible to see the words of this novel as constituting a form with any kind of significance, whether it be put in autobiographical, social, moral, or any other terms? Although we might say readings such as this can be judged by the extent to which they illuminate a particular text and, through this, other texts or materials of the time, this argument still passes over the question of the initial illumination.

Rereading the novel in terms of such questions will produce a somewhat different picture of the text. Within this picture, *Great Expectations* will not appear to be a reproduction of fictional conventions and rhetorical laws, nor will it appear a transcendent individual transformation of such conventions and laws. Instead, it will appear as a struggle to establish language as culture. In other words, it will appear as a political act: a struggle to establish language as a form of representation in which conventions and laws can find a solid ground. Thus, in addition to its appearance as feeling, character, ideology, truth, nature, transcendence, and history, the rule of irony will appear as *meaning* and *power*. And even though this view of the novel is only one way of addressing the text and does not invalidate the other readings *Great Expectations* may be given, it does expose the political relation between text and culture that is repressed when convention, law, creative genius, context, or some other variety of idealized authority is granted power over critical practice.

II

> *If we look into the grammar of the word, we shall find that it is no less astounding that men should have conceived of a deity of time than it would be to conceive of a deity of negation or disjunction.*
>
> —Wittgenstein[17]

In describing his first meeting with Estella at Satis House, Pip calls the feeling she inspired in him "the smart without a name." He says, "I was so humiliated, hurt, spurned, offended, angry, sorry—I cannot hit upon the right name for the smart—God knows what its name was—that tears started to my eyes"(*GE*, 70). The description asserts that his feelings were a mystery to him while giving this mystery the form of an asyndeton. And just as Pip asserts throughout the course of his narrative that he can neither describe nor adequately explain his feelings for Estella at the times of which he is writing, so he repeatedly supports his assertion in similar forms. "Once for all," he will say, "I knew to my sorrow, often and often, if not always, that I loved her against reason, against promise, against peace, against hope, against happiness, against all discouragement that could be" (*GE*, 270). Moreover, having been struck with this feeling of disconnection—"the madness of my heart," as he calls it (*GE*, 150)—Pip will suggest that its mystery is normative. As he comments, "But how could I, a poor dazed village lad, avoid that wonderful inconsistency into which the best and wisest of men fall every day?" (*GE*, 150). He even speaks directly to the reader on this point when he describes how he requested that Herbert refrain from speaking to him of Estella's marriage. In addition, he says he avoided reading any account of this event. "Why I hoarded up this last wretched little rag of the robe of hope that was rent and given to the winds," he comments, "how do I know! Why did you who read this, commit that not dissimilar inconsistency of your own, last year, last month, last week?" (*GE*, 444–45). His desire for Estella appeared a mystery to him, Pip says, and so he became—and, in relation to his older self, has remained—a mystery to himself. In this mystery he appears divided from himself and yet, insofar as he is divided, united with the readers he imagines for his story.

But what of actual readers? How are they to respond to this inconsistency, this division that is also a unity?

This stipulation of mystery might hardly be noticed by readers familiar with conceptions of romance common in the Western world since the Renaissance, whether this familiarity stems from an acquaintance with the relevant literature or simply from an upbringing in contemporary society. Students in literature classes, questioned about the way Pip describes his feelings—"I loved her simply because I found her irresistable" (*GE*, 270)—have assured me that "love is just that way sometimes . . . it isn't logical." These students, of course, were unknowingly repeating the wisdom of innumerable professors of literature.

This is not to say there is any sort of critical consensus over the question of this desire. The explanations critics have suggested for Pip's fascination with Estella are extremely varied. However, almost all are united in their divisions by the assumption that love, in a sense, explains itself: that love is love.

Estella has been seen as symbolically representing Pip's social aspirations, and she has been seen as representing Dickens's infatuation with Ellen Ternan (at the time he was writing *Great Expectations*) or with Maria Beadnell (when he was a boy). One critic has identified Pip's love as "pure romantic—erotic—infatuation,"[18] whereas another has said Pip's continued interest in Estella "suggests either irrational devotion or patent masochism."[19] His love has been termed "self-deception"[20] and self-abasement.[21] The relation between Pip and Estella has also been seen as "marked by the interdict, as well as the seduction, of incest."[22] At least one critic has found Estella simply incredible,[23] while another has taken the opposite position, complaining that there is an "unwillingness to grant life to Estella among critics."[24] This variety of responses leads to two conclusions. The first is that Pip's desire solicits explanation. "After all," as John Kucich says, "whether Pip marries Estella . . . is less interesting than why he still loves her at all."[25] The second conclusion is that professors, like students, are drawn to explaining love by love.

For all their sophistication, the explanations of these critics assume love makes sense. Even the critic who finds Estella incredible maintains this assumption by suggesting how she ought to have been portrayed: "In any case, would not this gloomy and solitary upbringing rather tend to encourage dreaming, a willingness to love, and even romantic illusions?"[26] Just as Pip's love for Estella is seen by both Pip and his readers as provoking questions, Pip and his readers also seem to agree in assuming that they can refer these questions to the psychology of love.

However, if we consider for a moment the rhetorical form given to this mystery, love loses its power to explain itself and Pip's narrative loses its ironic seed of integrity. It is true that those of us who are more like Pip than Estella can find in the word *love* a satisfying explanation of his emphasis on the mystery of his feelings. What this word cannot explain is the emphasis on lists with an absence of connectives in Pip's representation of this mystery. Pip's attraction to Estella can be explained psychologically only if we disregard his insistence on a psychological identity that cannot be represented, an identity that can establish its presence only in the absence of logical coordination and subordination in passages like those I cited. We can make sense of Pip's desire by accepting his rhetorical appeal to a human identity completely fractured in rhetorical reality,[27] but we can *explain* this love only by disregarding the rhetoric that has enabled it to make sense in the first place. Mystery becomes periphrasis and understanding, blindness, once we attend to the form of Pip's language on this point: "Truly it was impossible to dissociate her presence from all those wretched hankerings after money and gentility that had disturbed my boyhood—from all those ill-regulated aspirations that had first made me ashamed of home and Joe—from all those visions that had raised her face in the glowing fire" (*GE*, 274).

In place of a sense of familiarity, in place of a mystery so invisible as hardly to be noticed, we are left at a loss for a word that, perhaps, as Pip says, "God knows." In this case, the sunshine of a deity no longer casts an identity over the differences of this text. Along with associated terms such as *desire* and *feeling*, *love* becomes an arrangement of marks or sounds that we can only hope represents a foreign language that eventually can be mastered—although the reader is told by the mature Pip that he never has achieved this mastery, that he must trust in God's attention to this point. We may then remember Estella's words: "It seems . . . that there are sentiments, fancies—I don't know what to call them— which I am not able to comprehend. When you say you love me, I know what you mean, as a form of words; but nothing more. You address nothing in my breast, you touch nothing there. I don't care for what you say at all" (*GE*, 421).

Adopting a position like Estella's, we may ask why Pip cannot explain his desire for her. More specifically, we may ask why the question of desire appears in this novel in the form of an asyndeton that extends familiar feeling into alienated rhetorical form. But then there is a more basic problem: Why should desire pose any question at all in this novel? What mystery can there be about the explanation of this desire, which is described in terms common to Western literature at least since the Renaissance? "In a word," Pip tells the reader, "it was impossible for me to separate her, in the past or in the present, from the innermost life of my life" (*GE*, 274). "You," Pip tells Estella, "are part of my existence, part of myself" (*GE*, 423–25). As such quotations may indicate, the mystery in this novel is not this traditionally described desire with its equally traditional associations with a woman's beauty, social class, wealth, and emotional frigidity. Instead, the mystery itself is the mystery.

This mystery makes sense only if we take Pip's words to be directed toward a tradition to which he is expressing antagonism. What this mystery then describes is not desire itself but rather Pip's refusal to accept the traditional explanation of desire. He rejects the traditional forms of comedy and tragedy that could make desire explicable in terms of such attributes as wealth and beauty; in fact, he insists on the bankruptcy of such forms and thus calls into question the legitimacy of any authority founded on the reading of established conventions. He brings a different character to writing: the universal subject beyond such accidents of being as wealth and beauty or, one might say, the subject whose universality is proved by his vulnerability to such accidents and to the dramatic slapstick they inspire.

In this way Pip is spiritualized by the mystery of desire. (Think what a difference it would make to his character if he interpreted his desire for Estella as the critics of this novel have and, through this interpretation, cured himself of his confusion and ceased to have any romantic feeling for her.) Ironically, this mystery gives him mastery even as its most dramatic consequence seems to be various forms of humiliation. In the narrative past and present, this mystery continuously displaces him from himself and thus projects him into a state of being in which wealth, beauty, and social class are accidents and so may be transmuted into the overriding value of this form of subjectivity in which people connect face-to-face, stripped of everything but their spiritual being. In this way they step into the light of Dickens's culture. Heirs to this form of romance, which Dickens might be said to have read out of the history of sentimental middle-class literature beginning with works like *Pamela* and *The Spectator*, most of us need to be arrested by some formality, such as an asyndeton, to notice how *strange* this rule of irony is.

III

> *Quite generally, to complete a certain sentence, to speak*
> *without hesitation, to speak with perfect grammaticality, can,*
> *under certain conditions, be offensive.*
>
> —Hymes[28]

Dickens's use of asyndeton exemplifies his drive to define such issues as class, wealth, beauty, and birth as accidental. Thus it is that he seeks to open a linguistic space for the universal subject. He tries to create a language in which form will appear to be displaced onto an outmoded tradition or a vulgar conventional present so as to leave an indefinable subjectivity in its place. If the cultural light shines through, this subjectivity *is* his writing. Through his writing he seeks to create the culture of universality, the culture that is the denial of culture. It is to this culture that professors and students respond when they find that Pip's desire for Estella makes sense. Although the differences in the ways they describe this sense may be significant for some purposes, they become insignificant when we consider how all readers must submit themselves to Pip's inconsistency if they are to find meaning in his desire. They must accept an impression of tradition and an impression of Pip's opposition to this tradition, and in this process they must turn away from the bewildering figure of Estella, whose identity can be represented only in terms of absence and discontinuity. In other words, they must read a quality of necessity in the conclusion of this novel back through the entirety of the narrative—a circumstance reflected in the long critical controversy over the "two endings."

Thus, what I am calling Dickens's culture, this culture in which Pip and *Great Expectations* make sense, operates most dramatically through the trope of irony. As it weds criminality and legality, wealth and poverty, beauty and ugliness, and other contradictory qualities, this trope insists on the alienating effect of all social forms, including language. As a result, it produces an impression of the universal nature of subjectivity. Irony does not function in this way through a dialectical absorption of difference into identity or indeed through any sort of philosophical logic, as such logic is commonly conceived. It does so by becoming a value in itself, an enchantment, for the appropriate reader. In other words, it becomes a deity that presides throughout the novel in the reader's appropriation of a meaningful relation between its narrator and protagonist. In this role it allows readers to explain desire, which so baffles Pip's consciousness, by explaining Pip. "I never had one hour's happiness in her company," Pip writes after describing a visit to Estella at Richmond, "and yet my mind all round the four-and-twenty hours was harping on the happiness of having her with me unto death" (*GE*, 350). Insofar as it dominates his writing and produces the universal subject for the reader, this trope of irony serves the cause of meaning precisely because it does not specify the nature of the relations among such values as class, wealth, and beauty. As a result, it excludes any specification of being other than the impression of Pip's subjectivity.

On the one hand, this irony marks cultural fault lines, which are unevenly stressed and liable to move in ways only vaguely predictable. On the other, it establishes a basis for cultural understanding that is all the more valuable because it is fundamentally mysterious. We are drawn to grasp this irony in the same way that Pip is drawn to read the characters on his parents' tombstones. It calls to mind enchanting images and themes, all of which erase intractable historical discontinuities involving familial, economic, social, legal, and affective relations. By revealing the forms of plagiarism that corrupt the rule of authoritative origins, this irony creates an impression of universality that enables us ironically to master this corruption. Bafflement and error are turned to propriety.

IV

For if someone arouses great expectations in us with the telling of a story, and at the end we see its falsehood immediately, it displeases us.

—Kant[29]

If it makes any sense at all, Pip's rhetoric in this matter of desire suggests that he indeed appears in a middle-class novel. That is, his rhetoric emphasizes the absence of the authority of origins in his narrative and the absence, for the moment, of a new authority to replace the old. In this way his rhetoric is positioned at the beginning of a new authority just as Pip's life is carefully plotted to suggest its coincidence with the first two decades of the nineteenth century. Pip tries to establish a new form of law through writing his narrative or, in other words, through the function of culture; but in this struggle his rhetoric suggests a difference between two ways of grasping language that should lead the critical reader to question the meaning of this text.

The first involves the cultural assurance of a concept whose understanding is maintained by participation in the ceremonies, forms of speech, institutions, and other aspects of a community that enable us to identify it or to identify with it. In this situation, however mysterious it may appear, love has the comprehensibility created by the identification with a sense of society. Love in this cultural situation may be drawn from pastoral, philosophical, aristocratic, bourgeois, Romantic, patriarchal, or other conventions, but in any case the sense of conventional understanding is maintained as long as this cultural identification holds. Only when it is absent, however provisionally, can language be grasped differently.

This second situation involves the material sign as it is regarded without the faith of the identification of a community or, in other words, as language is historicized and culture is examined critically. This situation occurs when language and culture are grasped in a culturally deviant way: when language and culture are made imaginary.

One example of this situation is Wittgenstein's investigation of the grammar of words like *time*. Another is Freud's consideration of the grammar of childhood and abnormality:

> We can observe how pathological states of thought-activity, in which the possibility of concentrating psychical expenditure on a particular point is probably restricted, do in fact give this . . . sound-presentation of the word greater prominence than its meaning, and that sufferers in such states proceed in their speech on the lines (as the formula runs) of the "external" instead of the "internal" associations of the word-presentation.[30]

And a third example is Pip's dreamy reading of his parents' tombstones, which the grown-up Pip presents as something of a joke: "The shape of the letters on my father's, gave me an odd idea that he was a square, stout, dark man."

The effect, in all these cases, is to bring into relief language in its materiality or, as Freud put it, in its external associations. This foregrounding seems to call for the directing power of a culture (or an autobiographer, a psychoanalyst, a reader) to create a likeness between arrangements of letters and forms of consciousness. Otherwise, it seems that power may erupt anywhere, without rhyme or reason, like a convict leaping from behind a tombstone or a tailor's boy from a corner of the street. In that case, people would feel meaning to be out of their control, but the problem would go even further. They would also have no way of agreeing on what meaning is. They could not begin to recognize critical differences such as those between truth and lies or reality and imposture.

The letters on his parents' gravestones come alive for Pip as if he sees in their material form the rhetorical nature of meaning. It is as if his imagination is grasped by the arbitrariness of the culture-bound power of semantic conventions. This impression is strengthened by the fact that a moment later his neck is grasped by the hand of an escaped convict, whose transgression is defined by those conventions. Thus, from the very beginning of Pip's adventures we see the breach in language that constitutes these adventures. This breach between ways of understanding language might better be called, simply, language, for Pip is launched into the life of language, into cultural difference, as we all are despite the neverending efforts of dictators of various sorts to legislate us into absolute identification with communities. Language is never utterly homogenous, even in the dead and learned languages that Kant said should be used for models of taste because they were not disturbed by semantic innovation and grammatical fashion. Although it always exists in a culture, language is never identical to itself, without change, because no culture can exclude all difference from itself.

Notice in this respect that Pip's ''odd idea'' is a culturally deviant reading, yet one that seems given to him. It seems to be developed under the cultural compulsion of the letters. His reading has the form of a cultural conception of meaning even though we, with the mature Pip, are led to recognize it as personal ''fantasy'' or ''feeling,'' not ''knowledge.'' Through just this sort of profound inconsistency, love appears as a question of language in the novel. Love appears as the rhetorical site, the form and forum of words, at which community is instituted or, conversely, is seen as being without any founding authority.

Through the confusions around love, the difference of language in this novel appears as an argument between two conceptions of culture. One is instituted spiritually, beyond the inventions of humanity, and so is presided over by a deity of identity. The other is subject to intractable divisions because it is a human creation authorized merely by conventional forms, such as those that characterize both the aristocratic story of origins and the middle-class story of progressive accomplishment. If the reader is to make sense of Pip's love of Estella, spiritual identity must assert itself through cultural difference without returning to the rule of origins. Dickens's culture then appears as the denial of culture. It appears as the culture of the middle classes that will not recognize the politics of its own creation and practices, recognizing only an ironic power over feeling, character, ideology, truth, nature, transcendence, and history.

Love appears as the site that articulates the potential of middle-class authority, the opening of its history, and the contest over its destiny. In other words, the question of authority in this novel is inseparable from the formal arrangement of categorical distinctions—emotional, psychological, cognitive, social, and so on—that all depend on the sense made or not made of the word *love*. The confusion this situation creates in Pip's affections is captured wonderfully (albeit unintentionally) in one of E. D. Hirsch's expressions of anxiety: "Once it is admitted that a meaning can change its characteristics, then there is no way of finding the true Cinderella among all the contenders. There is no dependable glass slipper we can use as a test, since the old slipper will no longer fit the new Cinderella."[31]

I do not suggest that Dickens's portrayal of different ways of grasping language is a portrayal of a universal situation of meaning. What I have described is just one way to represent the complex implications of the desire for, recognition of, and resistance to social change. The example of Pip reading the gravestone is not exemplary of the problem of all interpretation throughout all time but only one instance of the ways language may become a problem for people. It *is* an important instance, one relevant to interpretive concerns in contemporary intellectual life associated with names like Wittgenstein and Freud. But why this difference in ways of grasping language is marked so dramatically in this novel, why it is focused especially on the issue of desire, why this mystery is recognized by a desiring boy but not by the girl he desires—these and similar questions must be pursued if we are not to replace an idealized conception of subjectivity with an idealized conception of language and critical practice.

Still, one conclusion does follow from this analysis of language: to examine the form of Pip's rhetoric is to point out the politics of conceptual understanding, since only by identifying with a particular vision of culture can we insert the missing connections into Pip's representation of desire and make it appear a coherent experience rather than an intersection of diverse and conflicting values.

In Conrad's "Heart of Darkness," Marlow's relation to his own sleeping beauty dramatizes a problem similar to that in Pip's relation to the unresponsive Estella. "The approach to this Kurtz grubbing for ivory in the wretched bush," Marlow says, "was beset by as many dangers as though he had been an enchanted princess sleeping in a fabulous castle." In his need for a rule by which he can resolve the contradiction, if it is a contradiction, of a report filled with "burning noble words" and yet concluded with the addendum "Exterminate all the brutes!" Marlow, too, must deal with the politics of "the idea" and with associated questions of social order and national destiny. In both cases we can see how irony can turn a social class, the middle class, into a spiritual agency. In both cases the writer self-consciously focuses on the question of the external form of language and, through the childish problem of representation exemplified by Pip's reading of gravestones and Marlow's boyhood reading of a map of the world, dramatizes the godlike power of rhetoric to create and uncreate identity; to elevate and victimize; to invent, awaken, and condemn to death.[32]

As it enables us to see the difference between these two ways of understanding language—or, more exactly, to see this difference of language—the rhetoric of love in *Great Expectations* marks the implication of culture in the text as a contested basis of meaning. Most generally, this challenge appears in the change that the narrative implies is underway from a former order of representation regulated by the rule of origins to Dickens's new order of democratic spirituality, regulated by the rule of irony. The rhetoric of love thus is the hinge on which history turns in this novel. Origins are denied so that the compulsion of the new may be asserted. The entire narrative of *Great Expectations* turns on the way the progress of history, which will make Pip a middle-class businessman and reconcile him with Estella, and the regress of origins, which opposes this progress with the threats of aristocratic posturing and class antagonism, are represented in the issue of desire, which is also the issue of reading.

Culture is called into being by this language of love because love is not taken for granted but rather is repeatedly declared a mystery impossible to describe: "What I wanted, who can say? How can *I* say, when I never knew?" (*GE*, 124). In addition, Pip's equivocations on this point are instructive. For example, he appeals to his readers' understanding of his experience and yet contrasts this experience to "the conventional notion of a lover" (269).[33] Furthermore, although Pip insists on the unusual nature of his feelings, any reader familiar with Victorian literature can see the attraction he describes as fulfilling traditional images, some of which are noted specifically in his references to fairy tales and knightly adventure. Equivocations such as these are not evidence of faults in the design of the narrative. They represent the way meaning is called into question in this narrative as culture, which is always at issue in the practice of interpretation, is made a dramatic issue by Dickens. It is the contest established in this way between the appearance of social conventions and the absence of social understanding that indicates an argument over culture concentrated in the representation of desire. (And this situation, too, is replayed in "Heart of Darkness," in which Marlow is continually concerned at once to assert and to deny the arbitrary power of convention.)

So the slippage between identity and rhetoric suggested by Pip's origin—"I was always treated as if I had insisted on being born in opposition to the dictates of reason, religion, and morality, and against the dissuading arguments of my best friends" (*GE*, 25)—appears again when Pip is made the subject of romance. Desire, too, appears as an orphan in the "universal struggle" (*GE*, 1) that occurs when the traditional image of authority is lost. It, too, appears to be up for grabs. It is a sign whose meaning must be put into question if a certain difference (which will call forth a certain kind of feeling, character, ideology, truth, nature, transcendence, history, and overall power) is to be articulated. Like Pip, desire appears in this novel as the difference that will be formed into an identity if the novel successfully appeals to conventions that are at once quite minimal (basic matters of a lexicon and grammar) and very great indeed (for is any expectation greater than the assumption that we may draw together words and forms of consciousness across a whole community?). The issue of desire is the issue of making sense in this novel according to conventions that must be formulated persuasively within the novel itself.

The examination of culture on this point is further marked through Miss Havisham, who speaks of love in a way that seems at once antithetical to Pip's concept and identical to his experience with Estella. As Pip comments, "She said the word often enough, and there could be no doubt that she meant to say it; but if the often repeated word had been hate instead of love—despair—revenge—dire death—it could not have sounded from her lips more like a curse" (*GE*, 278–29). The same crumbling of cultural understanding into the form of the asyndeton appears in Estella's speech about love being "a form of words." It appears as well in an earlier response to Pip just after her return from her education in France: "Oh! I have a heart to be stabbed in, I have no doubt . . . and, of course, if it ceased to beat I should cease to be. But you know what I mean. I have no softness there, no—sympathy—sentiment—nonsense" (*GE*, 276).

The significance of this rhetorical form to the institution of culture is also emphasized by the other aspects of Pip's narrative that place desire in the company of a radical confusion. For example, Miss Havisham appears most excited when Estella's moods are "so many and so contradictory of one another" that Pip is "puzzled what to say or do" (*GE*, 109); Pip describes the way love makes him the "restless aspiring discontented" individual who was so feared by the moralists of the social order in nineteenth-century England (*GE*, 124); and many other incidents in the novel, from Pip's first encounter with escaped convicts to his attempt to help Magwitch escape the officers of the law, dramatize for him the dissonance between the stable values represented by Joe's "dear old home-voice" (*GE*, 541) and the flux of appearances represented by Estella, London, and the glamorous heights of society.

Given such a context, the significance of this rhetorical form can be specified even more precisely. Within Pip's narrative, it represents an absence of connection, hierarchy, and totality—all the forms Pip needs to make sense of himself within his society. His use of asyndeton symbolizes the danger that identity (a spiritual likeness) may fall into synonymy (a linguistic or material association). The threat being dramatized is that love may indeed appear as just "a form of words" that will suffer a vertiginous metonymic transformation into concepts such as softness, sentiment, nonsense, and hate—and thus into an unavoidable and permanent source of existential confusion—if it is not regulated by the power of culture. "Replacing the feudal index," Roland Barthes suggests, "the bourgeois sign is a metonymic confusion."[34] This drive to overcome the threat of confusion is the reason for Pip's desire for Estella. His desire for her is the desire to identify with a culture that cannot exist as long as her lack of feeling is truth. Language itself is at stake in this desire.

This threat of metonymic transformation might be compared to those works by Escher in which leaves turn into fish, ascending into descending stairs, with the blink of an eye. Another comparison might be to word games, such as Lewis Carroll's "doublets," in which we are allowed a number of transformations of a specified kind to change one word, such as *love*, into another, such as *hate*. Some children's rhymes also play on this kind of confusion, such as the riddle that asks, "Why are fire engines red?":

> One and one are two.
> Two and two are four.
> Three times four is twelve.
> There are twelve inches in a ruler.
> Queen Mary was a ruler.
> Queen Mary ruled the sea.
> There are fish in the sea.
> The fish have fins.
> The Finns fought the Russians.
> The Russians are red.
> Fire engines are always rushin'.
> That's why fire engines are red.[35]

Or perhaps an even better comparison, because it illustrates dramatically the question of mastery, is the "preriddle." This is the kind of joke that occurs when young children are first introduced to "knock-knock" jokes and other forms of riddling and take the "external" form of the joke for its meaning. ("Knock-knock," such a child may say. "Who's there?" "Banana." "Banana who?" "Banana dog-face!")

No matter how we may describe it, the threat of this situation disables the grown-up sense of culture by which we customarily determine the proper context for meaning in any situation. One consequence may be a compulsion like that Pip feels as a youth and as a narrator, a compulsion to force into being a safely grown-up understanding. Just as he tries to get Estella and other people in his world to recognize specific forms of meaning, such as *love* and the *gentleman*, so does Pip appeal to the reader to come around to his retrospective grasp of these forms: to find in this grasp an ironic identity. To the extent that this appeal is accepted (and this is not an all-or-nothing proposition, as the critic who judged Estella incredible illustrates), what I have called the rule of irony provides the "likeness" that orders representation in this novel. The apparent opposition between the rule of origins and the rule of irony then is based from the beginning on the ironic resolution of this opposition. Irony is dematerialized, spiritualized, in the reading of the text. It becomes an invisible god of culture.

If a sense of recognition, the light of culture, should arise out of this work, then Pip's writing, and Dickens's, will be a successful piece of communication. If it should not, then communication in general will be made to appear something like the situation in which two Englishmen found themselves, as the joke goes, when they were traveling on a very noisy train. The first one said, "I say, is this Wembly?" His neighbor replied, "No, Thursday." "I am too," said the first. And so even the externals of words, their "mere" forms, would escape from us and leave us most baffled when we thought ourselves most secure in fellow feeling. Reading this novel, we would be like Pip in his first readings of his parents' gravestones, or of Satis House, or of Wemmick and Jaggers.

By sowing confusion through the rhetorical form in which desire appears, Dickens designed a way to counter the accidents of classes—even of the middle classes to which Pip would belong—with the divine power of rhetoric to create and uncreate all social confusions. His meaning is political, an issue of power, before it is an issue of the various opinions, images, dramatic emphases, and other textual features readers form into an allegory of such things as feeling, character, identity, truth, nature, transcendence, and history. The struggle to institute culture thus appears in this novel as a battle of tropes in which Dickens counters the danger of asyndeton with the recuperative trope of irony. Insofar as Pip's romantic and narrative desire makes sense, irony acts as the spiritual essence of language that saves it from being trapped in the world of material forms and thus allows it to manipulate these forms. It makes some invisible, alters others, creates new ones, and, in short, invents a middle-class world that seems to be the universal world of nature. This trope of irony in Pip's narrative serves as the prediction of its eventual payoff or progress (we may imagine a game in which *profit* is transformed into *progress*).[36] In doing so it differentiates Dickens's work from earlier novels—*Tom Jones*, for instance—in which the ending has the appearance of divine intervention rather than divine inevitability. The ending of a middle-class novel must not appear to intervene, or as in the case of George Eliot's *The Mill on the Floss*, it will prove disturbing to readers. It must develop, grow, in accordance with the progressive rule of irony rather than the static rule of origins.

The fact that Pip can experience desire in this context only in terms of contradictory feelings and qualities does not really make desire a problem, then. It makes desire the saving grace of his history, for these contradictions are the means of producing the god of irony. Irony becomes the trope through which culture is produced and cultural recognition given to the individual. It marks the *invisibility* of culture, the disappearance of cultural power into the seemingly neutral form of understanding or reading. It marks as well the *difference* of culture: the appearance of value in the differentiation of culture from nature that makes it possible for either category to be used to criticize the other. This materialization of value through the dematerialized form of irony is what is required to make Dickens's narrative coherent as a narrative, a Victorian novel, a fictional autobiography, a psychological journey, a type of literature of any sort. It is what gives desire the power of meaning in *Great Expectations* and, in fact, what makes it possible to read the words of this novel. It is the self-effacing interlocutor between the words of the text and the cultural sense made of the text. It is the trope that leads us forward (if it does lead us forward) into entire programs of reading in which the rhetorical elements of the text are organized and thematized. In short, it is a form of unconsciousness. It is the unconsciousness of social life as it and we are caught up within the politics of rhetoric in which various figures, like this figure of irony, this *grown-up* figure, have a material force that is no less powerful for being generally invisible. It is the rhetoric we must not recognize as such, the rhetoric we must recognize instead as things such as feeling, character, and truth, if we are to see this narrative as something other than nonsense. Thus, its role in this novel may be taken to exemplify the implication of politics as rhetorical power in any form of representation.

In this argument I concentrate on some aspects of the text to the exclusion of others and emphasize some figures over others, although it would be entirely possible to select textual elements different from those isolated and to analyze them in terms of the basis of meaning in the novel. I chose my players in this way for purposes that can, presumably, be read in this work by those inclined to do so. The fact that I have made this choice needs no argument—this is a necessary act, whether it is acknowledged or not—and the value of the choice I have made will be established by means largely beyond my control. Still, it may be useful here to illustrate this choice with an anecdote that is, in a sense, both autobiographical and historical.

The anecdote involves what at first was a puzzling situation to me in the classroom or, one might say, a situation I could not read. The puzzle was that the students I teach generally have a much more difficult time in trying to put desire into question than they have in dealing with God or the State. Even though most of the students in the school where I currently teach are politically conservative and more than nominally religious, most are able to regard political and religious beliefs as historical constructions (at least for the purposes of the classroom) with an ease that vanishes when I ask them to consider how, why, and what people desire. Perhaps I am not as good at "teaching desire" as in engaging them in political and religious questions, or it may be that Church and State are easier to historicize than subjectivity because their material nature seems more obvious; but I think the reason for the difference is elsewhere. For despite the apocalyptic pronouncements on the family and feeling made by Christopher Lasch and his ilk, it seems clear to me that the sentimental love that came to be identified popularly as the heart of society during the eighteenth and nineteenth centuries still largely plays this symbolic role, even with all the other differences between Victorian and late twentieth-century American society. Hence this resistance that arises at the thought of putting desire into words. (That is, into words that are critical and historical, not cushioned within the vocabularies and themes of such popular psychologies as Lasch's.) To materialize the source of symbolic order in this way still appears a threat to identity, despite the way Pip's associated concerns with social class, wealth, and gentility differ from the issues environing love for my students. And, of course, it must be remembered that this resistance to the materialization of desire appears not only among my students but throughout the profession of literary studies, in which the tradition of humanism (as well as some Leftist and Utopian challenges to that tradition) insists on identifying, controlling, and continuing a spiritual consciousness of desire.

So it makes some sense that *Great Expectations* should be interesting today for the way it portrays the implication of politics in this language of desire, which still has such force, for college students and for college professors, as an unconscious compulsion and a symbolic recuperation of social conflict, uncertainty, and alienation. It makes some sense, too, that an analysis of the materiality of language should provoke the self-consciousness of this description, even though at issue here is merely a matter of academic lit-crit—"merely" a form of words.

V

Varium et mutabile semper femina.
—Mercury in *The Aeneid* (4:569–70)

After all, words initiate the mystery for Pip. Unlike Estella, who clings to conventional form, attributing her identity to the woman who raised her—"I must be taken as I have been made" (*GE*, 356)—Pip dismisses the significance of others in creating the sense of identity that alienates him from his younger self and makes him ashamed of the home in which he was raised. Although he notes the influences that might be said to have played upon him, especially his sister's behavior, he comments, "How much of my ungracious condition of mind may have been my own fault, how much Miss Havisham's, how much my sister's, is now of no account to me or to any one. The change was made in me; the thing was done. Well or ill done, excusably or inexcusably, it was done" (*GE*, 123). In place of the scheme of human influence that Pip continues to resent whenever Estella suggests it later in the novel—"Her reverting to this tone as if our association were forced upon us and we were mere puppets, gave me pain" (*GE*, 312)—Pip asserts that language is responsible for the way he is.

To be more exact, a consciousness of language, a recognition of language as cultural rather than natural power, is what Pip sees as having made all the difference: "what would it signify to me, being coarse and common, if nobody had told me so!'' (*GE*, 149). Once Pip has recognized language as the institution of cultural differences rather than the undifferentiated stuff of being, the comic mispronunciation that gave him his name and the confusion he felt over the meaning of the words on his parents' tombstones (''I read 'wife of the Above' as a complimentary reference to my father's exaltation to a better world'' [*GE*, 48]) appear trivial indeed compared to the associations of words he begins to produce almost obsessively. Returning from his first visit to Miss Havisham's, he invents outrageous stories about the appearances inside her home and the events in which he participated there. As he finds that his stories are believed, he feels himself driven to pile on ever more incredible details. In effect, he is driven to test the recognition of language as the issue of difference, as an absence of unconscious wholeness, that has just been impressed on him. He finds that language passes not only with flying colors—with a blue flag and a red flag and one with gold stars—but also with a black velvet coach, cake and wine, dogs fighting for veal cutlets in a silver basket, swords, pistols, jam, pills, and all the other things his words can bring to life.[37]

Pip is not frightened by his linguistic inventions simply because they are lies that prove to be amazingly convincing to people in authority. He is frightened because he cannot account for their origins, even though he associates this institution of language with Estella's influence over him. If he can materialize reality through language in this way, he must feel that he is being materialized, or mastered, through language—and through Estella. ''I don't know what possessed me, Joe,'' Pip says of these lies. His inventions seem to be generated out of his new consciousness of language and yet seem to spin out of his control and beyond the conscious agency of others. As he goes on to tell the reader,

> And then I told Joe that I felt very miserable, and that I hadn't been able to explain myself to Mrs. Joe and Pumblechook, who were so rude to me, and that there had been a beautiful young lady at Miss Havisham's who was dreadfully proud, and that she had said I was common, and that the lies had come of it somehow, though I didn't know how.
>
> This was a case of metaphysics, at least as difficult for Joe to deal with, as for me. But Joe took the case altogether out of the region of metaphysics, and by that means vanquished it.
>
> ''There's one thing you may be sure of, Pip,'' said Joe, after some rumination, ''namely, that lies is lies.'' (*GE*, 79–80)

Like Matthew Pocket, who asserts that ''no man who was not a true gentleman at heart, ever was, since the world began, a true gentleman in manner'' (*GE*, 209), Joe goes ''out of the region of metaphysics'' by dogmatically asserting an identity—''lies is lies''—that Pip accepts. (In so doing, of course, Joe follows the strategy of many more eminent philosophers.) The problem is that this statement does vanquish the case instead of solving it.[38]

Joe says all lies "come from the father of lies" (and this *of* seems the genitive of material in a novel in which the protagonist's father is dead, his substitute father lacking in authority, his "fairy godmother" in fact another father who once had threatened the life of his own child, and all paternal authority, in effect, categorically challenged).[39] However, a question still remains. How did Pip touch upon this origin if not in his new consciousness of himself as a creature of language? If words are the devil, and Pip a creature of words, then salvation can lie only in Joe's inarticulate place virtually outside of language. One possible terminus for the plot of the novel is thus sketched out, and one that will maintain some force in Dickens's design;[40] but from his first meeting with Estella, Pip already has gone too far into language for this plot to satisfy him. Even the case of Joe is not as simple as it initially may appear; it is not too long in the novel before the reader and the young Pip observe him lying to Mrs. Joe when he says Miss Havisham sent her greetings. As Pip will learn, it is not by imitating Joe that he can overcome the confusion of origins and the threat of a confusing identification with origins that is represented by Estella. Only an idealization of language through a new form of discourse, a form that turns upon its opposition to the rule of origins, will allow him to master himself.

This emphasis on the question of language is further reinforced by situations involving other characters in the novel. For instance, there is Pip's first description of Orlick: "Now, Joe kept a journeyman at weekly wages whose name was Orlick. He pretended that his christian name was Dolge—a clear impossibility—but he was a fellow of that obstinate disposition that I believe him to have been the prey of no delusion in that particular, but wilfully to have imposed that name upon the village as an affront to its understanding" (*GE*, 130). This "disposition" of Orlick's is further illustrated in Pip's comment on an encounter with him when he and Biddy were out for a walk:

> "Well, then," said he, "I'm jiggered if I don't see you home!" This penalty of being jiggered was a favourite suppositious case of his. He attached no definite meaning to the word that I am aware of, but used it, like his own pretended Christian name, to affront mankind, and convey an idea of something savagely damaging. When I was younger, I had had a general belief that if he had jiggered me personally, he would have done it with a sharp and twisted hook. (*GE*, 153)

As Pip associates it with his childish propensity to invent figures out of words without any conscious rule of "likeness" to regulate these inventions, Orlick's linguistic character appears to embody the "savagely damaging" threat that culture may be dissolved into meanings associated only through chance or arbitrary power, unresponsive to the "understanding" of a community. The irony is that

Orlick's threat to Pip may be seen to resemble the threat of Pip's childish use of language. This also may be seen as the threat posed by the use Joe makes of language as throughout his life words become things in his mouth, resulting in coinages like "unacceptabobble" and "coddleshell" (for codicil), to name just two among many (*GE*, 542, 544).

In fact, although Joe lectures Pip about lies, his own speech shows signs not only of ineptitude but also of the compulsion that so bewilders Pip. Once Joe is struck by language—as he remembers the epitaph he spontaneously composed for his father—he, too, is overcome with the wonder of invention. Describing this epitaph ("Watsume'er the failings on his part, Remember reader he were that good in his hart"), Joe says, "I made it . . . my own self. I made it in a moment. It was like striking out a horseshoe complete, in a single blow. I never was so much surprised in all my life—couldn't credit my own ed—to tell you the truth, hardly believed it *were* my own ed" (*GE*, 52–53).

Throughout the rest of the novel, like a bumpkin Ancient Mariner, Joe periodically appears compelled to reproduce the form of this epitaph, as when he describes to Pip how Orlick had attacked Pumblechook: "And wotsume'er the failings on his part, he were a corn and seedsman in his hart" (*GE*, 545). In other words, like Coleridge's storyteller, Joe appears driven by the invisible difference of culture, a compelling power producing comedy or tragedy, as the case may be, but in any case appearing as a supernatural language essential to the coherence of a narrative. In effect, Joe must appear as a bumbling poet to the reader if Pip is to appear a successful autobiographer and Dickens, a successful novelist. Joe's place in literature, like Wopsle's in theater, must be classified, assigned a cultural category, if the rule necessary to meaning in this novel, and to *Great Expectations* being a novel, is to appear. Joe experiences his language in this novel as an unconscious rhetorical compulsion and thus leads the reader toward the unconscious, the cultural identity, that gives meaning to this novel.

Moreover, since Pip's childish use of words appears only heightened once he is awakened to language as a cultural rather than natural power, he seems to be accusing Orlick of his own linguistic practice. In his lumbering, uneducated, violent person, Orlick appears as a material form unnrestrained by the authority of origins (as his disrespect for law and for Joe's position indicates) and ungraced by any sort of transcendent identification (as his uncomplicated lust for Biddy suggests). Haunting Pip throughout the novel, identifying himself as the double whose place Pip has usurped, Orlick represents the far side of the politics of culture in *Great Expectations*. In one sense the threat he poses is entirely conventional, as he represents the violent figure of the unenlightened working class that appears throughout Dickens's work, as in so many novels and other literary works of this time. In another sense, however, he is not common at all, as Pip's characterization of him makes him a specifically linguistic threat.

There is no accounting for Pip's assertion that Orlick's Christian name was "a clear impossibility" except in terms of the more general contention in his narrative among political conceptions of language that results in the problems of dissimulated identities, displaced authorities, and figures of speech run wild. This impossibility makes sense only in terms of the concern of this novel to turn the political statement of the case, in its conventional and unconventional aspects, into a spiritual impression of the nature of language. Irony is called on as the answer to the sterility of metaphysical tautology and to the wilderness of figures of speech. If it is to be read as a coherent whole, the procedure needed to draw *Great Expectations* together is for the reader to be able to identify Pip, for Pip to make sense; and for this act to be possible, this trope of irony that appears even in the title of this book (in which great expectations are also great disappointments) must be recognized as representing the spiritual institution of culture. It must give meaning to incongruity, as a "good" joke does, instead of leaving it a puzzle, or "muddle," as Stephen Blackpool would say. (Hence the way students and professors rationalize the irrationality of desire in this narrative.) The reader who makes sense of this novel must buy into or get a purchase upon a certain form of politics. This does not necessarily involve specific political positions but rather the differences of power, the values, comprised within the rule of irony: the formal distinctions separating concepts like feeling, character, and ideology.

Of course, there are many ways of reading this novel without making sense of it and without simply turning it into nonsense, including the present reading, which recognizes the imaginary nature of its authority and so allows the text to appear in its diversity: object of literary criticism, source of quotations, fable of history, expression of desire, representation of social conflict and confusion, and so on. However, one truly has to work at such a reading; for in our present circumstances, the attraction of this irony is very strong for students and teachers alike.

Because of the role played by irony, it is not enough that Orlick should be defeated in his ultimate attack on Pip's life. In addition, he must be discredited, his linguistic disposition proven "obstinate" and unjustified, as the figural power of language in general is recuperated and regulated within this rule of irony, which is not simply a trope but rather the institution of cultural meaning. The unimaginable alternative, to those who make sense of this novel—who project any reading, be it historical, psychological, formal, or whatever—is that Orlick truly would be Pip's double, the differences between them would dissolve and, with them, every distinction we perceive in the text so as to make our reading something other than the idiosyncratic musing upon letters that gives the youthful Pip the image of his father as "a square, stout, dark man." Pumblechook, for example, would no longer be seen as a plagiarized version of Joe—"The falser he, the truer Joe; the meaner he, the nobler Joe" (*GE*, 490)—because words like *false* and *true, mean* and *noble*, would not body forth a coherently organized culture through the reader's sense of irony, appearing instead as bewildering metonyms or synonyms, as *love* and *hate* are in Miss Havisham's speech.

If we were to imagine this alternative, we could imagine Pip's narrative, the educated discourse of the mature Victorian merchant, metamorphosing or dissolving into something resembling the text the youthful Pip presents to his guardian: "mI deEr JO i opE U r krWitE wEll i opE i shAl soN B haBelL 4 2 teeDge U JO aN theN wE shOrl b sO glOdd aN wEn i M preNgtD 2 u JO woT larX an blEvE ME inF xn PiP" (*GE*, 50). And then, perhaps, blurring further into the experience of reading described by the then analphabetic Joe, with his "oncommon" fondness for literature: " 'Give me,' said Joe, 'a good book, or a good newspaper, and sit me down afore a good fire, and I ask no better. Lord!' he continued after rubbing his knees a little, 'when you *do* come to a J and a O, and says you, "Here, at last, is a J-O, Joe," how interesting reading is!' " (*GE*, 51).

For Joe in a sense is the exemplary civilized reader, in this as in other respects most civilized when he appears most primitive, in accordance with the usual logic of nostalgia. He reads for the sheer pleasure of experiencing a sense of cultural identity. He recognizes his name, or a reasonable facsimile thereof, and feels he has accomplished a great deal — as he has. Although at this point he has not had Pip's experience with the elements of language ("I struggled through the alphabet as if it had been a bramble-bush" [*GE*, 50]), he has something else. He has a sense of belonging among these elements, however foreign they may be to him according to conventional standards of literacy. Pip has already lost this sense (although he does not recognize the loss until he is insulted by Estella), and he spends his entire narrative, literally and figuratively, comically and tragically, striving to recapture himself in words.

All the while, then, it could be that the sense Pip wants to make is the nonsense of writing as it appears to Joe before he is finally educated by Biddy. To borrow a term from Michel Charles, it could be that in the progress of his education he really is looking for a passage from knowledge to naïvité, a kind of "deapprenticeship."[41] This might be the case — if it were not for the example of Orlick, who has a way with nonsense very different from Joe's. Because of the threat represented by Orlick, Pip must make sense and Joe must finally be taught the elements of reading and writing. For Orlick dramatizes the consideration that identity, if it is a founding or foundling thing, can, like the youthful Pip, find comfort, pleasure, and recognition only by chance. In this respect Orlick is but a figure of that "universal struggle" in which Pip is, by chance, the only one of his siblings to live; a figure as well of the family battles in which Pip is bandied about and allowed no identity beyond that ascribed to him by the character momentarily assuming power over him; a figure of all the nonsense Pip must put up with in relation to Estella, and in the revelation of Magwitch as his benefactor, and thus in all the language of desire for which he must devise a cultural discipline if he is to represent Joe as an innocent reader and himself as a meaningful character and readable writer. Orlick is Pip without irony and thus stands in the same relation to him as Pumblechook stands to Joe and Compeyson to Magwitch. Or, to put it in other words, the rule of irony arises in this novel, in part, from readers seeing morally weighted parallels in the relations between Orlick and Pip, Pumblechook and Joe, and Magwitch and Compeyson.

Although he is otherwise so different from Estella, Orlick also represents the linguistic threat engaged by the very possibility of this novel as a meaningful "form of words." It only makes sense that Estella should marry Bentley Drummle, for Drummle is a more genteel Orlick. It only makes sense, too, that Estella should be regenerated spiritually through the brutal treatment Drummle accords her. As she meets her match in him and as the arbitrary violence of chance that he represents proves compelling to her, she becomes a woman bound by the necessity of feeling; and so she is drawn, inevitably, to trace this feeling back through her earlier relationship with Pip. As in so much Victorian literature, suffering gives meaning to the form of words and thus becomes the means for identifying with the past. Once the external, the material, the "merely" rhetorical, is identified as the form of suffering, the difference and invisibility of culture also are identified. For this reason, Victorian writing can fasten its sentiment on criminals, whores, and other deviants and yet remain profoundly conservative in its attitude toward society. This is another reason that a rhetorical reading is so important, because other sorts of reading are liable to mistake the formal institution of culture (suffering Jo in *Bleak House*, suffering Maggie in *The Mill on the Floss*, and so on) for a radical critique of culture.

Orlick's significance in this respect may be further clarified if we consider the aphasia that afflicts Mrs. Joe as a result of his attack on her. As Pip describes her condition after this attack,

> When, at last, she came round so far as to be helped down-stairs, it was still necessary to keep my slate always by her, that she might indicate in writing what she could not indicate in speech. As she was (very bad handwriting apart) a more than indifferent speller, and as Joe was a more than indifferent reader, extraordinary complications arose between them, which I was always called in to solve. The administration of mutton instead of medicine, the substitution of Tea for Joe, and the baker for bacon, were among the mildest of my own mistakes. (*GE*, 142)

Similar examples of these complications are noted when Pip receives his great expectations:

> Infinite pains were then taken by Biddy to convey to my sister some idea of what had happened. To the best of my belief, those efforts entirely failed. She laughed and nodded her head a great many times, and even repeated after Biddy, the words "Pip" and "Property." But I

doubt if they had more meaning in them than an election cry, and I cannot suggest a darker picture of her state of mind. (*GE*, 167)

What Orlick communicates to Mrs. Joe through his violence are the arbitrary uses to which he puts language. These uses "affront mankind" by allowing for semantic substitutions that threaten social order as they frustrate cultural understanding. Significantly enough, near the end of the novel, when Orlick is boasting to Pip of Compeyson and the gang with which he is associated, he refers to "them that writes fifty hands," adding, "that's not like sneaking you as writes but one" (*GE*, 550). Again, plagiarism is the opposite of mastery.

To be sure, in one sense the threat posed by Mrs. Joe's aphasia is a simple one that seems to have nothing to do with politics. The situation in question appears purely an educational one as problems with handwriting, spelling, and memory lead to "the substitution of Tea for Joe" and similar linguistic associations. If love were a problem in this context, the metonymic displacements by which it is threatened elsewhere in Pip's story might appear either tragic or comic but in any case remediable on the basis of an educated conception of language. There would be pathos, perhaps, or absurdity but no threat to the understanding of the village if Mrs. Joe were to substitute *mutton* for *love*. This substitution would be regarded simply as a mistake, an error induced by neurological trauma and perceptible by means of tests for linguistic appropriateness and coherence.

When Mrs. Joe gives no more meaning to the words *Pip* and *property* than one can find in "an election cry," however, a different case is suggested. The "dread of not being understood" hidden in Pip's childhood breast (*GE*, 74) becomes a more serious matter. If *Pip* and *Property* might be exchangeable terms, Pip's identity might be merely a matter of external associations—in this case, an economic association—and the question of spiritual understanding throughout the novel an attempt to substantiate a plot whose only ground is in a haphazard scheme of material coincidence or disjunction. The manipulation of these words would indeed be comparable to the election cry that serves Pip as an emblem of meaningless rhetoric. It would be a form of words that is accepted but without any value or power as communication except, perhaps, to the mob (the criminal "them that writes fifty hands," the audience that assaults Wopsle, the rising "rebel" and his cohorts feared by Mrs. Joe and so many others in these times).

In this situation, love would merely be a political discourse. It would be nothing more or less than a socially unifying form of words designed to make certain likenesses and differences appear as if they represent a necessary cultural order rather than historical contingencies of secrecy, pain, conflict, and death. One can see, then, that if Pip "cannot suggest a darker picture" of his aunt's "state of mind" than by this example of *Pip* and *property* and its comparison to an election cry, it is because the rhetoric he is pursuing is meant to repress the language of the state from consciousness. Political language without transcendent sanctification poses just as much of a threat in this novel and in Dickens's other works as does poetical language without political order. It may be the threat of the mob, the machinery of state, or the glowering lout, just as the threat of poetical language may be variously an issue of lies, desire, meter, or madness, because at stake in either case is an overriding question of topical organization: a question of a system of cultural classification that must be persuasively formulated, performed, through this text if it is to have the power of meaning as a power over its readers.

We could enumerate many other features of *Great Expectations* that focus on this question of words: for example, the aforementioned Mr. Wopsle's love of histrionic reading. This leads him into embarrassment not only on the stage but also in The Three Jolly Bargeman, where he entertains his audience with a dramatic account of what is described, in a significant ambiguity, as a "highly popular murder" (*GE*, 155). As he is taken up short by Mr. Jaggers for presuming that the man accused of the crime is guilty, his experience perfectly illustrates the conflict in this novel among political uses of language, with Wopsle here suffering the consequences of allowing figures of speech a liberty that, to Jaggers, sounds devilish. Of course, the politics represented by Jaggers's meticulous legalism also do not promise salvation for Pip in the novel. However, like his adventures on the stage, Wopsle's encounter with the lawyer directs Pip's audience toward a recognition that the very same words can either alienate a group of people or bind it together, depending on the situation of the performance. The same audience that had given Wopsle its rapt attention turns on him after Jaggers's intervention transforms his rhetoric into a different kind of figuration. In the same way, the word *love* in this novel can be received as "love" or as "hate" depending on the situation involved. As long as one lacks a rhetoric that will bind these conflicts, these proliferating figures, into a unified cultural form, such transformations of context are bound to continue and with them transformations of being: fairy godmother into condemned felon, cold princess into suffering wife, and so on.

Another example arises from Herbert's decision to call Pip "Handel," after the composer of "The Harmonious Blacksmith." In addition to the emphasis it places on the new process of acculturation to which Pip delivers himself when he goes to London, this act eventually has a consequence unintended by Herbert. When Pip is returning home to visit Estella and has to ride on a coach with two convicts, he discovers to his horror that one of them is a figure out of the past he is trying to transcend: the emissary Magwitch sent with two pound notes to reward him for his theft of "wittles" and a file. Pip describes his attempt to remain inconspicuous and tells of the following event: " 'Good-bye, Handel!' Herbert called out to me as we started. I thought what a blessed fortune it was, that he had found another name for me than Pip" (*GE*, 265).

In this case, Pip's assumed name saves him from embarrassment just as Mag-witch's alias, "Provis," will help to delay his capture and death; but it does so at the cost of a sense of alienation from his friend and the world at large. Pip never had gone by his "proper" name—"Pip" is his mispronunciation of "Philip" and a name he was told by his benefactor he should keep—but this scene helps to show the social pressures on the desired stability of all proper names in the novel. A man for whom "lies is lies" may always remain himself, Biddy may never be "insulting, or capricious, or Biddy to-day and somebody else to-morrow" (*GE*, 152), and Matthew Pocket may remain faithful to himself, like his son, Herbert; but this stable identity simply does not seem possible when it comes to dealings with convicts, the law, and the trials of the past that made Estella the "orphan" whom Pip and Jaggers decide never to enlighten about her "true" identity. More-over, one remembers that Joe is *not* Joe when he appears in London or elsewhere in his Sunday clothes, that Biddy cannot be herself with Pip for much of the novel because he cannot perceive and she not speak her desire, that the cost Matthew must pay for maintaining his identity is to be misrecognized by his wife and most of the world, and that Herbert fulfills himself only because Pip hides his contri-bution to his friend's successful entry into business. In this context, Pip's unnameable desire for Estella is not aberrant. Rather, it is symptomatic of a con-testation in social understanding clearly manifested, if rarely recognized, throughout this text.

Perhaps the most telling situation in which this emphasis on language is played out in other terms besides desire, however, occurs when Magwitch first reveals himself to Pip and then admires his apartment: " 'And your books, too,' turning his eyes round the room, 'mounting up, on their shelves, by hundreds! . . . You shall read 'em to me, dear boy! And if they're in foreign languages wot I don't understand, I shall be just as proud as if I did' " (*GE*, 372–73). As with the situations of desire, aphasia, proper names, and so on, Magwitch's approach to Pip's linguistic proficiency represents an unnerving recognition that linguistic value depends more on the situation of power established for words than on some power of meaning intrinsic to them.[42] Thus formulated, this recognition would hardly be disturbing to contemporary linguists. However, it must be so to Pip, whose desire to create an idealist conception of language is represented by his insistence that he cannot name the cause or causes of his desire for Estella, that it is simply love, that "love is love." Understandably, he is distressed to have his educated proficiency in languages regarded as if it might add up to nothing more than a sign of gentility. In other words, he is distressed at the thought that he might not be able to win anything through language. If words have a meaning assigned only by social circumstances, as Estella implies when she speaks of love, then Pip must feel that all categorical distinctions are liable to fall, that there is no way to distinguish his identity from this convict's, that love might well be dire death or hate, and that there is no way to unify the experiences of the life of an orphan who has left the community in which he was born—left the rule of origins—to venture into the bewildering, painful, and tawdry play of identities that appears as modern English society.[43]

Furthermore, even linguists of the present day might be given pause if they were to recognize the implications of Magwitch's love of foreign literature. It is one thing to develop speech-act theories or some other approach to the issue of cultural normality and competency, quite another to recognize how Magwitch represents the law. That is to say, in the society of this novel it is only an illiterate criminal or the like who is innocent enough to speak the truth of language. It is only through the contradiction of cultural values that the law of culture can be instituted, for this institution requires recognition, which can come only from someone excluded from it. Hence Estella can be brought to recognize feeling only when she is barred from Pip by her marriage to the heartless Drummle. Hence, too, the way Joe feels for Mrs. Joe even when she is on the rampage because, when he was a boy, he saw his father abuse his mother. A woman needs to be beaten for culture to be instituted in this novel—a point to which I will return.

Those within the culture Pip projects must be fundamentally unconscious of it because their recognition of it would imply it was not spiritual, not transcendent, but rather a wholly human or political affair. Therefore, the identity of culture must appear, ironically, through the contradiction of nonidentity represented by figures like Magwitch and Joe. Once again, then, we can see how exemplary are Pip's confusion and his continuing unconsciousness even as a narrator of the reasons for his love of Estella. And we can also see the corollaries to this unconsciousness: that in this scheme of things the agency of cultural solidarity is cultural deviancy; that this deviancy speaks and bodies forth the power of the supernatural; and that the business of culture is to turn on this deviancy so as to institute itself by making sense of nonsense. Hence the irony by which Magwitch, who embodies the contradictions of fairy godmother and murderous father, convict and patron, and so on, is turned in Pip's experience from a source of fearful confusion to a figure producing order—"I only saw in him a much better man than I had been to Joe" (GE, 521).

"Magwitch," as I am describing him here, is only a figure of the god of rhetoric, the god that is revealed so as to open this narrative, the god that must be made invisible once again if this narrative is to be brought to a meaningful conclusion. (Magwitch, the fairy godmother, like Estella, Miss Havisham, Molly, Mrs. Joe, and Joe's mother, is a beaten woman by the end of the novel.) It is this god of rhetoric, especially through the leading trope of irony, that reads this text, that makes sense of it, that assures us, insofar as we do find sense in this novel, that words are something other than utterly foreign sounds or marks on a page whose value is determined solely by the power brought to bear on them at a particular moment. It is this god that puts us in a culture and in history and so rescues us from the paralyzing linguistic confusions that bedevil Pip. As long as the text (as long as the reader) is read by this trope and the forms of understanding to which it leads, desire makes sense, however unaccountable, unnameable, and confusing its effects it may be. Value is produced as long as this trope reigns, while value is traduced, dissimulated, and put up for grabs if its reign should end.

To make this analysis of rhetorical enchantment is not to revive that philosophical and literary tradition in which rhetoric is seduction, bewitchment, betrayal, pornography, or in some other way a source of error. In this tradition, there is always another side to language, while there is no such victim and no rhetorical crime in my analysis. In describing the rhetorical conditions necessary to make sense of Pip in *Great Expectations*, my aim is not to save readers from the novel or from criticism written on the novel. My aim is rather to explore the inescapability of politics in reading: the contest over forms of power that constitutes the reading and understanding of texts in any form. The importance of this exploration does not lie in any release from rhetoric, which in a sense is only a fashionable term for the limits we imagine to our powers. It lies in the recognition that the institution of reading creates meaning by repressing the difference of language, a difference that takes form in cultural history, cultural differences and conflicts, and the possibility of cultural change. This exploration of reading and repression, then, may help to change this grown-up, this rhetoric, this god, but not by an identification with an Other (the child, the reality, the imaginary, the semiotic . . .). To do so would be to identify with a narrative such as Dickens's in which deviancy speaks a supernatural language. The point is rather to demonstrate the repression of difference even within the acknowledgment of difference, to show how representations of the child and the grown-up, the deviant and the normal, and the like are implicated in each other. To show, in other words, how a cultural analysis of meaning—an analysis of the historical conditions of meaning within discourse, as it is characterized by the production of differences between such figures as the child and the grown-up—can allow us to contest the power of culture and history precisely to the extent that we can appreciate their imaginary necessity.

Of course, there is no reason we cannot simply ignore or deny this necessity, or at least think we are doing so, as long as we are not concerned to change the established conditions of social life. And, of course, there is no guarantee that the critical activity of historical reflection will lead to satisfying change in these conditions. However, the possibility of change simply does not appear without a political challenge to meaning. Without such a challenge we do not see how the presence and absence of meaning are not simply found, like a rock on the ground or a god from the sky, but rather are made through the social relations of men and women in the world.

VI

I felt the firm ground of my homeland sinking under my feet, I felt myself falling, clarinet in hand, falling into the depths of years and centuries past, fathomless depths (where love is love and pain pain).

—Ludvik Jahn in *The Joke*[44]

At one point in *Great Expectations*, Pip challenges Estella's claim that love is just a form of words to her. "Surely it is not in Nature," he says. Estella first replies, "It is in *my* nature." She then adds, "with a stress upon the words," according to the narrator, "It is in the nature formed within me. I make a great difference between you and other people when I say so much. I can do no more" (*GE*, 422).

From one perspective, this passage is rather simple. Estella draws two distinctions familiar to philosophical tradition. She distinguishes the universal from the particular and the essential from the accidental. Thus, even as she denies the nature Pip would find within her, she might yet be said to be implicitly acknowledging the propriety of that nature. Viewed in this way, the difference Estella makes between Pip and other people, her willingness even to engage in this dialectic, may be seen as tipping us off to the likelihood of the eventual reconciliation in which essence will slough off accident, the particular will merge with the universal, and Pip and Estella will meet within a proper apprehension of each other and the world.

And yet the matter is not so simple. For the philosophical rhetoric that would rationalize this scene, and with it the entire history of the relationship between Pip and Estella, can do so only by distinguishing certain features of this scene and of the novel as a whole to the exclusion of others. In other words, it can do so only through politics.

Consider what happens when Estella's statement, "It is in *my* nature," gives way to her statement, "It is in the nature formed within me." The shift from one statement to the other, she tells Pip, represents a change in the audience to which she is speaking. The peculiar "stress" of her words represents her transformation of Pip from "other people" to something apart from that category. If she is to differ from him in this matter of feeling and yet still to acknowledge the possibility of a shared identity, it appears she can do so only by making this rhetorical change, contrasting Pip to other people. In other words, she can meet Pip on the ground of universality only by denying that ground. She can acknowledge Pip's insistence on the difference between proper and improper nature only by inflecting her words in such a way as to refuse them any universally proper meaning. The peculiar stress on her words is nothing more or less than the stress of cultural context, the boundary of identity and difference that cannot be asserted without putting into play a rhetoric that violates context.

This analysis will seem overwrought, or so I expect. It may seem that I am taking this scene too seriously, developing critical generalizations on the basis of a very brief passage in a rather long novel, a passage never meant to be analyzed so rigorously. Or it may seem that the premise of my entire analysis here is exorbitant, that no one would take such a passage as this and seek to draw out of it the rationality I have imagined in the reading opposed to my version. In developing this idea about the stress of context, it may seem that I am going far beyond any reasonable context for the activity of literary criticism. At least I can imagine that this entire analysis might seem like a joke. I can remember the frustration when, as a teacher, I pushed students to think further about issues they had already accounted for to their own satisfaction. This imagination, feeling, or memory is, of course, not unlike Pip's descriptions of his situation as a narrator. In trying to show the strangeness of the words of this novel, I, too, am insisting on a certain opposition to conventional understanding.

And yet Dickens's words are always being caught up in this joke of interpretation. Is not *Great Expectations* one long joke: the supposed autobiography of a man whose main theme is his inability ever to come to a satisfactory understanding of himself? Is Pip really so different from Tristram Shandy in this respect? What does Dickens do in his writing other than belabor the obvious, such as the difficulty of defining nature, so as to question the distinction between the superficial and the profound, the obvious and the compelling? The obvious *is* the compelling, as Dickens portrays it, and never more so than when it appears in the form of words, which his characters so frequently take to be the most obvious of all cultural forms, comprehensible in any context.

Consider this form of words, this irony, that looms so large in Pip's narrative. Early in the narrative, appealing to his readers to identify with him, Pip introduces this trope that will signify order if his appeal is successful. If his readers will agree to be as Pip wants them—if Pip can imagine this agreement without any fear of aphasia, childishness, criminality, or other sorts of deviancy creeping in—then this trope will be recognized as controlling his life. To put it another way, if this trope can be successful in making conditions such as aphasia and childishness appear deviant, subordinate to its power of order, then Pip will be Pip, the narrative of his life will be coherent, a sense of cultural universality will be established, and the life of the individual will appear as the life of society. Of course, this rhetorical work of subordination cannot be accomplished within a single passage; but this oft-quoted passage illustrates very well the leading form of identification that must be brought to *Great Expectations* in order to create a sense of unity and necessity within Pip's narrative. "Pause you who read this," Pip writes, "and think for a moment of the long chain of iron or gold, of thorns or flowers, that would never have bound you, but for the formation of the first link on one memorable day'' (*GE*, 82).

The ironic equivocation here—"iron or gold . . . thorns or flowers"—is echoed in the multitudinous examples of this figure that Pip describes himself meeting at every stage of his adventures. In addition to those previously noted, there is Pip's description of Joe as "a sort of Hercules in strength, and also in weakness" (*GE*, 7). When Pip first learns of his great expectations, we find him "feeling very sorrowful and strange," as he says, "that this first night of my bright fortunes, should be the loneliest I have ever known" (*GE*, 169). Not long afterward, Pip meets Wemmick, the living contradiction of the private and public man. Given such a context, it is no wonder the following dialogue should occur between Herbert and Pip:

> "I was a blacksmith's boy but yesterday; I am—what shall I say I am—to-day?"
> "Say, a good fellow, if you want a phrase," returned Herbert, smiling, and clapping his hands on the back of mine: "a good fellow, with impetuosity and hesitation, boldness and diffidence, action and dreaming, curiously mixed in him." (*GE*, 288)

But identification through the form of irony in this narrative does not end with the recognition Herbert offers Pip. There is the further example of Mr. Pocket, whose homelife is a monstrous shambles even as he is known to be "a most delightful lecturer on domestic economy" whose "treatises on the management of children and servants were considered the very best text-books on those themes" (*GE*, 315). In reference to his dining club, The Finches of the Grove, Pip speaks of "a gay fiction among us that we were constantly enjoying ourselves, and a skeleton truth that we never did" (*GE*, 318–19). Pip meets Magwitch, and Magwitch tells him, "I lived rough, that you should live smooth; I worked hard that you should be above work" (*GE*, 372). And in his description of the way he hid Magwitch from the authorities, Pip touches on yet another irony:

> I was always full of fears for the rash man who was in hiding. Herbert had sometimes said to me that he found it pleasant to stand at one of our windows after dark, when the tide was running down, and to think that it was flowing, with everything it bore, towards Clara. But I thought with dread that it was flowing toward Magwitch, and that any black mark on its surface might be his pursuers, going swiftly, silently and surely, to take him. (*GE*, 443)

How to read marks on any surface, signs in any form, when such ironies seem to be spawned by the very nature of social life in such a way as to frustrate that life completely? When signs of life may just as well be read as signs of death, as in the view of the marshes Pip had as a child? It might seem from such a passage that irony produces disorder rather than order in this novel, steps that lead down rather than steps that lead up. But that is just the point. Only by identifying with this trope, bringing to it a sense of what is obvious and what is not, of what is and is not feeling, character, truth, and so on, can the reader turn this text into a meaningful form of words. This irony must be read as a culture, a context of meaning, if this novel is to make any sense. That context will differ according to the political predilections of the reader (using *political* in the broadest sense), but only by supplying such a stress to this trope can we read this text.

Many more examples of this trope of irony in Pip's narrative could be adduced, but perhaps just one more example will suffice to explain the role it plays for those able to make sense of the novel. In this passage Pip describes his experience after Magwitch has died and he has been arrested for debt and fallen ill while in custody:

> That I had a fever and was avoided, that I suffered greatly, that I often lost my reason, that the time seemed interminable, that I confounded impossible existences with my own identity; that I was a brick in the house wall, and yet entreating to be released from the giddy place where the builders had set me; that I was a steel beam of a vast engine, clashing and whirling over a gulf, and yet that I implored in my own person to have the engine stopped, and my part of it hammered off; that I passed through these phases of disease, I know of my own remembrance, and did in some sort know at the time. That I sometimes struggled with real people, in the belief that they were murderers, and that I would all at once comprehend that they meant to do me good, and would then sink exhausted in their arms, and suffer them to lay me down, I also knew at the time. But, above all, I knew that there was a constant tendency in all these people — who, when I was very ill, would present all kinds of extraordinary transformations of the human face, and would be much dilated in size — above all, I say, I knew that there was an extraordinary tendency in all these people, sooner or later, to settle down into the likeness of Joe. (*GE*, 540–41)

Like many dreams in narratives, such as the one Victor Frankenstein has just after he has created his monster, this passage seems designed to double the text, to transform our reading of it by drawing our attention to the pulsing of a grammar of incident, idea, and imagery that otherwise might not be perceived as clearly as other narrative patterns. As it both asserts and denies this textual difference, the conventional innocence of the dream — its formal subordination to the representation of consciousness — is one means of opening the question of representation or, in the language of this novel, of likeness. (Some other means of marking this question have already been noted: the foregrounding of certain tropes or a certain style through repetition, the intratextual manipulation of "other" texts or of exercises in writing and reading, the use of various forms of literary allusion, the employment of unreliable or self-questioning narrators, and so on.) In the case of this dream—or, more properly, this dreamlike hallucinatory experience—the "normal" reading it puts into the shade is any based on linear time, fixed identities, coherent social relations, and the difference of properties (in all senses of the word) from persons. In other words, this passage would seem to discount any reading like the one I imagined as my first reading of this novel, in which the narrative of Pip's experiences takes on an evolutionary form that is also a middle-class record of social change and projection of national destiny. In the place of such readings, this passage suggests a meaning expressible as a formal transformation. An apparently negative relation between subject and world (in which neither term is stable but the latter is always threatening to the former) is revealed as being in reality a positive relation (in which the security of the subject is assured by a constant form of "likeness").

Such a reading would seem to make the novel perfectly circular or tautological in form, as it suggests we return to the point in Pip's experiences before his sense of identity was disturbed by convicts, Estella, gentlemen, and the like. As some critics have suggested, Pip's palindromic identity would lead him to end where he began. But the matter is not so simple. For when Pip, in effect, tries to extend this reading by going home to marry Biddy and thus recover his life as it would have been without the influences that so upset it, he finds Joe has stolen the march on him. It appears Joe is not only a reassuring likeness, a comforting model of identity, but also a difference that literally displaces Pip into another country for eleven years. Moreover, it may be recalled that even before Pip was disturbed by convicts and Estella's words, his life already was an issue quarreled over by relatives and even by nature, insofar as he belonged to its "universal struggle." He may never have become conscious of it until later, but he already was torn by the difference of language even before he met the representatives of this difference in their sexual, familial, social, and other forms.

Consider in this regard Pip's earlier allusion to Mary Shelley's novel: "The imaginary student pursued by the misshapen creature he had impiously made, was not more wretched than I, pursued by the creature who had made me, and recoiling from him with a stronger repulsion, the more he admired me and the fonder he was of me" (GE, 392). In this revision of Victor Frankenstein's tale that he describes as his own life, this revision in which pursuer and pursued become interchangeable figures, as they do in Mary Shelley's novel, what is Pip representing but the weird grammar that results from the implication of desire within a rhetoric shot through with irony? Here, Pip seems to be Estella, and Magwitch, the pursuing Pip. Later, Pip will yield to Magwitch's advances, by which time Magwitch will have become less of a pursuer as he is chased by the authorities of the state. Later still, Estella will, in a sense, yield to Pip's pursuit when he no longer is pursuing her. These plots and others seem to double each other in this novel and yet through this doubling seem only to reproduce desire as ironic contradiction: expectation as disappointment. They seem to reproduce the ending of *Frankenstein*, in which Victor's ambivalence about his creation is matched by the monster's sorrowful eulogy for the man he has hounded to death.

How can this novel be read if irony is always to appear just when we have, at last, believed in an unchanging identity? Or how are we to read this irony? Only by the reader's interpretation of irony as a rule of order (a form of feeling, character, truth . . .). While such an interpretation may serve many purposes (such as the production in readers of things such as feeling, character, and truth), it always turns the imaginary rule of culture into an unconscious compulsion and thus makes us unconscious of the politics of reading as a social practice open to social change.

This possibility of change is apparent in all the questions about language raised in *Great Expectations* and in Dickens's other works. Consider the situation in *David Copperfield* when the young protagonist of that novel has been sent to Salem House by Mr. Murdstone, his new stepfather, who has ordered the schoolmaster to make David wear a sign on his back to punish him for an alleged misdeed. David describes this experience as follows:

> There was an old door in the playground, on which the boys had a
> custom of carving their names. It was completely covered with such
> inscriptions. In my dread at the end of the vacation and their coming
> back, I could not read a boy's name without inquiring in what tone and
> with what emphasis *he* would read, "Take care of him. He bites."
> There was one boy—a certain J. Steerforth—who cut his name very
> deep and very often, who, I conceived, would read it in a rather strong
> voice, and afterwards pull my hair. There was another boy, one Tommy
> Traddles, who I dreaded would make game of it, and pretend to be
> dreadfully frightened of me. There was a third, George Demple, who I
> fancied would sing it. I have looked, a little shrinking creature, at that
> door, until the owners of all the names—there were five-and-forty of
> them in the school then, Mr. Mell said—seemed to send me to Coventry
> by general acclamation, and to cry out, each in his own way, "Take
> care of him. He bites." (*DC*, 1:94)

The passage is similar to that in which Pip meditates on the characters of another public text, the tombstone. Here, too, written characters appear to have a living character, a personality and influence, once we regard them closely. Here, too, a boy senses an intimate connection between the acts of writing and reading, on the one hand, and the conduct of life, on the other, which it seems would not be apparent to the normal grown-up, who would take them as neutral acts of communication. David literally has been marked as a deviant—even questioned as to his species, one could say—just as Pip was said to be deviant just because he had survived his siblings, even aside from the other attributions of delinquency he had to suffer. And, like Pip, David is tormented here and else-where by the fact of other readings, by the fact that different readings create a cacophony of stresses on a text, all of which seem directed against him.

A conventional way to dismiss the topic of language in this scene would be to introduce the name of imagination (as an accepted, classified, deviation) and to compare David's perception in this scene with flights of rhetoric indulged in by other characters in Dickens's works. However, even aside from the way it seems to compel critics into their own constructions of living beings out of written char-acters (an interesting phenomenon in itself),[45] the problem with this category of imagination is that it obscures the contest between deviant and proper uses of language with chat about "sensitivity," "perception," "innocence," and the like. That is, analysis in terms of imagination typically turns representations, such as those involving David before the door and Pip before his parents' grave-stones, into universal expressions of individual consciousness, even though these representations have as their premises the issue of language as a matter of irre-ducible social differences. Thus, as it is used traditionally in works of criticism, the word *imagination* constitutes — or, perhaps more accurately, is divinely com-pelled by — a complicated rhetorical order that this term is supposed to explain. Readings of Dickens's works in terms of the author's imagination may be excel-lent, but only as David's reading of the door, Pip's reading of the gravestones, and, say, Matthew Arnold's reading of history may be called excellent.

Another way to approach this issue would be through a consideration of the specific images involved in the readings within these scenes. We could discuss the significance of the fact that David's reading of Steerforth's and Traddle's sig-natures in some part anticipates the plot of the novel in which they all appear. Similarly, we could consider the significance of the fact that Pip's construction of his parents' appearances creates a more "normal" image of the Victorian father and mother than that provided by Joe and Mrs. Joe. By limiting the critical focus to the problem of understanding specific forms of representation, this approach would avoid some of the critical disabilities that come about when gods like imagination are called into play as explanatory mechanisms but would probably end up calling on gods of a more modern sort. These are not the gods of the universe or of universal human nature but those of a specific culture. They are gods of social, literary, or representational convention — gods that may be re-vealed under close analysis to be the attributes of an unexpressed deity of uni-versality.

The point of my analysis is to call into question this rhetorical unconscious-ness, which plays a role in all reading, through a concentration on the politics of rhetoric: on the differences of power instituted in rhetoric and on the possibility of changing the act of reading through a political criticism. No doubt it is impos-sible to contest this unconsciousness to its limits, or we would not be in the prov-ince of communication. However, my reading of *Great Expectations* to this point may be extended by considering two ways Dickens often calls attention in his other novels to communication as a process pursued by and pursuing differences that cannot be neutralized. The first involves questions over nouns, one of the major categories given to experience within society, whereas the second involves questions over the relation between symbolic and referential uses of language.

Consider the situation in *Nicholas Nickleby*, for instance, when Nicholas says he can hardly believe Snawley is Smike's father, since nature does not appear to have put any affection for Smike within him. Charles Cheeryble replies, "Men talk of nature as an abstract thing, and lose sight of what is natural while they do so" (*NN*, 2:214). This problem is driven home when it is discovered that Smike is really Ralph Nickleby's son, unbeknownst to him, so that Ralph appears as "a man who, in the hot pursuit of his bad ends, has persecuted and hunted down his own child to death" (*NN*, 2:447). Thus, Dickens's joke: Nicholas's doubt is proven correct at the very moment when it is proven false. The situation resembles the plot in *Dombey and Son* that leads Dickens to comment, "It might be worthwhile, sometimes, to inquire what Nature is, and how men work to change her, and whether, in the enforced distinctions so produced, it is not natural to be unnatural" (*DS*, 2:254).

It makes no more sense to argue for the philosophical depth of such passages than it does to criticize them for being insufficiently philosophical in one way or another, as in their placement within narratives that may appear to assert very obviously a simple form of Christian sentimentality and bourgeois liberalism. (I will never forget a student in one of my classes in graduate school, confronted with one of Dickens's more outrageously sentimental exclamations, who exploded, "What can you do with that?") Dickens's genius (to use an obvious term) is in his insistence on the obvious. His writing can be seen as an extended description of the irrationality of cultural forms even in their simplest, most superficial, most agreeable, and most trivial appearances. Objects such as the buttons on a boy's coat may be as fascinating as a character's gestures, a social institution, a building, a word, a piece of trash, or a habitual expression. This is not to say that his writing does away with all "enforced distinctions" but rather that it describes the supernatural effect, the irrational compulsion, drawn through all such distinctions, no matter how they may be debated and fought, transformed and institutionalized, trivialized, elaborated, and magnified. Dickens's writing does not simply represent Christian sentimentality and bourgeois liberalism, then; but it does represent these related nineteenth-century ideologies complexly, and most notably in the way it calls on the trope of irony to stress them within the irrational differences of language.

One cannot simply appeal to words as the young Pip would like to do: "Surely it is not in Nature." What one can do in Dickens's writing, however, is to achieve irony. Mrs. Rudge says, in words that resemble the opening of *A Tale of Two Cities*, "I am guilty, and yet innocent; wrong, yet right; good in intention, though constrained to shield and aid the bad'' (*BR*, 1: 256); and if Dickens's writing has any meaning at all, she is not trapped by these contradictions but rather is put on the side of the angels. On the other hand, when Mr. Dombey asks his son what he would like to do in response to Walter Gay's plea for money, the opposite situation occurs. "Give it to his old uncle," Paul says. When Dombey echoes, "Lend it to his old uncle, eh?" (*DS*, 1:162), his failure to acknowledge the contradiction in his revision helps to damn him for most of the novel.

Adopting Dickensian rhetoric, I write of angels and damnation in describing the order suggested by such passages; but the significance of the appearance of contradiction within Dickens's writing is that angels and devils appear in this writing, as Pip, similarly, appears as a coherent figure and comprehensible narrator, only insofar as this trope ironically bodies forth a culture for readers and so provides them with a rule of likeness. At the same time, however, the working of this trope may suggest a criticism that emphasizes the heterogeneity of culture and of the practice of reading.

This consideration may be further clarified by a glance at the second way Dickens's works commonly dramatize language as the basis and product of social contestation, by raising the issue of symbolic as opposed to referential uses of language. Probably the most famous dramatization of this issue in Dickens's novels occurs in *Bleak House*, in which the legal contest of Jarndyce and Jarndyce stands as "a monument of Chancery practice" in which, as Conversation Kenge says, "every difficulty, every contingency, every masterly fiction, every form of procedure known in that court, is represented over and over again" (*BH*, 1:25). In this case, language consumes its ostensible referent. Language within this institution has no other purpose than to perpetuate itself and thus to perpetuate the irrational forms and procedures of this institution. A less famous case, though arguably as significant, can be seen in the way a distaste for the United States is figured in *Martin Chuzzlewit* through an emphasis on the mispronunciations and sundry other abuses of language that make American rhetoric all but incomprehensible to Mark Tapley and Martin Chuzzlewit. If Chancery might be taken to represent a special case of institutional abuse (despite all the indications in *Bleak House* that it is meant to represent a general state of affairs), we may see in *Martin Chuzzlewit* that politics in the narrow, institutional sense cannot be isolated from questions of social definition and national destiny. As this novel makes clear, the relation between symbolic and referential uses of language has to be decided according to a certain institutional system if language is to have any comprehensibility whatsoever; and as this novel also makes clear, a system cannot be instituted without continuing conflicts. This is yet another banality that Dickens belabors until the objects, characters, scenes, conversations, and other features of his writing may seem to escape the rule of representation that we unconsciously presume to be containing them.

The description of Mr. Micawber in *David Copperfield* illustrates very well this vexing situation: this challenge, in the form of irrational display, to any sort of rule. As the narrator describes Micawber in the act of declaiming his charges against Uriah Heep toward the end of the novel,

> Again, Mr. Micawber had a relish in this formal piling up of words, which, however ludicrously displayed in his case, was, I must say, not at all peculiar to him. I have observed it, in the course of my life, in numbers of men. It seems to me to be a general rule. In the taking of legal oaths, for instance, deponents seem to enjoy themselves mightily when they come to several good words in succession, for the expression of one idea; as, that they utterly detest, abominate, and abjure, and so forth; and the old anathemas were made relishing on the same principle. We talk about the tyranny of words, but we like to tyrannise over them too; we are fond of having a large superfluous establishment of words to wait upon us on great occasions; we think it looks important, and sounds well. As we are not particular about the meaning of our liveries on state occasions, if they be but fine and numerous enough, so, the meaning or necessity of our words is a secondary consideration, if there be but a great parade of them. And as individuals get into trouble by making too great a show of liveries, or as slaves when they are too numerous rise against their masters, so I think I could mention a nation that has got into many great difficulties, and will get into many greater, from maintaining too large a retinue of words. (*DC*, 2:383)

The "general rule" described in this passage, the idea that "the meaning or necessity of our words is a secondary consideration," threatens a Frankensteinian reversal of the master–slave relationship, an *unironic* confusion. (In terms of bourgeois economy, it is significant, too, that it is the prodigal Micawber who occasions this passage and that its imagery is related to aristocratic display and thus to the bankrupt rule of origins.) Just as Dickens will describe how the propriety of words yields to the irrational stress of context, so he will describe how the dream of meaning yields to the irrational stress of symbolic form. On the one hand, observing the weakness of contextual limits, David Copperfield observes "that conventional phrases are a sort of fireworks, easily let off, and liable to take a great variety of shapes and colours not at all suggested by their original form" (*DC*, 2:185). Plagiarists, forgers, bogus ectypes arise from this lack of mastery, in *David Copperfield* and elsewhere in Dickens's works. On the other hand, we see form itself become a compulsion outrunning questions of meaning, as in Pip's lies, Joe's rhymes, Micawber's rodomontade, or Mr. Dick's memorial of his life, which the figure of Charles I persists in disturbing. As David's Aunt Trotwood explains the problem, "That's his allegorical way of expressing it. He connects his illness with great disturbance and agitation, naturally, and that's the figure, or the simile, or whatever it's called, which he chooses to use." "It's not a business-like way of speech,'' she adds, ''nor a worldly way'' (*DC*, 1:245); and yet Dickens's emphasis in this novel and elsewhere is on the ways the discourse of business and other areas of the world is captive to forms that seem inevitably to confuse meaning and necessity.

To a certain extent, this is an obvious point, again, however eloquently Dickens makes it. Dickens shows himself aware that language has both symbolic and referential functions, as in the speech Mary makes to Martin Chuzzlewit about his father when the younger Martin is about to depart for America:

> ''Martin! If you would but sometimes, in some quiet hour; beside the winter fire; in the summer air; when you hear gentle music, or think of Death, or Home, or Childhood—if you would at such a season resolve to think but once a month, or even once a year, of him, or any one who ever wronged you, you would forgive him in your heart, I know!''
> (*MC*, 1:296)

So Dickens comments on Martin's return to England, ''And though home is a name, a word, it is a strong one; stronger than magician ever spoke, or spirit answered to, in strongest conjuration'' (*MC*, 2:160). This recognition of a symbolic function allows for ironies like the definition of a girl in the Dombey household as ''a bad Boy—nothing more'' (*DS*, 1:4) and for the transformation marked by Miss Tox's comment that ''Dombey and Son . . . is indeed a daughter . . . after all'' (*DS*, 2:493).

The problem is that this symbolic function may interfere with the referential function of language to such an extent that it becomes questionable whether words do not, indeed, rise up and master people. Chancery seems more a metaphor of society than an isolated institution; David Copperfield sees Micawber as an exemplary figure rather than an eccentric; and as he is driven to logorrhea Pip finds that lies, the mere display of words, may prove as convincing as words actually meant to have a referent. Just as a cultural context cannot be stressed without putting into play a rhetoric that violates context, so, too, it seems impossible to place the stress of symbolic form or language, or to recognize it in language, without sending this form off on a career of its own that threatens the meaning that was supposed to be gathered within it. Just as context is self-contradictory because, in drawing a boundary around identity, it represses the difference of identity from itself, so is form self-contradictory because it pretends to master meaning while yet being the servant of that meaning. In the former case, the contradiction becomes apparent in situations such as Pip's introduction to Estella, in which the rightness of one context becomes all wrong in another and there appears no way of reconciling the two, not to mention the many other contexts that will assert themselves. In the latter case, the contradiction becomes apparent in situations such as Magwitch's discussion with Pip about foreign literature, in which knowledge appears as a purely symbolic function, its ideal identity nothing but the tautology that knowledge is knowledge.

In any case, Dickens's comments on language in his other works, as in *Great Expectations*, suggest that if there is to be coherent meaning—a very big *if*—it must come through the rule of irony. The display of words and symbolic forms cannot guarantee meaning and, indeed, appears at least as likely to traduce it as to communicate it. One can master language only by identifying with the rule of irony in which master and slave, truth and falsity, Joe and Pumblechook, criminal and gentleman, and similarly opposed phenomena meet within a tacit system of understanding. In this way irony, as the reader identifies with it and thus creates it, represses such differences as those of class, sex, power, birth, and wealth in favor of a spiritual identity of some sort. In other words, when Dickens designs Joe as "a Hercules in strength, and also in weakness," Pip's life as a composition of flowers and thorns, great expectations as great disappointments, a criminal as a truer gentleman than the model gentleman, knowledge as ignorance, and so on through every example of this figure in *Great Expectations*, his critique of idealist conventions, traditions, and language makes conflicting social values disappear within the very irony that forms them into the appearance of contradiction, the irony that can belong in his writing only to a consciousness that bears the features of certain middle-class values. Only for someone composed of these values—which include, for instance, an abhorrence of violence, an acquiescence to state power, and a patriarchal definition of love—can this novel appear a coherent organization of psychological, social, historical, or other kinds of meanings. Only someone who identifies, at least provisionally, with the rule of irony in this text can see its conflicts as figuring any necessary meaning.

In terms of this understanding of irony, we can make sense of many features of Dickens's work that otherwise might be incomprehensible, if they are not simply ignored. For instance, we can make sense of a psychology such as that assumed by Dickens in *A Tale of Two Cities* when he writes that "a species of fervour or intoxication, known, without doubt, to have led some persons to brave the guillotine unnecessarily, and to die by it, was not mere boastfulness, but a wild infection of the wildly shaken public mind. In seasons of pestilence some of us will have a secret attraction to the disease—a terrible passing inclination to die of it" (*TTC*, 328). We can compare this passage to Miss Flite's description of the "dreadful" and "cruel attraction" of Chancery (*BH*, 2:67) and to the description Dickens gives in *Barnaby Rudge*, in reference to the interest in the countryside in news of the Gordon Riots, of "that appetite for the marvellous and love of the terrible which have probably been among the natural characteristics of mankind since the creation of the world" (*BR*, 2:116). In these instances, as in Pip's love for the punishing Estella or as in the "popular murder" recounted by Wopsle, we see desire arise through irony, desire compelled by irony even to the point of the ultimate irony of self-destruction, because only this crucible is intense enough to purge desire of its discontinuous and conflicting material associations. Notice, too, that in all these cases the persons experiencing the desire are in the position of observing suffering—a point that will bring us, again, to the curious fact that a woman must be beaten to produce culture in Dickens's writing.

VII

Perhaps what is inexpressible (what I find mysterious and am not able to express) is the background from which whatever I could express receives meaning [den Hintergrund, auf dem das, was ich aussprechen konnte, Bedeutung bekommt].

Wittgenstein[46]

Something more remains to be said of this writing of desire. Until this point I have set aside the consideration that this mysterious desire, although feminine in its properties and effects (softening, domesticating, sacralizing), is a masculine desire designed to awaken a cold woman. In other words, it is a desire designed to prove the authority of desire over women, including Miss Havisham, who finally exchanges her misanthropy for the philanthropy of making Herbert (and thus, eventually, Pip) a partner in a business firm. Moreover, as previously noted, it appears in this novel that women must be beaten in order for culture to be instituted. We might consider, too, as I have only in passing, how Pip labors to trace Estella's parentage by Magwitch and Molly and yet decides to keep this information from her.

This stressing of power in terms of sexual difference illustrates, again, why a word like *desire* cannot be read with any kind of neutrality. It must be read in context and as a kind of symbolic form and yet must also exceed the stress of that context and form, which does not take account of the distaste this conception of desire may arouse. Nor can neutrality be achieved through a qualification like "masculine desire," since this modification of our understanding would ignore the interdependency of the categories of the male and female in this text, not to mention their complex relations with other terms.

This stress on the sexual differentiation of power emphasizes once again the politics of reading and returns me to the reading I initially imagined of this novel. That reading developed into a question about the justice of a term like *middle-class discourse* and then into my assertion that the terms of cultural understanding are as inescapable as the challenges to those terms are imperative. What, then, have my reading and rereadings of this novel produced?

First, the idea that texts can appear as such only within a culture, which is a form of understanding ruled by political differences. Therefore, a text is always already a reading, as I indicated by asking the reader to "imagine" a first reading of this novel. We do not read abstract characters on an abstract page but a text as it becomes historically available to us as readers within history. As my reading of *Great Expectations* shows, the theoretically infinite varieties of sense readers may make of texts is testimony not to the impossibility of interpretation but rather to the reality of the politics that produce such limited ranges of sense in reading and other social practices.

Second, the idea that culture, as semantic context and symbolic form, is always at issue in texts. As I have tried to show through my analysis of irony in *Great Expectations*, no text can give us the definitive rule for its comprehension. It can yield only certain figural relations that *may* make sense, if the reader interprets those relations in certain ways. For this reason, my reading of *Great Expectations* has been divided between a description of the meaningful relations in the novel and a critique of that reading based on the same novel. This self-critical approach is not arbitrary but rather the kind of approach that must be taken (though not necessarily in this form) if we are not to be so enchanted by culture that we are read by the very language we think we are reading.

Third, the idea that the historical nature of texts is apparent in the rhetorical scheme, the discourse, needed to make sense of them. *Great Expectations*, I have argued, cannot make sense to a reader unless that reader brings to the text certain conceptions of feeling, character, ideology, truth, nature, transcendence, and history. These conceptions need not be conscious, and my specification and description of them certainly are not definitive; but the value of my analysis in terms of historical understanding may be judged by the extent to which it comprehends relations that must be repressed in other readings, as the beating of women sometimes is rationalized in criticism of this novel as a symbolic return for the abuse Pip suffers as a boy. From this perspective, the only unity of a text is in the conditions of its historical possibility.

Fourth, the idea that the critical value of this political interpretation of texts lies in its insistent questioning of that which goes without question in our cultures and the cultures of the past. Its value lies in its questioning of the very idea of culture and thus of any form of understanding taken to be natural, obvious, inevitable, eternal, and so on. Without needing to make any claim that other readings are wrong—in fact, while rejecting any such argument by showing the politics that construct such judgments—I am arguing that the critical analysis of history in this kind of interpretation is the approach to understanding that can help us most in challenging political oppression in the cultural institutions of the modern world, in which I especially include the modern university, in which the business of interpretation is so largely concentrated today.

"A woman must be beaten for culture to be instituted" is one way I summarized the historical nature of *Great Expectations*. "Middle-class discourse" is another phrase under which I tried to describe the historical conditions legible in the language of this text. And, of course, these descriptions are not exclusive. In fact, another way of describing the value of political interpretation is to say it gives us a means for describing relations among different historical figurations such as these without reducing them to an identity. It gives us a history as full of discontinuity, confusion, loss, and inequality as our own time, while also giving us a history as open to change as we must consider the present to be if we are not to be subtle exegetes of our own acquiescence to oppression.

Notes

Notes

Chapter 1. What Is a Joke?

1. Henri Bergson, *Le Rire: Essai sur la signification du comique, Oeuvres*, with an introduction by Henri Gouhier and notes by André Robinet (Paris: Presses Universitaires de France,1970), p. 389. (Translations not otherwise noted are my own.)

2. Quoted by Neil Schaeffer, *The Art of Laughter* (New York: Columbia University Press, 1981), p. 44

3. In his analysis of "pre-riddles" (riddles invented by young children that have the form but not the semantic logic of "mature" riddles) Brian Sutton-Smith suggests these children's implicit definition of the riddle as a "puzzling question with an arbitrary answer" is related to the cultural articulation of authority in adult–child relationships, among which teacher–student relationships are especially important. See "A Developmental Structural Account of Riddles," *Speech Play: Research and Resources for Studying Linguistic Creativity*, ed. Barbara Kirshenblatt-Gimblett, University of Pennsylvania Publications in Conduct and Communication, ed. Erving Goffman and Dell Hymes (Philadelphia: University of Pennsylvania Press, 1970), esp. pp. 114–15.

4. George Meredith, *An Essay on Comedy and the Use of the Comic Spirit* (New York: Charles Scribner's Sons, 1923), p. 91.

5. Ludwig Wittgenstein, *Philosophical Investigations*, trans. G. E. M. Anscombe, 3rd ed. (New York: Macmillan, 1969), p. 47e. Cf. Wittgenstein's comment that "a serious and good philosophical work could be written that would consist entirely of jokes," quoted by Walter Redfern, *Puns* (New York: Basil Blackwell, 1984), p. 40.

6. Walter Benjamin, "Surrealism: The Last Snapshot of the European Intelligentsia," *One-Way Street and Other Writings*, trans. Edmund Jephcott and Kingsley Shorter (London: NLB, 1979), p. 239.

7. See Mikhail Bakhtin, *Rabelais and his World*, trans. Helene Iswolsky (Cambridge: M.I.T. Press, 1968).

8. See, for instance, John Paulos, "The Logic of Humour and the Humour in Logic," *It's a*

Funny Thing, Humour, ed. Anthony J. Chapman and Hugh C. Foot (Oxford: Pergamon Press, 1977), p. 113; and Cicero, *De Oratore*, 2:217–18.

9. Two otherwise inconsequential books on the philosophy of humor—Mari Collins Swabey's *Comic Laughter: A Philosophical Essay* (New Haven: Yale University Press, 1961) and John Morreall's *Taking Laughter Seriously* (Albany: State University of New York Press, 1983)—are notable for their identification of the laugher with the philosopher who transcends ordinary reality. This context, as well as the sillier aspects and uses of Bakhtin's work, invites Terry Eagleton's comment in "Wittgenstein's Friends," *New Left Review* 135 (1982):90: "Any politics which predicates itself on the carnivalesque moment alone will be no more than a compliant, containable libertarianism."

On this point, see also Dominick LaCapra's comment on the way the subversion of categories in contemporary literary studies may "facilitate a return to institutional practice as usual" in *History and Criticism* (Ithaca, NY: Cornell University Press, 1985), p. 110.

10. Ludwig Wittgenstein, *The Blue Book, The Blue and Brown Books* (New York: Harper and Brothers, 1958), p. 27.

11. For an example of this verse, see Susan Stewart, *Nonsense: Aspects of Intertextuality in Folklore and Literature* (Baltimore: Johns Hopkins University Press, 1978), p. 70. Stewart's entire book is relevant to my analysis in this essay.

To see how the reading of a joke differs according to situational variables, such as whether a man is described as telling an anti-women's liberation joke to liberated or conservative women or whether the audience is described as laughing or not, see, for instance, Lawrence LaFave,"Humor Judgments as a Function of Reference Group and Identification Classes," *The Psychology of Humor*, ed. J. H. Goldstein and P. E. McGhee (New York: Academic Press, 1972). See also Chris Powell, "Humour as a Form of Social Control: A Deviance Approach," *It's a Funny Thing, Humour*, pp. 53–55, where he describes how a scene from Chaplin's *Modern Times*, presented to right-wing and left-wing groups, is received by both groups as a joke—though a very different joke. Another study especially valuable for its analysis of the issue of aggressiveness as it is perceived by and in relation to men and women is Carol Mitchell's "Some Differences in Male and Female Joke-Telling" in *Women's Folklore, Women's Culture*, ed. Rosan A. Jordan and Susan J. Kalčik, Publications of the American Folklore Society, n.s., 8 (Philadelphia: University of Pennsylvania Press, 1985), pp. 163–86.

Of course, there are some problems with studies like these, especially in the simplistic idea of identification that is often assumed. However, as they are relatively unencumbered by idealist assumptions about meaning, their conception of the text corresponds more closely to the version that is read and taught than to the canonized and fetishized version that is the usual object of even the most sophisticated literary criticism. In "Theoretical Notes on Humor," *Journal of Communication* 26 (1976):104–12, J. H. Goldstein points out some of the problems with group-identification theories of joking, although his own analysis still idealizes the process of joking as play.

12. Michael Gregory and Susanne Carroll, *Language and Situation: Language Varieties and their Social Contexts*, Language and Society (London: Routledge and Kegan Paul, 1978), p. 50.

13. Bergson, *Le Rire*, p. 406. See also Richard Boston's comment on the fact that "Hazlitt, Bergson, and Beerbohm all list Negroes amongst laughable objects" in *An Anatomy of Laughter* (London: William Collins and Son, 1974), p. 54.

14. Stewart notes in passing (*Nonsense*, p. 42 n) another way Bergson's argument may suggest the importance of historical analysis: "It is interesting that Bergson's definition of humor as the mechanical encrusted on the living comes on the heels of the Industrial Revolution."

15. Stephen Leacock, *Humor: Its Theory and Technique* (New York: Dodd, Mead and Company, 1935), pp. 181–82.

16. William Labov, *Sociolinguistic Patterns* (Philadelphia: University of Pennsylvania Press, 1972), p. 317.

17. Cf. Roberta Salper's comment that the women's movement is distinctive in the way it is regarded by its opponents as a joke, quoted by Carolyn Korsmeyer, "The Hidden Joke: Generic Uses

of Masculine Terminology," *Feminism and Philosophy*, ed. Mary Vetterling-Braggin et al. (Totowa, NJ: Littlefield, Adams and Company, 1978), p. 141.

18. Franz Kafka, "The Metamorphosis," *The Complete Stories*, ed. Nahum N. Glatzer (New York: Shocken Books, 1946), p. 104.

19. J. G. A. Pocock, *Politics, Language and Time: Essays on Political Thought and History* (New York: Atheneum, 1971), p. 29.

20. For a striking example of how the institution of literature is political, see Lionel Gossman's description of the institutionalization of the teaching of English literature in English and American schools, "Literature and Education," *New Literary History* 13 (1982):352–53.

Also, cf. Jacques Derrida's comments on the implication of critical theory in politics, especially in the humanities, in "The Principle of Reason: The University in the Eyes of its Pupils," trans. Catherine Porter and Edward P. Morris, *Diacritics* 13 (1983):13.

21. M. A. K. Halliday, *Language as a Social Semiotic: The Social Interpretation of Language and Meaning* (Baltimore: University Park Press, 1978), p. 232.

22. Jonathan Culler, *The Pursuit of Signs: Semiotics, Literature, Deconstruction* (Ithaca, NY: Cornell University Press, 1981), p. 125. All further references to this work, abbreviated *PS*, will be included in the text.

23. For a criticism of such notions of consensus, see Pierre Bourdieu and Jean-Claude Passeron, *Reproduction in Education, Society and Culture*, trans. Richard Nice, Sage Studies in Social and Educational Change, 5 (London: Sage Publications, 1977), p. 35. The entire book is relevant to the issues with which I am concerned in this study.

24. Stanley Fish, *Is There a Text in This Class?: The Authority of Interpretive Communities* (Cambridge: Harvard University Press, 1980), pp. 320–21. All further references to this work, abbreviated *ITT*, will be included in the text.

25. See Fish, "Profession Despise Thyself: Fear and Self-Loathing in Literary Studies," *Critical Inquiry* 10 (1983):349–64.

26. On the analysis of literature in terms of its historical readership, see Hans-Robert Jauss, *Towards an Aesthetic of Reception*, trans. Timothy Bahti, Theory and History of Literature, 2, ed. Wlad Godzich and Jochen Schulte-Sasse (Minneapolis: University of Minnesota Press, 1982).

27. John R. Searle, *Speech Acts: An Essay in the Philosophy of Language* (Cambridge: Cambridge University Press, 1970), p. 70. All further references to this work, abbreviated *SA*, will be given within the text.

28. J. O. Urmson, "J. L. Austin," in *The Linguistic Turn: Recent Essays in Philosophical Method*, ed. Richard Rorty (Chicago: University of Chicago Press, 1967), p. 233.

Also, cf. David Silverman and Brian Torode's description of how Austin's writings depend on a conception of the *I* akin to that of bourgeois law in *The Material Word: Some Theories of Language and Its Limits* (London: Routledge and Kegan Paul, 1980), *p. 219.*

29. See David Kairys, ed., *The Politics of Law: A Progressive Critique* (New York: Pantheon Books, 1982). Also, see Paul Ricoeur's use of an idealized image of the legal forum as a model for the situation of interpretation, which he categorically separates from acts of violence, in *Hermeneutics and the Human Sciences: Essays on Language, Action and Interpretation*, ed. and trans. John B. Thompson (Cambridge: Cambridge University Press,1981), p. 215.

30. Of course, the teller of a joke may also be the audience—one may amuse oneself—but the factors involved in this situation do not differ essentially from those in the more general situation I describe.

31. Milan Kundera, *The Joke*, trans. Michael Henry Heim, Writers from the Other Europe, ed. Philip Roth (New York: Penguin Books, 1982), p. 26. All further references to this work, abbreviated *J*, will be included in the text.

32. See Joan P. Emerson, "Negotiating the Serious Import of Humor," *Sociometry* 32 (1969):179. Although she follows Erving Goffman's type of analysis, Emerson concentrates on the

risks of telling jokes, including the possibility that "retrospective definitions" may be applied to them and may determine whether they are bad jokes, good jokes, or even jokes at all.

33. Milan Kundera, *The Unbearable Lightness of Being*, trans. Michael Henry Heim (New York: Harper and Row, 1984), p. 86.

34. Cf. Wittgenstein's description of a joke that does not depend on surprise in *On Certainty*, ed. G. E. M. Anscombe and G. H. von Wright, trans. Denis Paul and G. E. M. Anscombe (Oxford: Basil Blackwell, 1974), pp. 60–61: "This is certainly true, that the information 'That is a tree', when no one could doubt it, might be a kind of joke and as such have meaning. A joke of this kind was in fact made once by Renan." (Of course, one could say the surprise lies in the absence of surprise, but then one still surrenders the possibility of any formal definition of *surprise*.)

35. Erving Goffman, *Frame Analysis, An Essay on the Organization of Experience* (Cambridge: Harvard University Press, 1974), p. 325 n. All further references to this work, abbreviated *FA*, will be included in the text.

36. Quoted by Susan Rubin Suleiman, "What Can Structuralism Do for Us?" in *What is Criticism?*, ed. Paul Hernadi (Bloomington: Indiana University Press, 1981), p. 81 n.

37. Mary Douglas, "The Social Control of Cognition: Some Factors in Joke Perception," *Man* n. s., 3 (1968):372. All further references to this article, abbreviated "SCC," will be included in the text.

38. Robert Darnton, *The Great Cat Massacre and Other Episodes in French Cultural History* (New York: Basic Books, 1984), p. 100. All further references to this work, abbreviated *GCM*, will be included in the text.

39. For another side of this problem, see Carolyn J. Allen's warning about the problem involved when feminists posit a women's culture in "Feminist(s) Reading: A Response to Elaine Showalter," in *Writing and Sexual Difference*, ed. Elizabeth Abel (Chicago: University of Chicago Press, 1982), pp. 298–303.

40. It might be thought that in this argument I am failing to see what philosophers refer to as the difference between the use and mention of an expression. However, my point is that this difference, in discourse, is not self-evident. It is a matter of interpretation that is negotiated or struggled over in our social relations. Witness the debate over the placement of *Huckleberry Finn* on school reading lists, with some people arguing that racist language and stereotypes are used in this novel while others argue that they are only mentioned or, in other words, used ironically, at least to some extent. See the discussion of this issue in Lillian S. Robinson's *Sex, Class, and Culture* (Bloomington: Indiana University Press, 1978), pp. 34–35.

41. Norman N. Holland, *Laughing: A Psychology of Humor* (Ithaca, NY: Cornell University Press, 1982), p. 191.

42. Sigmund Freud, *Jokes and Their Relation to the Unconscious, The Standard Edition of the Complete Psychological Works of Sigmund Freud*, ed. and trans. James Strachey in collaboration with Anna Freud, assisted by Alix Strachey and Alan Tyson, 24 vols. (London: The Hogarth Press and the Institute of Psychoanalysis, 1960), 8:15. All further references to this work, abbreviated *JRU*, will be included in the text. I have given the original language in those places where I have modified translations.

43. The book's editors note (*JRU*, 94 n) that this should perhaps be spelled *Roulade*.

44. John Stuart Mill, "The Subjection of Women," in John Stuart Mill and Harriet Taylor Mill, *Essays on Sex Equality*, ed. Alice S. Rossi (Chicago: University of Chicago Press, 1970) p. 187.

45. Cf. Jurgen Habermas's analysis, in a discussion of Wilhelm Dilthey, of the way hermeneutic understanding "bans the dangers of communication breakdown" between the individual and culture and between different cultures, in *Knowledge and Human Interests*, trans. Jeremy J. Shapiro (Boston: Beacon Press, 1971), p. 176.

46. Michael S. Duchowny, "Pathological Disorders of Laughter," in *Handbook of Humor Research*, ed. Paul E. McGhee and Jeffrey H. Goldstein (New York: Springer-Verlag, 1983), 2:92.

47. Cf. Stewart's comment (*Nonsense*, p. 64) on the phrase "I was just joking" as a way of framing "reversible events."

48. Enid Welsford, *The Fool: His Social and Literary History* (Gloucester, MA: Peter Smith, 1966), p. 7.

49. William Hazlitt, "On Wit and Humour," *The English Comic Writers and Miscellaneous Essays*, Everyman's Library (London: J. M. Dent and Sons, 1919), p. 9.

50. Immanuel Kant, *Kritik her Urteilskraft*, in *Immanuel Kants Werke* (Berlin: Bruno Cassirer, 1922), 5:411.

51. Ibid., 5:409–10.

52. See J. Huizinga, *Homo Ludens* (Boston: Beacon, 1955); Roger Callois, *Man, Play and Games* trans. Meyer Barash (Glencoe, IL: The Free Press, 1961); and Kirshenblatt-Gimblett, ed., *Speech Play*. For an interesting critique of Huizinga and Callois, see Jacques Ehrmann, "Homo Ludens Revisited," *Yale French Studies* 41 (1968):31–57.

53. See Jurij Lotman's description of joking as "biplanar behavior" in *The Structure of the Artistic Text*, trans. Gail Lenhoff and Ronald Vroon, Michigan Slavic Contributions, 7 (Ann Arbor: University of Michigan, 1977), p. 62.

54. Derrida, "Où commence et comment finit un corps enseignant," *Politiques de la philosophie*, ed. Dominique Grisoni (Paris: Bernard Grasset, 1976), p. 74. For a critique of the way traditional and contemporary literary history is set up in contrast to the political, see Mark Seltzer, "Reading Foucault: Cells, Corridors, Novels," *Diacritics* 14 (1984):84–85. Also, on the way mutual displacements of sense and nonsense generate sense within textual structure as it is conceived by structuralist theories, see Gilles Deleuze, *Logique du sens* (Paris: Les Editions de Minuit, 1969), pp. 84–89.

Cf. also Evan Watkins's comment on criticism as an activity that cannot be totalized in "The Politics of Literary Criticism," *The Question of Textuality: Strategies of Reading in Contemporary American Criticism*, ed. William V. Spanos et al. (Bloomington: Indiana University Press, 1982), p. 36.

55. Edward Sapir, "Cultural Anthropology and Psychiatry," *Selected Writings of Edward Sapir on Language, Culture, and Personality*, ed. David G. Mandelbaum (Berkeley: University of California Press, 1949), pp. 514–15.

56. Bronislaw Malinowski, *The Dynamics of Culture Change: An Inquiry into Race Relations*, ed. Phyllis M. Kaberry (New Haven: Yale University Press, 1945), p. 59.

57. Hazlitt, "On Wit and Humour," p. 19.

58. All quotations are taken from A. R. Radcliffe-Brown, "On Joking Relationships," *Structure and Function in Primitive Society: Essays and Addresses* (New York: The Free Press, 1952), pp. 91–95. (See also, in the same volume, "Further Note on Joking Relationships.")

59. See, for instance, Ann Sharman's argument that the "misconception that all behaviour described by Radcliffe-Brown as 'joking' forms a single category of behaviour, and the continued attempt to find a satisfactory single explanation, has inhibited rather than promoted analysis" in "Joking in Padhola: Categorical Relationships, Choice and Social Control," *Man* n.s. 4 (1969):114. Also, for a critique of Radcliffe-Brown's assumptions as well as an overview of the generally uncritical acceptance of those assumptions by succeeding anthropologists, see John G. Kennedy, "Bonds of Laughter among the Tarahumara Indians: Toward a Rethinking of Joking Relationship Theory," *The Social Anthropology of Latin America: Essays in Honor of Ralph Leon Beals*, ed. Walter Goldschmidt and Harvey Hoijer, Latin American Studies, 14 (Los Angeles: Latin American Center–UCLA, 1970), pp. 36–68. It should be noted, however, that the alternative Kennedy proposes to Radcliffe-Brown's theory follows writers like Huizinga and Callois and so tends to assume an idealist view of art and play despite its quasi-psychoanalytic approach to the significance of joking.

For a recent overview of the anthropological literature on joking relationships, see Mahadev L.

Apte, *Humor and Laughter: An Anthropological Approach* (Ithaca, NY: Cornell University Press, 1985), Chapter 1, "Joking Relationships," pp. 29–66.

60. In his "Further Note," Radcliffe-Brown also suggests that relationships of solidarity based on the exchange of gifts should be compared to joking relationships.

61. Peter Hammond, "Mossi Joking," *Ethnology* 3 (1964): 259, 264.

62. Quoted in Sir Richard Blackmore, *Essay upon Wit, Essays on Wit*, No. 1 (Ann Arbor, MI: Augustan Reprint Society, 1946), p. 207.

63. All references to *King Lear* are taken from *The Complete Signet Classic Shakespeare*, ed. Sylvan Barnet (New York: Harcourt Brace Jovanovich, 1963).

64. Frank Whigham, *Ambition and Privilege: The Social Tropes of Elizabethan Courtesy Theory* (Berkeley: University of California Press, 1984), p. 51. Whigham's entire study is valuable for its explorations of issues I only touch upon here. For instance, see his comment (p. 39) on the "evacuated authority" that may be implied in courtly performance. On the topic of power and authority in Shakespeare, see also the essays in, *Political Shakespeare: New Essays in Cultural Materialism*, Jonathan Dollimore and Alan Sinfield, eds. (Manchester: Manchester University Press, 1985).

65. See Rosalie L. Colie's comment on the way "the fractionating by Goneril and Regan of their father's train . . . echoes the same habit of mind and spirit exercised by the king himself" in "*King Lear* and the 'Crisis' of the Aristocracy," *Some Facets of* King Lear: *Essays in Prismatic Criticism*, ed. Rosalie L. Colie and T. T. Flahiff (Toronto: University of Toronto Press, 1974), p. 213.

66. This is a frequent description, but see, for instance, Edwin Muir, "The Politics of *King Lear*," *Essays on Literature and Society*, rev. ed. (Cambridge: Harvard University Press, 1965). For a criticism of this view, see the comment Stephen Orgel makes in his analysis of the masque in *The Illusion of Power: Political Theater in the English Renaissance* (Berkeley: University of California Press, 1975), p. 40: "Philosophically it is both Platonic and Machiavellian: Platonic because it presents images of the good to which the participants aspire and may ascend; Machiavellian because its idealizations are designed to justify the power they celebrate."

67. Cf. Dollimore's comment that "the paradoxical leap of faith which protestantism finally and crucially demanded proved impossible for many" and that "the anxious might dwell *dis*obediently upon the very alienation and ambiguity which was supposed to make them acquiesce" in *Radical Tragedy: Religion, Ideology and Power in the Drama of Shakespeare and his Contemporaries* (Brighton, Sussex: The Harvester Press,1984), p. 105. On *King Lear* in particular, see Chapter 12, "*King Lear* and Essentialist Humanism" pp. 189–203. Also, cf. Colie's comment that in *King Lear* "the language of number is dissolved into paradoxes of 'all' and 'nothing,' thereby running out into areas of meaninglessness and incalculability" in "*King Lear* and 'Crisis' of the Aristocracy," p. 213; and, in the same volume, Martha Andresen's description (" 'Ripeness is all': *Sententiae* and Commonplaces in *King Lear*," p. 163) of the way "*sententiae* and their tradition are immersed in the paradoxicality of the play."

68. See Jonathan Goldberg's analysis of this motto in *James I and the Politics of Literature: Jonson, Shakespeare, Donne, and Their Contemporaries* (Baltimore: Johns Hopkins University Press, 1983), p. 68.

Chapter 2. *Ethnographia Mundi*

1. Bronislaw Malinowski, *A Scientific Theory of Culture and Other Essays* (Chapel Hill: University of North Carolina Press, 1944), p. 60.

2. Martin Heidegger, "Words," *On the Way to Language*, trans. Peter D. Hertz (New York: Harper and Row, 1982), p. 145.

3. Cicero, *Tusculan Disputations*, 2. 5. 13.

4. A. L. Kroeber and Clyde Kluckhohn, with the assistance of Wayne Untereiner, *Culture: A Critical Review of Concepts and Definitions* (New York: Vintage Books, 1969), p. 3.

5. See the brief summary of uses of "culture" from the eighteenth century to the present day by Raymond Williams, *The Sociology of Culture* (New York: Schocken Books, 1982), pp. 10–13. See also George W. Stocking, Jr., *Race, Culture and Evolution: Essays in the History of Anthropology* (New York: The Free Press, 1968), esp. Chapter 4, "Matthew Arnold, E. B. Tylor, and the Uses of Invention," pp. 69–90, and Chapter 9, "Franz Boas and the Culture Concept in Historical Perspective," pp. 195–233.

6. See Hans-George Gadamer, *Truth and Method*, trans. William Glen-Doepel (London: Sheed and Ward, 1975), esp. p. 244.

7. Marvin Harris, *The Rise of Anthropological Theory: A History of Theories of Culture* (New York: Thomas Y. Crowell, 1968), pp. 100-101, 516-17.

8. See, for instance, the introduction to Marc J. Swartz et al., eds., *Political Anthropology* (Chicago: Aldine Publishing, 1966), pp. 26–27: "In the political process the concepts we have been examining—in their ideal purity and abstraction—become, as it were, fragmented and contaminated from their exposure to human interests, passions, and desires."

9. Richard A. Shweder, "Preview: A Colloquy of Culture Theorists," *Culture Theory: Essays on Mind, Self, and Emotion*, ed. Richard A. Shweder and Robert A. LeVine (Cambridge: Cambridge University Press, 1984), p. 7. Of course, many others have suggested this idea; see, for instance, Paul Veyne's comments on the contemporary intersection of history, descriptive ethnography, and sociology in *Writing History: Essay in Epistemology*, trans. Mina Moore-Rinvolucri (Middletown, CT: Wesleyan University Press, 1984), p. 23.

10. Marshall Sahlins, *Culture and Practical Reason* (Chicago: University of Chicago Press, 1976), p. 2.

11. For a brief overview of the various contemporary definitions of culture among anthropologists, see Roy G. Andrade, "Cultural Meaning Systems," in *Culture Theory*, pp. 114-16.

12. Roland Barthes, *The Pleasure of the Text*, trans. Richard Miller (New York: Hill and Wang, 1975), p. 38.

13. Ludwig Wittgenstein, *The Brown Book, The Blue and Brown Books* (New York: Harper and Brothers, 1958), p. 134.

14. Quoted by Anthony Giddens, "Introduction: Durkheim's Writings in Sociology and Social Philosophy," *Emile Durkheim: Selected Writings*, ed. and trans. Anthony Giddens (Cambridge: Cambridge University Press, 1972), p. 18.

15. C. Wright Mills, *The Sociological Imagination* (New York: Oxford University Press, 1959), p. 137.

16. Robert Darnton, *The Great Cat Massacre and Other Episodes in French Cultural History* (New York: Basic Books, 1984), p. 23.

17. But see Ludwig Wittgenstein, *Philosophical Investigations*, trans. G. E. M. Anscombe, 3d ed. (New York: Macmillan, 1969), p. 139e: "When a sentence is called senseless, it is not as it were its sense that is senseless. But a combination of words is being excluded from the language, withdrawn from circulation." As I note in my discussion of Clifford Geertz, I do not suggest that the writings of Wittgenstein, or the other figures I mention, are all of a piece.

18. Jonathan Lear, "Moral Objectivity," *Objectivity and Cultural Divergence*, ed. S. C. Brown, Royal Institute of Philosophy Lecture Series, 17 (Cambridge: Cambridge University Press, 1984), pp. 148–49.

19. For instance, for the critique of the metaphor of totality in philosophy, see the works of Jacques Derrida, including though not limited to those cited elsewhere in this book. In law, see David Kairys, ed., *The Politics of Law: A Progressive Critique* (New York: Pantheon Books, 1982); and Roberto Unger, *The Critical Legal Studies Movement* (Cambridge: Harvard University Press, 1986). In sociology and anthropology, see Pierre Bourdieu, *Outline of a Theory of Practice*, trans. Richard Nice, Cambridge Series in Social Anthropology, 16 (Cambridge, Cambridge University Press, 1977). This critique of explanation in the human sciences is apposite to my own in many ways, although it

treats unconsciousness, misrecognition, common sense, and like phenomena as structural aspects of sociality in a way I find insufficiently critical toward its own sociological method. In sociology, see also William Labov's analysis, in *Sociolinguistic Patterns* (Philadelphia: University of Pennsylvania Press,1972), especially p. 203, of heterogeneity as a condition of speech communities. In Marxist theory, see, for instance, Rosalind Coward and John Ellis, *Langugage and Materialism: Developments in Semiology and the Theory of the Subject* (London: Routledge and Kegan Paul, 1977), especially pp. 82–86; and Paul Q. Hirst, *Marxism and Historical Writing* (London: Routledge and Kegan Paul, 1985). In feminist theory, see Mary Jacobus, "The Difference of Views," *Women Writing and Writing about Women*, ed. Mary Jacobus (Totowa, NJ: Barnes and Noble, 1979), pp. 10–21; the essays by Toril Moi ("Sexual/Textual Politics," pp. 1–14), Terry Lovell ("Writing Like a Woman: A Question of Politics," pp. 15–26), and Mary Russo ("Notes on 'Post-Feminism,' " pp. 27–37) in *The Politics of Theory*, ed. Francis Barker et al. (Colchester: University of Essex, 1983); Toril Moi, *Sexual/Textual Politics* (London: Methuen, 1985); and Teresa de Laurentis, ed., *Feminist Studies/Critical Studies* (Bloomington: Indiana University Press, 1986). Also relevant to Marxism and feminism is Catherine Belsey's *Critical Practice*, New Accents (London: Methuen, 1980). In history, see Dominick LaCapra, *History and Criticism* (Ithaca, NY: Cornell University Press, 1985), especially Chapter 3, "Is Everyone a *Mentalité* Case? Transference and the 'Culture Concept,' " pp. 71–94. In history and social theory see the works of Michel Foucault. In anthropology, see Edmund Leach, *Social Anthropology* (New York: Oxford University Press,1982), pp. 35–37, 142. Leach describes how the naive notion of a homogenous or homeostatic society appears in the works of early and contemporary anthropologists, including the works of those who are not functionalists or structural-functionalists. See also Steve Barnett and Martin G. Silverman, *Ideology and Everyday Life: Anthropology, NeoMarxist Thought, and the Problem of Ideology and the Social Whole*, Anthropology Series: Studies in Cultural Analysis, ed. Vern Carroll (Ann Arbor, University of Michigan Press, 1979); and for the best and most recent approaches to this issue, see James Clifford and George E. Marcus, eds., *Writing Culture: The Poetics and Politics of Ethnography* (Berkeley: University of California Press, 1986). In literature, see Jeffrey L. Sammons, *Literary Sociology and Practical Criticism: An Inquiry* (Bloomington: Indiana University Press, 1977), pp. 16–38; Christopher Butler, *Interpretation, Deconstruction, and Ideology: An Introduction to Some Current Issues in Literary Theory* (Oxford: Oxford University Press, 1984); and Allon White, "Bakhtin, Sociolinguistics and Deconstruction," *The Theory of Reading*, ed. Frank Gloversmith (Totowa, NJ: Barnes and Noble, 1984), pp. 123–46. See also the essays in *Culture in the Social Sciences*, ed. Louis Schneider and Charles Bonjean (Cambridge; Cambridge University Press, 1973), particularly the contributions by Lucien W. Pye ("Culture and Political Science: Problems in the Concept of Political Culture," especially p. 76) and by Robert F. Berkhofer,Jr. ("Clio and the Culture Concept: Some Impressions of a Changing Relationship in American Historiography," pp. 77–100).

Of course, this is just a sampling of the work relevant to this subject, some of which I avoid mentioning here because I refer to it elsewhere in this study. For a succinct theoretical statement of the problem of the metaphor of totality in all these fields, see Gayatri Chakrovorty Spivak, "The Politics of Interpretation," *Critical Inquiry* 9 (1982):259: "It is impossible, of course, to mark off a group as an entity without sharing complicity with its ideological definition. A persistent critique of ideology is thus forever incomplete. In the shifting spectrum between subject-constitution and group-constitution are the ideological apparatuses that share the condition/effect oscillation."

20. Clifford Geertz, *The Interpretation of Cultures: Selected Essays* (New York: Basic Books,1973), p. 10. All further references to this work, abbreviated *IC*, will be included in the text.

21. Clifford Geertz, *Local Knowledge: Further Essays in Interpretive Anthropology* (New York: Basic Books, 1983), p. 156. All further references to this work, abbreviated by *LK*, will be included in the text.

22. Norman A. McQuown, "The Nature of Culture," *Language, Culture and Education*, ed. Anwar S. Dil (Stanford, CA: Stanford University Press, 1982), p. 52.

23. Hilary Putnam, *Meaning and the Moral Sciences*, International Library of Philosophy and Scientific Method (London: Routledge and Kegan Paul, 1978), p. 89.

24. On this problem of interpretive neutrality, c.f. Alan Ryan, *The Philosophy of the Social Sciences* (New York: Random House, 1970), Chapter 7, "The Social Sciences as Sciences," pp. 149–72. Also cf. Walter Benn Michaels, "The Interpreter's Self: Peirce on the Cartesian 'Subject,' " *Reader-Response Criticism: From Formalism to Post-Structuralism*, ed. Jane P. Tompkins (Baltimore: Johns Hopkins University Press, 1980), pp. 185–200.

25. Williams, *The Sociology of Culture*, p. 28.

26. The significance of these protocols recently has been highlighted in the case of the Stanford graduate student, Stephen Mosher, who was banished from his doctoral program in anthropology for his "unprofessional" activities.

27. On this point, see Harris's comment on the politics inherent in "emicized and mentalistic cultural anthropology" in "History and Ideological Significance of the Separation of Social and Cultural Anthropology," *Beyond the Myths of Culture: Essays in Cultural Materialism*, ed. Eric B. Ross, Studies in Anthropology (New York: Academic Press,1980), p. 404.

28. Dell Hymes, *Foundations in Sociolinguistics: An Ethnographic Approach* (Philadelphia: University of Pennsylvania Press, 1974), p. 123. All further references to this work, abbreviated *FS*, will be included in the text.

29. Robert A. LeVine, "Properties of Culture: An Ethnographic View," in *Culture Theory*, p. 68.

30. Gadamer, *Truth and Method*, p. 271.

31. Sahlins, *Culture and Practical Reason*, p. 123.

32. Marshall Sahlins, *Islands of History* (Chicago: University of Chicago Press, 1985).

33. Edward Sapir, "Culture, Genuine and Spurious," in *Selected Writings of Edward Sapir on Language, Culture, and Personality*, ed. David G. Mandelbaum (Berkeley: University of California Press, 1949), p. 308. All further references to this work, abbreviated *SW*, will be included in the text.

34. See Sapir's statement in "Group": "If one looks beyond the groups which are institutionally defined—in other words, beyond associations in the narrow sense of the word—any society, above all the complex society of modern times, has many more groups of more or less psychological significance than it possesses individuals who participate in groups" (*SW*, 362).

35. See also Sapir's "Why Cultural Anthropology Needs the Psychiatrist" (*SW*, 569–77), for another brilliant excursus into the limits of the concept of culture; and "Psychiatric and Cultural Pitfalls in the Business of Getting a Living," an essay on the relation between economics, personality, and the concerns of the psychiatrist, for the way it raises and then represses the question of politics in its concluding lines: "It is conceivable that good mental hygiene, even expert psychiatry, may find it proper to recommend some share of income reduction for the sake of the mental health of those who are too heavily burdened by a material prosperity that far outruns their needs or, if the truth were known, their secret desires. In this mysterious realm we need further light" (*SW*, 589).

36. Jacques Derrida, "Force and Signification," *Writing and Difference*, trans. Alan Bass (Chicago: University of Chicago Press,1978), pp. 17, 19.

37. Heidegger, "The Nature of Language," *On the Way to Language*, p.83.

38. Wittgenstein, *Philosophical Investigations*, p. 56e.

39. Jacques Derrida, "Signature Event Context," *Margins of Philosophy*, trans. Alan Bass (Chicago: University of Chicago Press, 1982), p. 320. All further references to this work, abbreviated *MP*, will be included in the text.

40. See Peter Brooker's description of how Derrida's writings are "politically unfocused" in "Post-structuralism, Reading and the Crisis of English," in *Re-reading English*, ed. Peter Widdowson, New Accents (London: Methuen, 1982), p. 67.

41. Basil Bernstein, *Class, Codes and Control, Primary Socialization, Language and Education*,

(London: Routledge and Kegan Paul, 1971), 1:108. All further references to this work, abbreviated *CCC*, will be included in the text.

42. For an example of this "misunderstanding," see Claus Mueller with the assistance of Carol Coe Conway, *The Politics of Communication: A Study in the Political Sociology of Language, Socialization, and Legitimation* (New York: Oxford University Press, 1973). Of course, Bernstein is not alone among sociologists in this use of context; such use is "normal." Compare Michael Gregory and Susanne Carroll, *Language and Situation: Language Varieties and Their Social Contexts*, Language and Society (London: Routledge and Kegan Paul, 1978).

43. See, for instance, the statement that in sociolinguistics "inequality is neutralized as variety" in Roger Fowler and Gunther Kress, "Critical Linguistics," *Language and Control*, ed. Roger Fowler et al. (London: Routledge and Kegan Paul, 1979), p. 193. This entire book is valuable in relation to the analysis of topics like competence and context. See also Susan Stewart's observation that "as the abstract objectivists tend to hypostatize grammar, the sociolinguists tend to hypostatize rules for speech behavior" and "do not seem to realize that such rules are not simply located *behind* the historical process of social life but are also *emergent* in them" in "Shouts on the Street: Bakhtin's Anti-Linguistics," *Critical Inquiry* 10 (1983):269.

On Bernstein in particular, see Noëlle Bisseret's statement that "Bernstein separates and dichotomizes so as to compare, as if it were a question of comparing, like an ethnologist, heterogeneous cultural systems and not two subsystems which define each other" in *Education, Class Language and Ideology*, trans. M. P. Eisele et al. (London: Routledge and Kegan Paul, 1979), p. 103. Also, for a critical analysis of the use of context in literary theory, see Steven Mailloux, "Historical Hermeneutics," *Critical Inquiry* 11 (1985):620–28.

44. M. A. K. Halliday, *Language as Social Semiotic: The Social Interpretation of Language and Meaning* (Baltimore: University Park Press, 1978), p. 34.

45. In relation to this point and others in this section, c.f. Foucault's description of his work's critical relation to the usual conception of context in *The Archaeology of Knowledge*, trans. A. M. Sheridan Smith, World of Man (New York: Pantheon Books, 1972), esp. pp. 97–99.

46. Derrida perhaps approaches this point in a footnote to "Cogito and the History of Madness," *Writing and Difference*, p. 310: "In short, Descartes knew that, without God, finite thought never had the *right* to exclude madness, etc. Which amounts to saying that madness is never excluded, except *in fact*, violently, in history; or rather that this exclusion, this *difference* between the fact and the principle is historicity, the possibility of history itself." See also Jacques Derrida, "Où commence et comment finit un corps enseignant," *Politiques de la Philosophie*, ed. Dominique Grisoni (Paris: Bernard Grasset, 1976), pp. 55–89.

47. Walter Benjamin, "Theses on the Philosophy of History," *Illuminations*, ed. Hannah Arendt, trans. Harry Zohn (New York: Harcourt, Brace and World, 1968), p. 258.

48. For a particularly striking example of this abuse of statistics in an anthropological work, which includes among its conclusions from these statistics a standpoint of irony and political apathy, see Pierre Maranda, "The Dialectic of Metaphor: An Anthropological Essay on Hermeneutics," *The Reader in the Text: Essays on Audience and Interpretation*, ed. Susan R. Suleiman and Inge Crosman (Princeton: Princeton University Press, 1980), pp. 183–204.

49. See Edward Said's description of culture as "a boundary by which the concepts of what is extrinsic or intrinsic to culture come into forceful play" in *The World, the Text, and the Critic* (Cambridge, MA: Harvard University Press, 1983), p. 9. Also, on the role of the deviant "inmate alien," "inside outsider," and "hybrid," see Zygmunt Bauman, *Culture as Praxis*, Monographs in Social Theory (London: Routledge and Kegan Paul, 1973), pp. 129–33.

50. E. S. Craighill Handy and M. Kawena Pukui, "The Polynesian Family System," quoted by Claude Lévi-Strauss, *The Savage Mind*, The Nature of Human Society Series (London: Weidenfeld and Nicolson, 1972), p. 37. All further references to this work, abbreviated *SM*, will be included in the text.

51. Labov, *Sociolinguistic Patterns*, p. 268.

52. Anthony Giddens, *Central Problems in Social Theory: Action, Structure and Contradiction in Social Analysis* (Berkeley: University of California Press, 1979), p. 71. On this point, see also Jack Goody, *The Domestication of the Savage Mind*, Themes in the Social Sciences (Cambridge: Cambridge University Press, 1977).

53. For an example of how this category of the native can flaw even a sophisticated investigation of historical explanation, one that takes account of the idea of cultural heterogeneity, see Rex Martin, *Historical Explanation: Re-enactment and Practical Inference*, Contemporary Philosophy (Ithaca, NY: Cornell University Press, 1977), Chapter 11, "Other Periods, Other Cultures," pp. 215–40. Also see Barthes's comment on how value always is produced through the opposition between the exception and the rule in *The Pleasure of the Text*, p. 41.

54. Clyde Kluckhohn, *Culture and Behavior*, ed. Richard Kluckhohn (New York: The Free Press, 1962), p. 251.

55. For a critique of Lévi-Strauss's description of exchange and women as commodities, see Bridget O'Laughlin, "Mediation of Contradiction: Why Moum Women Do Not Eat Chicken," *Women, Culture and Society*, ed. Michelle Zimbalist Rosaldo and Louise Lamphere (Stanford, CA: Stanford University Press, 1974), pp. 301–18. Sherry B. Ortner's essay in this volume, "Is Female to Male as Nature is to Culture?" also addresses this issue as it tries to modify Lévi-Strauss's argument, although its good points tend to get lost in a confused conception of culture.

See also Gayle Rubin's critical appropriation of Lévi Strauss and Freud to analyze sexism, including Lévi-Strauss's and Freud's, in "The Traffic in Women: Notes on the 'Political Economy' of Sex," *Toward an Anthropology of Women*, ed. Rayna R. Reiter (New York: Monthly Review Press, 1975), pp. 157– 210; Joke Schrijvers, "Viricentrism and Anthropology," *The Politics of Anthropology: From Colonialism and Sexism Toward a View from Below*, ed. Gerrit Huizer and Bruce Mannheim, World Anthropology (The Hague: Mouton, 1979), especially p. 105; and Carol P. MacCormack's criticism of Lévi-Strauss for making men active and women passive and for implying that those women who do not fit this mold are "conceptually aberrant, if not 'unnatural,' " in "Nature, Culture and Gender: A Critique," *Nature, Culture and Gender* (Cambridge: Cambridge University Press, 1980), esp. pp. 11–27.

56. Victor Turner, *Dramas, Fields, and Metaphors: Symbolic Action in Human Society*, Symbol, Myth, and Ritual Series (Ithaca, NY: Cornell University Press, 1974), pp. 16–17.

57. Mary Douglas, *Implicit Meanings: Essays in Anthropology* (London: Routledge and Kegan Paul, 1975), p. 228.

58. Stanley Diamond, *In Search of the Primitive: A Critique of Civilization* (New Brunswick, NJ: Transaction Books, 1974), p. 146. All further references to this work, abbreviated *ISP*, will be included in the text.

59. Jean Baudrillard, *The Mirror of Production*, trans. Mark Poster (St. Louis: Telos Press, 1975), especially pp. 93–96.

60. Robert A. Levine, *Culture, Behavior, and Personality* (Chicago: Aldine Publishing Company, 1973), pp. 138–39, 154.

61. Talcott Parsons, "Culture and Social System Revisited," *Culture in the Social Sciences*, pp. 42–43. All further references to this work, abbreviated "CSSR," will be included in the text.

62. Halliday, *Language as Social Semiotic*, p. 24.

63. Quoted by Roy G. D'Andrade, "Cultural Meaning Systems," in *Cultural Theory*, p. 89. Cf. Goodenough's definition of culture as "a set of standards that seems to be authoritative" according to "local authorities" and as a "game" in *Description and Comparison in Cultural Anthropology* (Chicago: Aldine Publishing Company, 1970), pp. 103–5.

64. Umberto Eco, *The Role of the Reader: Explorations in the Semiotics of Texts*, Advances in Semiotics (Bloomington: Indiana University Press, 1979), pp. 9–10.

65. Julia Kristeva, *Desire in Language: A Semiotic Approach to Literature and Art*, ed. Leon S. Roudiez, trans. Thomas Gora (New York: Columbia University Press, 1980), p. 36. See also the way she compares nature and culture to desire and law in *Desire in Language*, p. 97.

66. Melville J. Herskovits, *Cultural Relativism: Perspectives in Cultural Pluralism* (New York: Random House, 1972), p. 31.

67. Putnam, *Meaning and the Moral Sciences*, p. 45. For a discussion of the question of relativism and universality in the analysis of speech, see also Fred R. Dallmayr, *Language and Politics: Why Does Language Matter to Political Philosophy?*, Loyola Lecture Series in Political Analysis (Notre Dame: University of Notre Dame Press, 1984), especially p. 115.

68. Kluckhohn, *Culture and Behavior*, pp. 284, 295.

69. See Ernest Gellner's comments on the paradox of liberal thinking on relativity in *Cause and Meaning in the Social Sciences*, ed. I. C. Jarvie and Joseph Agassi (London: Routledge and Kegan Paul, 1973), especially p. 28.

70. Foucault, *The Archaeology of Knowledge*, p. 44.

71. Derrida, "Structure, Sign and Play in the Discourse of the Human Sciences," *Writing and Difference*, p. 282. It should be noted, however, that Derrida's succeeding judgment (p. 282), "The quality and fecundity of a discourse are perhaps measured by the critical rigor with which this relation to the history of metaphysics and to inherited concepts is thought," is perhaps more self-serving than analytically or politically compelling. The same is true of his conclusion in this essay (p. 293) that "we are in a region (let us say, provisionally, a region of historicity) where the category of choice seems particularly trivial." These statements are symptomatic of a disciplinary compulsion that appears within Derrida's writing despite all its violations of traditional philosophical discourse.

72. Diamond, *In Search of the Primitive*, p. 110.

73. See Roy Wagner's comment that textbook anthropology "is a catalogue of the devices that theory has used to check and overcome relativity" and his comment that "academia has been the handmaiden of other interests committed to the invention of our secular reality" in *The Invention of Culture*, Prentice-Hall Anthropology Series (Englewood Cliffs, NJ: Prentice-Hall, 1975), p. 157; and Geertz's criticism of universals as "a lowest-common denominator view of humanity" in *The Interpretation of Cultures*, p. 43.

74. Stanley Fish, *Is There a Text in This Class?: The Authority of Interpretive Communities* (Cambridge, MA: Harvard University Press, 1980), p. 309.

75. E. D. Hirsch, Jr., *Validity in Interpretation* (New Haven: Yale University Press, 1967), p. 158.

76. Franz Kafka, "In der Strafkolonie," *Erzählungen und Kleine Prosa, Gesammelte Schriften*, ed. Max Brod (New York: Schocken Books, 1946), 1:206.

77. On this point, see John Brenkman, "Theses on Cultural Marxism," *Social Text*, 3 (1983).

78. Wittgenstein, *Philosophical Investigations*, p. 50e.

79. Coward and Ellis, *Language and Materialism*, p. 37. Cf. the comment on Barthes's privileging of the avant-garde in David Silverman and Brian Torode, *The Material Word: Some Theories of Language and Its Limits* (London: Routledge and Kegan Paul, 1980), p. 267.

80. Cf. Harold Garfinkel's analysis of logic and methodology as "glasses for organizational phenomena" in "Remarks on Ethnomethodology," *Directions in Sociolinguistics: The Ethnography of Communication*, ed. John J. Gumperz and Dell Hymes (New York: Holt, Rinehart and Winston, 1972), p. 322.

81. Francis Sparshott, "The Problem of the Problem of Criticism," in *What Is Criticism?*, ed. Paul Hernadi (Bloomington: Indiana Univerity Press, 1981), p. 12.

82. Hirsch, *Validity in Interpretation*, p. 5.

83. Tzvetan Todorov, *The Poetics of Prose*, trans. Richard Howard (Ithaca, NY: Cornell University Press, 1977), p. 87.

84. Malinowski, *A Scientific Theory of Culture*, p. 14.

85. Bronislaw Malinowski, *The Dynamics of Culture Change: An Inquiry into Race Relations*, ed. Phyllis M. Kaberry (New Haven: Yale University Press, 1945), p. 3.

86. "At Radio Free Europe, A Few Changes of Pace," *The New York Times*, 6 June 1984, sec. 1, p. 16, col. 2.

87. M. M. Bakhtin, *The Dialogic Imagination: Four Essays*, ed. Michael Holquist, trans. Caryl Emerson and Michael Holquist, University of Texas Press Slavic Series, 1 (Austin: University of Texas Press, 1981), p. 294.

88. Umberto Eco, *Semiotics and the Philosophy of Language*, Advances in Semiotics (Bloomington: Indiana University Press, 1984), p. 84.

89. Dell Hymes, "Sociolinguistics and the Ethnography of Speaking," *Social Anthropology and Language*, ed. Edwin Ardener (London: Tavistock Publications, 1971), pp. 48–49.

90. Turner, *Dramas, Fields, and Metaphors*, p. 14.

91. Kristeva, *Desire in Language*, p. 133.

92. Fredric Jameson, *The Political Unconscious: Narrative as a Socially Symbolic Act* (Ithaca, NY: Cornell University Press, 1981), pp. 282–83 n. For Jameson's description of a theory of cultural revolution that takes account of the heterogeneity of culture, see especially pp. 94–99.

93. Cf. Alwin Baum's reference to the "semiotic map of culture, a map which traces paths and intersections, but which is itself only the code of codes" and his comment: "It is ironic but ultimately logical that the tradition of modern literary theory should presume to decipher that map even as it stands at the crossroads of this textual interplay of cultural consciousness." "The Crossroads of Critical Consciousness: A Response to Jonathan Culler's 'Structuralism and Grammatology,' " *The Question of Textuality: Strategies of Reading in Contemporary American Criticism*, ed. William V. Spanos (Bloomington: Indiana University Press, 1982), p. 92. Also, for an analysis of some of the problems in current critical attempts to articulate culture as "the socially and historically situated process of production of meanings," see Michèle Barrett et al., eds., *Ideology and Culture Production* (New York: St. Martin's Press, 1979).

Chapter 3. Paranomasia, Culture, and the Power of Meaning

1. Sigmund Freud, *Jokes and Their Relation to the Unconscious*, in *The Standard Edition of the Complete Psychological Works of Sigmund Freud*, ed. and trans. James Strachey and Alan Tyson, 24 vols. (London: The Hogarth Press and the Institute of Psychoanalysis, 1960), 8:120.

2. For an excellent recent example of this kind of reading, see Robin Gilmour's description of the "ways in which Pip's story can be seen as representative of early nineteenth-century experience" in *The Idea of the Gentleman in the Victorian Novel* (London: George Allen and Unwin, 1981), p. 135.

3. All references to Dickens's *Works* are taken from the Gadshill Edition, ed. Andrew Lang, 38 vols. (London: Chapman and Hall, 1897–1919). References are given within the text according to the following abbreviations: *Great Expectations* as *GE*; *David Copperfield* as *DC*; *Nicholas Nickleby* as *NN*; *Dombey and Son* as *DS*; *Barnaby Rudge* as *BR*; *Bleak House* as *BH*; *Martin Chuzzlewit* as *MC*; and *A Tale of Two Cities* as *TTC*.

On the topic of the interrelation of life and death, see Colin N. Manlove, "Neither Here nor There: Uneasiness in *Great Expectations*," *Dickens Studies Annual* 8, ed. Michael Timko et al. (New York: AMS Press, 1980), pp. 61–72; Barry Westburg, *The Confessional Fictions of Charles Dickens* (DeKalb, IL: Northern Illinois University Press, 1977), pp. 124–25; and the letter from Carlyle that John Forster uses as the epigraph to his biography of Dickens, in which Carlyle writes of Dickens hiding, "amid dazzling radiances of the sun, the elements of death itself" (*The Life of Charles Dickens*, Gadshill Edition, 2 vols [London: Chapman and Hall, 1899]).

4. J. Hillis Miller, *Charles Dickens: The World of His Novels* (Bloomington: Indiana University Press, 1958), p. 253.

5. G. K. Chesterton, *Appreciations and Criticisms of the Works of Charles Dickens* (London: J. M. Dent and Sons, 1911), p. 202.

6. Forster, *The Life of Charles Dickens*, 2:341.

7. John O. Jordan, "The Medium of *Great Expectations*," *Dickens Studies Annual* 11, ed. Michael Timko et al. (New York: AMS Press, 1983), p. 85. In the same volume, see Robert Tracy's description of Dickens's evident distrust of writing and his suggestion that this stems from his unease over his role as a manipulator, or forger, of words and characters ("Reading Dickens' Writing," pp. 37–59). On this point, see also Westburg, *The Confessional Fictions of Charles Dickens*, p. 151.

8. See Georg Lukács, *The Theory of the Novel: A Historico-Philosophical Essay on the Forms of Great Epic Literature*, trans. Anna Bostock (Cambridge, MA: M.I.T. Press, 1971); and M. M. Bakhtin, *The Dialogic Imagination: Four Essays*, ed. Michael Holquist, trans. Caryl Emerson and Michael Holquist, University of Texas Press Slavic Series (Austin: University of Texas Press, 1981).

9. See D. C. Muecke's distinction between specific and general irony in *The Compass of Irony* (London: Methuen, 1969), especially Chapter 6, "General Irony," pp. 119–58; Wayne Booth's distinction between stable and unstable irony in *A Rhetoric of Irony* (Chicago: University of Chicago Press, 1974); and Lilian R. Furst's commentary on this distinction in *Fictions of Romantic Irony* (Cambridge: Harvard University Press 1984), especially Chapter 2, "The Metamorphosis of Irony," pp. 23–48.

10. Dorothy Van Ghent, *The English Novel: Form and Function* (New York: Holt, Rinehart and Winston, 1953), p. 129.

11. Peter Brooks, "Repetition, Repression, and Return: *Great Expectations* and the Study of Plot," *New Literary History* 11 (1980):521.

12. Westburg, *The Confessional Fictions of Charles Dickens*, p. 122. On the complications of Pip's relation to language, see also Max Byrd, " 'Reading' in *Great Expectations*," *PMLA* 91 (1976):259–65; Melanie Young, "Distorted Expectations: Pip and the Problems of Language," *Dickens Studies Annual* 7, ed. Robert B. Partlow, Jr. (Carbondale and Edwardsville: Southern Illinois University Press, 1978), pp. 203–20; and Murray Baumgarten, "Calligraphy and Code: Writing in *Great Expectations*," *Dickens Studies Annual* 11, especially pp. 66–70. See also Ann B. Dobie's description of the ways Dickens suggests "the fluid, nonstatic nature of existence" in "Early Stream-of-Consciousness Writing: *Great Expectations*," *Nineteenth-Century Fiction* 25 (1971):405–16.

13. See, for instance, Sylvia Bank Manning's comment that at the end of the novel "Pip the protagonist and Pip the narrator have become one" in *Dickens the Satirist*, Yale Studies in English, 176 (New Haven: Yale University Press, 1971), p. 192; and Henri Talon's comment that to find his identity Pip "must embrace his whole career, totalize and interpret all that is significant," in "Space, Time, and Memory in *Great Expectations*," *Dickens Studies Annual* 3, ed. Robert B. Partlow, Jr. (Carbondale and Edwardsville: Southern Illinois University Press, 1974), p. 123.

14. Many critics have commented on the significance of Pip's name, but see F. S. Schwarzbach, *Dickens and the City* (London: Athlone Press, 1979), pp. 192–93; and Harry Stone, *Dickens and the Invisible World: Fairy Tales, Fantasy, and Novel-Making* (Bloomington: Indiana University Press, 1979), p. 311.

15. Henri Fluchère, "Lecture et relecture de 'Great Expectations,' " *Europe* 488 (1969):63. See also Brooks, "Repetition, Repression, and Return," p. 524: "The desire for meaning is ultimately the reader's, who must mime Pip's acts of reading, but do them better. Both using and subverting the systems of meaning discovered or postulated by its hero, *Great Expectations* exposes for its reader the very reading process itself: the way the reader goes about finding meaning in the narrative text, and the limits of that meaning as the limits of narrative."

16. Grahame Smith, *Dickens, Money, and Society* (Berkeley: University of California Press, 1968), p. 172.

17. Ludwig Wittgenstein, *The Blue and Brown Books* (New York: Harper and Brothers, 1958), p. 6.

18. Bert G. Hornback, "*Noah's Arkitecture*": *A Study of Dickens's Mythology* (Athens: Ohio University Press, 1972), p. 127.

19. E. Pearlman, "Inversion in *Great Expectations*," *Dickens Studies Annual* 7, p. 199.

20. Miller, *Charles Dickens*, p. 265.

21. See A. L. French, "Beating and Cringing: *Great Expectations*," *Essays in Criticism* 24 (1974).

22. Brooks, "Repetition, Repression, and Return," p. 515.

23. See A. O. J. Cockshut, *The Imagination of Charles Dickens* (New York: New York University Press, 1962), p. 60.

24. Lucille P. Shores, "The Character of Estella in *Great Expectations*," *Massachusetts Studies in English* 3 (1972):92.

25. John Kucich, *Excess and Restraint in the Novels of Charles Dickens* (Athens: University of Georgia Press, 1981), p. 156.

26. Cockshut, *The Imagination of Charles Dickens*, p. 160.

27. See Van Ghent's description of how Dickens's characters, because of their use of language, "suggest a world of isolated integers, terrifyingly alone and unrelated," in *The English Novel*, p. 127.

28. Dell Hymes, *Foundations in Sociolinguistics: An Ethnographic Approach* (Philadelphia: University of Pennsylvania Press, 1974), p. 148.

29. Immanuel Kant, *Kritik der Urteilskraft*, in *Immanuel Kants Werke*, 11 vols. (Berlin: Bruno Cassirer, 1922), 5:410.

30. Freud, *Jokes and Their Relation to the Unconscious*, 8:119.

31. E. D. Hirsch, Jr., *Validity in Interpretation* (New Haven: Yale University Press, 1967), p. 46.

32. Joseph Conrad, *Heart of Darkness*, ed. Robert Kimbrough (New York: W. W. Norton, 1963), pp. 7, 43, 51.

33. See Pip's description (*GE*, 49) of Wopsle's readings of Collins's "Ode on the Passions" during the quarterly examination given at his great-aunt's school when Pip was a child: "It was not with me then, as it was in later life, when I fell into the society of the Passions, and compared them with Collins and Wopsle, rather to the disadvantage of both gentlemen."

34. Roland Barthes, *S/Z*, trans. Richard Miller (New York: Hill and Wang, 1974), p. 40.

35. Quoted in *Speech Play: Research and Resources for Studying Linguistic Creativity*, ed. Barbara Kirshenblatt-Gimblett, University of Pennsylvania Publications in Conduct and Communication (Philadelphia: University of Pennsylvania Press, 1970), p. 92.

36. See Ross H. Dabney's note, "In a world of Joe Gargery's capital could never be amassed," in *Love and Property in the Novels of Dickens* (London: Chatto and Windus, 1967), p. 128 n.

37. Cf. the description in *Dombey and Son* (2:455) after the House of Dombey has fallen and people outside are clamoring for information: "Then, in short, would Mr. Perch, a victim to his position, tell all manner of lies; affecting himself to tears by those that were of a moving nature, and really believing that the inventions of yesterday had, on repetition, a sort of truth about them to-day."

38. See Garrett Stewart's comment that these "lies *are* lies, yet there is a troublesome 'metaphysical' residue in the preceding scene that simply cannot be reduced to moral certainty" in *Dickens and the Trials of Imagination* (Cambridge, MA: Harvard University Press, 1974), p. 189.

39. See Albert D. Hutter's reading of this novel in terms of Oedipal fears and aggression in "Crime and Fantasy in *Great Expectations*," *Psychoanalysis and Literary Process*, ed. Frederick Crews (Cambridge, MA: Winthrop Publishers, 1970), pp. 25–65.

40. See George Levine's argument that full communication in *Great Expectations* "comes usually through gestures, inarticulate noises, or ungrammatical and irrational speech" in "Communication in *Great Expectations*," *Nineteenth-Century Fiction* 18 (1963):179. On this topic, see also I. Ovsby, "Language and Gesture" in *Great Expectations*," *The Modern Language Review* 72 (1977):784–93.

41. Michel Charles, *Rhétorique de la lecture* (Paris: Editions du Seuil, 1977), p. 107 n.

42. In an amusing distorted fashion, this conflict is reproduced in one of the critical arguments over this novel. Whereas Dabney says "we cannot take Pip's learning seriously" because it is "arbi-

trarily" represented (*Love and Property in the Novels of Dickens*, p. 138 n), F. R. Leavis and Q. D. Leavis appeal to the authority of Pip's subjectivity ("Of course it is in his reactions and conversation that our conviction lies") in *Dickens the Novelist* (London: Chatto and Windus, 1970), p. 315 n.

43. Cf. Steven Connor's Lacanian argument in *Charles Dickens* (London: Basil Blackwell, 1985), esp. p. 136.

44. Milan Kundera, *The Joke*, trans. Michael Henry Heim, Writers from the Other Europe (New York: Penguin Books, 1982), p. 265.

45. In addition to Cockshut's revision of Estella, see, for instance, Robert Garis's comment that "it is literally inconceivable to us that Pip should think of marrying Biddy" in *The Dickens Theatre: A Reassessment of the Novels* (Oxford: Oxford University Press, 1965), pp. 202–3.

46. Ludwig Wittgenstein, *Culture and Value*, ed. G. H. Von Wright in collaboration with Heikki Nyman, trans. Peter Winch (Chicago: University of Chicago Press, 1980), p. 16e.

Index

Index

175

Theory and History of Literature

Daniel Cottom is an associate professor of English at the University of Florida. He received his doctorate in English from the State University of New York at Buffalo in 1978 and, until mid-1986, taught at Wayne State University. Cottom is the author of *Social Figures: George Eliot, Social History, and Literary Representation* (Minnesota, 1987) and *The Civilized Imagination: A Study of Ann Radcliffe, Jane Austen, and Sir Walter Scott.*